MONITORING LAWS

Our world, and the objects and people within it, are increasingly interpreted and classified by automated systems. At the same time, those automated systems and their classifications influence what happens in the physical world. In this cyber-physical world or 'world state', people are asking what law's role should be in regulating these systems. In *Monitoring Laws*, Jake Goldenfein traces the history of government profiling, from the invention of photography to create criminal registers, through the emerging deployments of computer vision for personality, emotion, and behavioral analysis. He asks what elements and applications of profiling have provoked legal intervention in the past, and demonstrates exactly what is different about contemporary profiling that requires a new legal treatment. This work should be read by anyone interested in how computation is changing society and governance, and what the law can do to better protect us from these changes now.

Jake Goldenfein is a Postdoctoral researcher at the Digital Life Initiative at Cornell University and a lecturer at Swinburne Law School. A law and technology scholar exploring governance in computational society, Goldenfein has published across disciplines, with work appearing in *Law and Critique*, the *Columbia Journal of Law and Arts*, the *Internet Policy Review*, and the *University of New South Wales Law Journal*.

Monitoring Laws

PROFILING AND IDENTITY IN THE WORLD STATE

JAKE GOLDENFEIN
Cornell Tech, Cornell University

CAMBRIDGE
UNIVERSITY PRESS

University Printing House, Cambridge CB2 8BS, United Kingdom

One Liberty Plaza, 20th Floor, New York, NY 10006, USA

477 Williamstown Road, Port Melbourne, VIC 3207, Australia

314–321, 3rd Floor, Plot 3, Splendor Forum, Jasola District Centre,
New Delhi – 110025, India

79 Anson Road, #06–04/06, Singapore 079906

Cambridge University Press is part of the University of Cambridge.

It furthers the University's mission by disseminating knowledge in the pursuit of education, learning, and research at the highest international levels of excellence.

www.cambridge.org
Information on this title: www.cambridge.org/9781108426626
DOI: 10.1017/9781108637657

© Jake Goldenfein 2020

This publication is in copyright. Subject to statutory exception and to the provisions of relevant collective licensing agreements, no reproduction of any part may take place without the written permission of Cambridge University Press.

First published 2020

A catalogue record for this publication is available from the British Library.

Library of Congress Cataloging-in-Publication Data
NAMES: Goldenfein, Jake, author.
TITLE: Monitoring laws : profiling and identity in the world state / Jake Goldenfein, Cornell Tech, Cornell University.
DESCRIPTION: New York, NY : Cambridge University Press, 2019.
IDENTIFIERS: LCCN 2019020265 | ISBN 9781108426626
SUBJECTS: LCSH: Electronic surveillance – Law and legislation. | Government information – Law and legislation. | Behavioral assessment. | Rule of law. | Biometric identification – Government policy. | Criminal behavior, Prediction of. | Electronic surveillance – Government policy. | Law enforcement – Government policy. | Civil rights. | Privacy, Right of.
CLASSIFICATION: LCC K3264.C65 G65 2019 | DDC 345/.052–dc23
LC record available at https://lccn.loc.gov/2019020265

ISBN 978-1-108-42662-6 Hardback

Cambridge University Press has no responsibility for the persistence or accuracy of URLs for external or third-party internet websites referred to in this publication and does not guarantee that any content on such websites is, or will remain, accurate or appropriate.

Contents

Acknowledgements		*page* viii
1	**Monitoring Laws**	1
	Profiling	3
	Information Law and Identity	6
	Building the World State	9
	Law in the World State	12
	Legal Identity in the World State	14
	Outline	17
2	**The Image and Institutional Identity**	21
	Photographic Knowledge	23
	Police Photography and Criminological Objectivity	28
	Police Photography and Identification	31
	The Measure of Criminality	34
	Police Photography and Human Knowability	38
	Conclusion	40
3	**Images and Biometrics – Privacy and Stigmatisation**	42
	Privacy and Police Photography	42
	Constitutional Privacy Protections	47
	Privacy, Identification, Stigmatisation	51
	Facial Recognition	58
	Conclusion	62

4	Dossiers, Behavioural Data, and Secret Speculation	64
	Detectives and Dossiers	66
	The Offence of Dossiers	71
	Inaccuracy, Secrecy, Inaccessibility	72
	Images and Text: Biology and Behaviour	73
	Conclusion	76
5	Data Subject Rights and the Importance of Access	78
	Privacy's Access Failure	80
	What Is a Data Subject?	82
	What Are Data Subject Rights?	88
	Consent	95
	Data Subject as Legal Subject	97
	Conclusion	98
6	Automation, Actuarial Identity, and Law Enforcement Informatics	99
	From Commerce to Crime	101
	Low-Level Automation	102
	High-Level Profiling	108
	Conclusion	113
7	Algorithmic Accountability and the Statistical Legal Subject	114
	Institutional Transparency	116
	Automated Decision-Making and Profiling in the GDPR and LED	119
	A Right to Explanation?	123
	Fairness	129
	The Technologies of Algorithmic Accountability	132
	Conclusion	134
8	From Photographic Image to Computer Vision: Neural Networks and Identity in the World State	135
	Personality Computation	137
	Computational Empiricism	143
	Measurement and Representation	146
	Computational Empiricism as a Dominant Epistemology	149
	Subjectivity and Cybernetics	152
	Conclusion	157

9	**Person, Place, and Contest in the World State**	158
	New Norms in the World State	159
	Contestation for Algorithmic Accountability	166
	Context as Normative Parameter in the World State	168
	(Legal) Identity as Interface	170
	Conclusion	177
10	**Law and Legal Automation in the World State**	178
	Profiling in the World State	182
Index		185

Acknowledgements

This text is the product of an enormous amount of teamwork, collegiality, and mentorship over many years, across various institutions. First, at Melbourne Law School, where I completed my PhD under Megan Richardson and Andrew Kenyon. Without their critical eyes, conceptual rigour, grammatical pedantry, heated debate, passion for the material, wisdom, life mentoring, generosity, kindness, and patience I would be absolutely nowhere. So much of my thinking and political disposition was shaped by conversations with my peers and colleagues there (and elsewhere in the Melbourne community), including Cait Storr, James Parker, Tom Andrews, Rose Parfitt, Sara Dehm, Maria Elander, Julia Dehm, Mark Trabsky, Laura Peterson, Adam Molnar, Pete Chambers, Julian Thomas, Ellie Rennie, and many more. I also need to thank my brilliant colleagues and mentors at Swinburne Law School, especially Dan Hunter for his guidance, as well as Amanda Scardamaglia, Jeremy Kingsley, and many others. I've also benefited hugely from the guidance of Helen Nissenbaum at Cornell Tech, along with my brilliant colleagues Michael Byrne, Elizabeth O'Neil, Yvonne Wang, Eran Toch, Erica Du, Laura Forlano, Lauren Van Haaften-Schick, and Marijn Sax, and been generously supported by the National Science Foundation under Grant SES-1650589. An incredibly special thanks to Jessie Taft whose assistance was invaluable. I also want to thank others in the community at NYU, including Julia Powles, Mark Verstraete, Ashley Gorham, Mason Marks, and Sebastian Benthall, as well as the Simons Institute for the Theory of Computing at UC, Berkeley, who briefly hosted me during their 2019 privacy programme. Since the beginning of this project, many significant life events passed including the coming of a daughter and the formation of a family. There is no way any of this would be possible without Lara Thoms and Alexandra Frith, and they have my love and respect. Without their support, motivation, general life-guidance, and the fact that they were willing to give up their own work to look after our child Goldie Thoms, this would have been impossible. I've also received incredible support from others in my family (and co-habitees), including Dia Goldenfein, Marc Goldenfein, Julias Rath, Stefan Grudza, Noni Simmons, and Colin Trechter.

1

Monitoring Laws

Part of this book was written at the State Library of Victoria in Melbourne and a small amount was written at the British Library in London. Designed by architect Joseph Reed (who also designed the UNESCO World Heritage Royal Exhibition Building in Melbourne), the Victorian library opened in 1856. The La Trobe Reading Room, or 'Dome Room', however, where the majority of my time was spent, opened in 1913. At the time it was the largest concrete dome in the world and an advanced piece of technology. The space is striking, not only for its scale and ambiance, but also for the arrangement of desks stretching outwards in rows from a central plinth towards the room's periphery. The configuration exposes each scholar to an (often absent) invigilator, capable of monitoring the entire area. Although several important features of Jeremy Bentham's panopticon are absent from this layout, there remains a gentle social pressure ensuring that nobody is talking or writing in the library books. In London, the British Library on Euston Road opened more recently, in 1998. Its reading rooms bear little resemblance to the historic style of the State Library in Victoria. There are no observation posts for staff nor are rooms arranged to ensure the visibility of readers to a central observer. Rather, each room is saturated with a grid of closed-circuit video cameras. Each row of desks is exposed to at least one camera mounted in the bulkhead, monitoring the length of the row, with more cameras on orthogonal walls. Under the electronic eyes of the British Library the feeling is that *you* are the one being read.

In contemporary life, individuals are exposed to *reading* – analysis and interpretation by an external agent – in multiple contexts, be it through ordinary human interaction or remotely via technological mediation. Pattern recognition and prediction are intuitive human decision-making processes, and individuals engage these cognitive exercises throughout their interaction with the world. But as our social environments are increasingly mediated by digital technologies, the character of the decision-making that reads and interprets us changes. One significant change is the degree to which those decisions and interpretations are performed by automated agents. Another change is the degree to which knowledge generated by autonomous agents is becoming a central way of understanding.

The integration of computation into everyday life has produced striking social transformations. We now inhabit new infrastructures of 'planetary scale computation' that involve massively complex systems of data collection, retention, and processing,[1] and generate immense quantities of knowledge about the world and the people within it. As Mark Andrejevic, Alison Hearn, and Helen Kennedy argue, 'it is now axiomatic to claim that we are in the "age of big data" and are witnessing a quantitative (and perhaps qualitative) "revolution" in human knowledge, driven by accompanying forms of data mining and analytics'.[2] As many contemporary scholars have shown, this type of knowledge-generating data analysis is visible in credit, and insurance scoring, healthcare, the provision of public services, behavioural advertising, law enforcement and policing, intelligence and security practices, criminal justice decisions like bail, sentencing and parole, employment and human resources practices, and many other areas.[3] Along with whatever benefits these tools might bring to scientific research, the application of methods from the physical sciences to human behavioural analysis means this computational society is also becoming one of social scoring, risk assessment, and predictive policing.

We are also entering a new phase in the nature and scale of data collection and analysis. For decades, the primary stuff of big data, at least for scholars of digital surveillance and privacy, has been the 'transactional' data typically created by interacting with online environments.[4] However, this data is increasingly supplemented with data captured directly from the 'real world' with sensors, and transformed into understanding through the unique statistical and pattern matching capacities of machine learning and neural networks. These technologies and practices translate the physical world into the symbolic register of computation, while simultaneously producing decisions and classifications that are expressed in the physical world and its objects. Automated agents now look, listen, measure, and act in ways that hybridise informational and physical environments into cyber-physical systems. When those systems include people and their behaviour, that hybridisation requires an understanding of individuals as compatible and co-extensive with the symbolic processing logics of computation and statistical knowledge systems. As the world is translated into computational registers, labelled, classed, categorised, and classified, we thus encounter new epistemologies premised on extremely granular measurement and extremely powerful computation. As the tools develop further,

---

[1] As described in Benjamin H Bratton, *The Stack: On Software and Sovereignty* (MIT Press, 2015).
[2] Marc Andrejevic, Alison Hearn, and Helen Kennedy, 'Cultural Studies of Data Mining: Introduction' (2015) 18(4–5) *European Journal of Cultural Studies* 379, 379.
[3] Cathy O'Neil, *Weapons of Math Destruction: How Big Data Increases Inequality and Threatens Democracy* (Crown Random House, 2016); Virginia Eubanks, *Automating Inequality: How High-Tech Tools Profile, Police, and Punish the Poor* (St Martin's Press, 2018); Danielle Keats Citron and Frank Pasquale, 'The Scored Society: Due Process of Automated Predictions' (2014) 89 *Washington Law Review* 1.
[4] Oscar H Gandy Jr, 'Statistical Surveillance' in Kirstie Ball, Kevin Haggerty, and David Lyon (eds) *Routledge Handbook of Surveillance Studies* (Routledge, 2012) 125.

rather than approximating people through reduction and heuristics, data science appears to be embracing a narrative of 'revelation' – of expressing the truth about its subjects. This logic of revelation, the idea that humans are best understood through the behavioural and informational patterns they generate, and that those behavioural patterns can be put to work or optimised towards certain goals, are becoming the defining characteristics of contemporary surveillance culture.

PROFILING

The primary data inputs for the automated analysis of people are biological and behavioural data. The creation and processing of those datasets, and the law's response, is the primary material of this book. But the information storage and processing that, it is argued here, began with photography, crude biometrics, and intelligence dossiers, are entering a new phase through the technologies, techniques, and philosophies of data science. The legal language for this type of decision-making, classification, and knowledge generation about people is 'profiling'. It is non-controversial that profiling as a form of knowledge production is an inherent and necessary element of ordinary decision-making. Reductionist thought processes enable quick, functional choices. The term profiling is etymologically connected to the artistic reproduction of a 'half face' (as opposed to a 'full face'),[5] as well as the more textual notion of summarising a person in writing – both suggesting reductive representations used to capture identity or character. At a broad social level, these decision-making processes include 'an ongoing distribution and cataloguing of information about the desires, habits, and location of individuals and groups'.[6] Within law enforcement specifically, that manifests as 'a process whereby behaviours and/or actions exhibited in crime are assessed and interpreted to form predictions concerning the characteristics of the probable perpetrator(s) of the crime'.[7] In certain administrative contexts, these profiling decisions constitute instances of states deploying technologies to count, tabulate, and classify (and thereby define) their subjects,[8] what Ian Hacking calls 'the idea of making up people'.[9] What profiling means in the context of contemporary computational environments is the subject of this book. It is argued that new profiling exercises, while building on the logics, politics, rationales, epistemologies, and techniques of older surveillance systems, also involve new knowledge paradigms and new consequences such as behavioural optimisation and other forms of manipulation. Beyond the epistemic features of 'big data' that have elsewhere been summarised as 'heterogeneous, unstructured, trans-semiotic,

---

[5] Samuel Johnson, *A Dictionary of the English Language* (London, 1755) 1580.
[6] Greg Elmer, *Profiling Machines: Mapping the Personal Information Economy* (MIT Press, 2004) 9.
[7] Richard Kocsis, *Criminal Profiling: Principles and Practice* (Springer, 2006) 2.
[8] Ian Hacking, *The Taming of Chance* (Cambridge University Press, 1990) 2.
[9] Ibid 6. See also Ian Hacking, 'Making Up People' (2006) 28(16) *London Review of Books* 23.

decontextualized, [and] agnostic',[10] the way these technologies are put to work, as particularly visible in the application of neural networks to image classification for instance, represents a new type of 'computational empiricism', buoyed by new relationships between states and private industry that produces computational products, services, and infrastructures. Profiling in the form of behaviour and personality computation is no longer about categorisation into consumer groups or the creation of credit risk scores, it is about building models of individuals that can direct behaviour towards any end.[11] It is about knowing people better than they can know themselves.

On one hand, some scholars reject any inherent problematisation of profiling as a decision-making practice, even in areas where they have been historically controversial like law enforcement.[12] For example, Frederick Schauer believes that profiling based on 'actuarial' processes (as opposed to 'clinical' methods which rely on subjective expert opinion) of 'attributing to the entire category certain characteristics ... that are probabilistically indicated by membership in the category, but that still may not be possessed by a particular member of the category'[13] are acceptable following an appropriate cost/benefit analysis. He believes only generalisations without sound statistical basis should be avoided, and accordingly argues that issues of 'racial profiling' by police, for instance, are actually problems of racism not of profiling.[14] On the other hand, scholars like Bernard Harcourt argue that reliance on statistics in profiling actually produces 'hidden distortions with significant costs for society'.[15] Others have also argued that purely numerical approaches may be 'iniquitously ideological' in their promotion of a particular worldview.[16] The position taken in this book is that there are consequences to embracing purely numerical and statistical approaches to understanding and assessing people, whether or not those assessments are true or statistically valid. Indeed, the nature of knowledge and decision-making has changed. Traditional opinion and subjective clinical decisions[17] are increasingly marginalised in favour

[10] Shoshana Zuboff, 'Big Other: Surveillance Capitalism and the Prospects of an Information Civilization' (2015) 30 *Journal of Information Technology* 75, 76.
[11] Maurits Kaptein and Dean Eckles, 'Selecting Effective Means to Any End: Futures and Ethics of Persuasion Profiling' (2010) *Persuasive Technology* 82.
[12] See, e.g., Tom Tyler and Cheryl Wakslak, 'Profiling and Police Legitimacy: Procedural Justice, Attributions of Motive, and Acceptance of Police Authority' (2004) 42(2) *Criminology* 253.
[13] Frederick Schauer, *Profiles, Probabilities, and Stereotypes* (Belknap Press, 2006) 4.
[14] Ibid, see, e.g., ch 7 'The Usual Suspects'.
[15] Bernard Harcourt, *Against Prediction: Profiling, Policing and Punishing in an Actuarial Age* (University of Chicago Press, 2006) 106. Harcourt argues, for example, that there is an overlooked social cost to profiling which includes the costs of additional incapacitation and incarceration, and that profiling problematically shapes conceptions of justice on the basis of a specific theory of punishment.
[16] Justin Clemens and Adam Nash, 'Being and Media: Digital Ontology after the Event of the End of Media' (2015) 24 *The Fibreculture Journal* 6, 19.
[17] See, e.g., Barbara Underwood, 'Law and the Crystal Ball: Predicting Behavior with Statistical Inference and Individualized Judgment' (1979) 88 *Yale Law Journal* 1408 where she defines 'clinical' approaches at 1432: 'One way to describe the difference between clinical and statistical methods is to

of 'machinic objectivity', and 'judgement' is replaced by computation.[18] The belief that purely computational mechanisms offer the most desirable pathways to knowledge also reflects an ideological and political commitment likely to favour entities with the largest computers. An all-out rejection of the actuarial or statistical paradigm, however, seems less and less realistic, indicating the need to conceptualise new mechanisms within this model of governing that show a capacity to reduce its problematic effects.

The legitimacy of a profiling exercise is the domain of law. Legal regimes form part of the environment in which the merit of particular ways of knowing are evaluated. Legal regimes facilitate or constrain technologies, practices, and ideas. This book accordingly examines contemporary profiling techniques, and their antecedents, as figures in the law and legal thinking, as well as the legal formulations that have emerged as a result. The legal fields in which these responses are most visible include the information law domains of 'privacy' and 'data protection', as well as the emerging paradigm of 'algorithmic accountability'. As the technologies, techniques, and narratives behind profiling change, we similarly see shifts in the legal doctrines addressing these systems. Legal limitations on surveillance and profiling have historically sought to reduce exposure to observation, increase transparency in data collection, retention, and profiling, and now, insist on fairness and interpretability in human computation. In other words, law has addressed profiling as a way of knowing by preventing access to individuals (or storage of information that might lead to certain decisions); by affording surveillance subjects the right to participate in the generation of knowledge about them; by ensuring that technical systems encode the world and the people within it according to certain statistical definitions of fairness; and potentially insisting on explanation of how automated profiling and decision-making systems achieve their outputs. Further, as the *substance* of legal protection has changed, we also see the actual formats and technologies of law evolve. For instance, whereas traditional privacy actions are connected to constitutionally protected individual rights, data protection also embraces diffuse bureaucratic compliance tools. The emerging fields of fairness and accountability change the nature of legal enforcement again, by embracing infrastructural and technological implementations that challenge traditional understandings of what constitutes law, legality, and legal subjectivity.

This book tries to account for, and contextualise, the emergence of these legal responses to profiling by understanding the technological narratives to which they are oriented. In doing so, the book also demonstrates how and why

---

say that clinical methods pay more attention to individual applicants, and statistical methods pay more attention to the rules for selecting them.'

[18] Hacking, above n 8, 3. The full quotation reads: 'Probability cannot dictate values, but it now lies at the basis of all reasonable choice made by officials. No public decision, no risk analysis, no environmental impact, no military strategy can be conducted without decision theory couched in terms of probabilities. By covering opinion with a veneer of objectivity, we replace judgment by computation.'

contemporary profiling practices transcend the legal tools we presently have to limit their effect. That transcendence, it is argued, is a product of the way contemporary profiling and data science practices construct and enact certain narratives of the self and identity. Those narratives, while increasingly accepted in the politics and practices of governing, are what the dominant legal paradigms reject, but with less and less success. How to re-think the shape and utility of legal notions of identity within a changing technological context is thus a critical question animating this book.

INFORMATION LAW AND IDENTITY

One influential understanding of privacy, data protection, and even algorithmic accountability, in their application to profiling, is that these legal systems protect individuals by protecting 'identity'.[19] That is, law operates to prevent an entity from *improperly* constructing a subject identity and making it the basis for further decision-making. For example, privacy law, at least in European privacy jurisprudence, has played a role in imposing limitations on what state entities can retain in administrative and law enforcement filing systems in order to prevent stigmatisation.[20] This is a different deployment of privacy law than preventing the unauthorised disclosure of private information, intrusion on seclusion, or even protections of reputation.[21] The protection of identity is not necessarily concerned with the dissemination of private information or the production of a problematic *public* image. Rather, these legal regimes operate to limit certain interpretive exercises by restricting what information can be used to make decisions. Data protection similarly protects identity by affording a degree of transparency over retained information. Data protection, or 'information privacy' regimes typically provide 'data subject rights' for eliminating inaccuracy or irrelevance in data holdings. Those rights enable individuals to impose their own self-image into data-processing environments by ensuring retained data somehow corresponds to the data subject's understanding of themself.

That in certain technological contexts, privacy might be best understood as a 'freedom from unreasonable constraints on the construction of one's own identity' has therefore been a theme in the information law scholarship since at least the 1990s.[22] For instance, Robert Post saw privacy's protection of 'autonomy' in 'the ability of persons to create their own identity and in this way to define

---

[19] See, e.g., Paul De Hert, A Right to Identity to Face the Internet of Things? (2007) UNESCO https://pure.uvt.nl/ws/portalfiles/portal/1069135/de_Hert-Paul.pdf, 1.
[20] S and Marper v. UK [2008] Eur Court HR 1581.
[21] See, e.g., Tanya Aplin and Jason Bosland, 'The Uncertain Landscape of Article 8 of the ECHR: The Protection of Reputation as a Fundamental Human Right' in Andrew Kenyon (ed) *Comparative Defamation and Privacy Law* (Cambridge University Press, 2016).
[22] Philip Agre and Marc Rotenberg, 'Introduction' in Philip Agre and Marc Rotenberg (eds) *Technology and Privacy: The New Landscape* (MIT Press, 1997) 7–8.

themselves'.[23] Benjamin Goold argued that privacy 'is not simply about the keeping of secrets or the restriction of access to information. Rather, it is also about maintaining a degree of control over one's identity'.[24] And Mireille Hildebrandt has claimed that in the era of profiling, privacy's connection to identity 'seems a more apt way to define privacy than definitions that focus on the sharing of personal data or on adherence to the purpose specification and the purpose limitations principles'.[25] However, 'identity' is also an exceedingly difficult concept to define, let alone operationalise in law. Indeed, it is argued here that the mismatch between notions of identity that animate existing legal protections and how contemporary data science conceptualises identity are causing what feels like a further loss of legal control over technological practices.

Ideas of identity deployed in the legal analyses are typically derived from certain philosophical models of identity, particularly 'narrative' theories. Scholars interrogating the relationship between information law and identity often invoke the work of Paul Ricoeur, and his notions of *ipse* and *idem* identity to provide an account of the multifaceted dimensions of identity construction.[26] This division between 'self' and 'sameness' identity, elsewhere contextualised as 'narrative' and 'categorical' identity, and even 'internal' and 'external' identity, structures the legal ideas that address when 'these two conceptions of identity come into competition', or 'when the categorical overlaps, contradicts and supplants the narrative'.[27] Goold, for instance, describes how certain surveillance practices generate a threat to identity that may be actionable in law, when 'an increasingly sophisticated array of surveillance and data processing techniques, which enable information to be acquired and shared at almost zero-cost ... threaten to establish the "categorical identity" as the primary means by which we are known – to the state and, more disturbingly, to each other.'[28]

The correspondence between internal and external life and appearance, the duality of identity, and its relationship to law and images, also has roots in psychoanalytic arguments by authors like French jurist Pierre Legendre. In retelling the story of Narcissus in his *Introduction to the Theory of the Image*, Legendre describes how the body is only presented for perception by others through means of an image.[29] He argues that through the body's translation into representation, it loses its status as a biological object and becomes something fictional or constructed, and

---

[23] Robert Post, 'Three Concepts of Privacy' (2001) 89 *The Georgetown Law Journal* 2086, 2092.
[24] Benjamin Goold, 'Privacy, Identity, Security' in Benjamin Goold and Liora Lazarus (eds) *Security and Human Rights* (Hart, 2007) 45, at 63.
[25] Mireille Hildebrandt, 'Legal Protection by Design: Objections and Refutations' (2011) 5(2) *Legisprudence* 223, 232.
[26] In particular, Paul Ricoeur, *Oneself as Another* (University of Chicago Press, 1992).
[27] Goold, above n 24, 63.
[28] Ibid 68.
[29] Pierre Legendre, 'Introduction to the Theory of the Image: Narcissus and the Other in the Mirror' (Peter Goodrich and Alain Pottage trans) (1997) 8(1) *Law and Critique* 3.

that the self-produced subject only emerges through being a target of seeing – that is, an object seen by someone else. Roland Barthes famously explored similar effects instituted by the camera in *Camera Lucida*, describing the photograph as the advent of the self as other – 'a cunning dissociation of consciousness from identity'[30] – and the experience of being photographed as a transformation from subject into object, whereby 'others – the Other – do not dispossess me of myself, [rather] they turn me ferociously, into an object, they put me at their mercy, at their disposal, classified in a file, ready for the subtlest deceptions'.[31] The reification and loss of control over those sites of outward appearance, and the transformation of an individual into an object and its classification in a file, thus threaten identity by being inimical to the way that subjects produce themselves – as argued by Cornelia Vismann, 'by administering themselves – by establishing a feedback with their own actions'.[32] Finding ways to give authority to that internal subjectivity has so far been the primary legal goal in this context.

For our purposes, there is also something significant in the relationship between images and data, especially images in the form of numerical data (i.e. as measurements). For instance, Giorgio Agamben identifies a turning point in the social and technological understanding of identity when individuals and their images were subjected to anthropometrics and biometrics.[33] The invention of photography and biometrics is where Agamben locates the end of external identity as a product of how we are recognised socially, and the beginning of a new institutional construction of identity informed by surveillance images and measurements. With the biometrics of Alphonse Bertillon (described in Chapter 2), Agamben argues 'for the first time in the history of humanity, identity was no longer a function of the social "persona" and its recognition by others, but rather a function of biological data, which could bear no relation to it'.[34]

For Agamben, biometrics represent a critical turning point in identity construction, especially in their function of making identity registers and archives searchable, and their being put in service of building institutional mechanisms for knowing people. That institutional capture of outward identity also commenced the elimination of space for an 'ethical' relationship to the image, a space for interpretation between the internal narrative of the individual and their outward appearance. It thus generated, in Agamben's words, 'naked life, a purely biological datum', or 'identity without the person'. This process of eliminating the interpretive space between individual and image that began with photography and anthropometrics has only amplified with the biometric and behavioural data analyses performed by

[30] Roland Barthes, *Camera Lucida* (Richard Howard trans, Vintage, 2000) [trans of *Camera Lucida* (first published 1980)] 12.
[31] Ibid 14.
[32] Cornelia Vismann, *Files: Law and Media Technology* (Geoffrey Winthrop-Young trans, Stanford University Press, 2008) 112 [trans of *Akten, Medientechnik und Recht* (first published 2000)].
[33] Giorgio Agamben, *Nudities* (Stanford University Press, 2010) at 46.
[34] Ibid 50.

machine learning, in the service of commercial, political, and law enforcement endeavours. Antoinette Rouvroy describes the result of this 'crisis of representation' in our contemporary political and economic paradigm, noting:

> There is no longer any subject in fact. It is not only that there is no longer any subjectivity, but it is that the very notion of subject is itself being completely eliminated thanks to this collection of infra-individual data; these are recomposed at a supra-individual level under the form of profile. You no longer ever appear.[35]

In many ways, the capture of biometric (as well as behavioural) data was the beginning of the end of identity defined by representation – that is, as defined by a separation between the thing and its appearance. That separation has only further disappeared in institutional identity's encounter with computation.

Since the Second World War, the discipline of cybernetics, in its various expressions and iterations, has generated new understandings of identity and self, technologically oriented more around computation than images. This intellectual tradition, informed by inter-disciplinary collaboration between communications, mathematics, biology, and engineering, as well as neuro, behavioural, and cognitive sciences, conceptualised the human mind as a symbolic information-processing machine, that could be modelled in purely informational and computational terms, and extended into information-processing networks.[36] As we will see, narratives of total human computability and control, but also new models of human autonomy, emerge from the shadow of cybernetic thinking. Central to these ideas however, in both their troubling and more emancipatory expressions, is a rejection of the person behind the mask as an unknowable and mysterious kernel of inward 'self' identity, and an embrace of identity as a systemic concept defined by dynamics of information flow.

BUILDING THE WORLD STATE

The 'world state' is a metaphor. It is not intended to denote the existence of a global single state or 'new world order'. That said, it does reference the changing nature of state-hood, the fact that geographic designations of jurisdiction and sovereignty have become increasingly strange, and that what we once associated with the state can now be described as a register of governance enacted by both traditional institutions as well as technology platforms. To that end, authors continue to explore how the ascendance of 'platform sovereignties', and the reality of infrastructures adopting sovereign registers of their own, means dealing with the challenges that planetary-

---

[35] Antoinette Rouvroy and Bernard Stiegler, 'The Digital Regimes of Truth: From the Algorithmic Governmentality to a New Rule of Law' (2016) 3 *La Deleuziana – Online Journal of Philosophy* 6, at 7 and 12.
[36] See, e.g., Paul N Edwards, *The Closed World: Computers and the Politics of Discourse in Cold War America* (MIT Press, 1997).

scale computation poses to law's geographic and jurisdictional legacies.[37] However, the primary use of the 'world state' metaphor here is to describe a process and condition by which the physical world, the objects and people within it, and their internal capacities and propensities, are translated into, and represented within, the symbolic register of computation. The phrase is taken from a computer vision textbook describing the outcome of an automated classification process.[38] The world (x) is measured and analysed, and a 'world state' (w) is produced. This metaphor also builds on long-standing thinking in media studies about how technologies and images that were intended to provide insight about the world ultimately end up blinding us. The 'world state' is what happens when the proliferation of technical images turns the world into an image, a collection of what Vilém Flusser calls 'states of things',[39] or where images become the only path to 'the real'.[40] This classic critique of technology insists that technological mediation inhibits access to 'the real' or 'the event'. In the case of photography, for instance, we are reminded that the images we create, while intended to be windows or maps for understanding the world around us, actually operate more like screens. Rather than expose the truth of the world, our images saturate the world, producing a veneer under which 'the real' slowly decays. A form of this critique is often levelled at profiling, wherein data produced through interactions with information environments are used as proxies for defining particular characteristics about us. Critiques of this 'scored society' describe how scores inadequately capture or represent us as individuals, and that proxies result in reduction, distortion, and error.[41] This intervention frames the harm to persons from profiling in terms of *loss* or reduction through representation.

In the computational society of the 'world state' – mapped by innumerable sensors that capture vision, sound, motion, and interactions with information systems – technology becomes *more* than a just system of representation. The 'world state' is not simply an informational layer that exists on top of, or adjacent to, the physical or 'real world' – it is enactive, it works, it governs, it decides. The result is a composite of physical and informational places, persons, and rules into networks of cyber-physical systems. The 'world state' is thus the dynamic and recursive cyber-physical reality that we increasingly inhabit and navigate. It is the contemporary iteration of

---

[37] Bratton, above n 1.
[38] Simon JD Prince, *Computer Vision: Models, Learning and Inference* (Cambridge University Press, 2012).
[39] Vilém Flusser, *Towards a Philosophy of Photography* (Anthony Mathews trans, Reaktion Books, 2000) originally published as *Für Eine Philosophie der Fotografie* (European Photography, 1983) 10.
[40] Jean Baudrillard, *Simulacra and Simulation* (Sheila Faria Glaser trans, University of Michigan Press 1994) originally published as *Simulacres et simulation* (Éditions Galilée, 1981).
[41] See, e.g., Cathy O'Neil, *Weapons of Math Destruction* (Crown Books, 2016); Virginia Eubanks, *Automating Inequality* (St Martin's Press, 2018); Danielle Citron and Frank Pasquale, 'The Scored Society: Due Process for Automated Decisions' (2014) 89 *Washington Law Review* 1.

a technological, social, political, and epistemological condition, that has been in development since the invention of photography. This book describes *some* of the technical, political, and regulatory logics that have played a role in building the 'world state', specifically in relation to profiling, and how those logics implicate human identity. Alongside insight into the character of the contemporary 'world state', the other goal of this book is to show how these logics have provoked or otherwise interacted with legal systems designed to constrain their effects. In other words, it describes law in the 'world state'.

Looking at the relationships between technology, profile, and law from the beginning of the transformations to identity outlined by Agamben, with the invention of photography and biometrics, demonstrates an ongoing dynamic between technological innovation, social narrative, political programme and legal response. Understanding that dynamic means understanding how the images registered by different surveillance technologies are each produced *and* read differently. These accounts show not only how such technologies register and record, but, following the work of Alan Sekula, how they establish the conditions and material sources from which knowledge and identity claims are derived, and how they have been, and continue to be, intrinsically connected to the production of political and juridical truths.[42]

Within the surveillance technologies and practices described in this book, the state remains a point of focus. The state has historically had a primary role in the systematic deployment of these profiling technologies, and pushed the narratives of necessity that led to their proliferation. The ascendance of statistical knowledge tools was similarly a product of early statecraft or the 'science of states', and the evolution of computation was a deeply military phenomenon.[43] However, the governing processes that began with text, filing cabinets, and photography in, for instance, law enforcement surveillance, have since been translated into contemporary exercises of data mining, predictive analytics, and machine learning – are increasingly the domain of the private sector. But while the contemporary dominance of data science is inextricably bound-up with private enterprise, it is also becoming difficult to meaningfully separate state and non-state entities and practices. States have increasingly become *users* of tech platforms with private companies offering data science-based profiling *services* to states, including in the domains of law enforcement, security, and criminal justice. Clearly commercial profiling practices have their own significant impacts and effects, but the relationships between state and private industry also implicates governance, and produces new sovereign formations. Both public and private entities are now participating in governmental decision-making and profiling, and at a level of significance that affects lives in meaningful ways. Determining the precise morphology of the private–public

[42] Allan Sekula, 'The Body and the Archive' (1986) 39 *October* 3.
[43] Edwards, above n 36.

complex is beyond the scope of this book. Instead, the focus is exercises of governance that have historically occurred at the register of the state, even if that governance is no longer performed exclusively by government as such. Profiling at this level defines access to the state's redistributive institutions, as well as law enforcement institutions' capacity to deprive liberty. As Walter Kirn wrote in *The Atlantic*, 'Google's data mines, presumably, exist merely to sell us products, but the government's models of our inner selves might be deployed to sell us stranger items. Policies. Programs. Maybe even wars.'[44] The reality, however, is that that Google's (and Amazon's, and Microsoft's, and Facebook's) data mines probably do that too. The focus here is thus shaped by the capacity to affect lives rather than the nature of the entity acting.

LAW IN THE WORLD STATE

The surveillance practices described in the following chapters typically involve creating representations for the sake of uncovering *who* a person is, what *type* of person they are, and *how* they might behave in the future. The laws that developed in response were accordingly concerned, at some level at least, about returning control of identity to the inner self by enforcing a correspondence between 'narrative' and 'categorical' notions of identity. The invention of photography and biometrics, however, initiated the institutional belief that the image or index may be what really matters in the determination of identity. Data science, in certain applications, extends this further, rejecting the separation between narrative and categorical, and promoting the position that patterns of behaviour can be the critical determinants of legal and political subjectivity.[45]

As these surveillance practices become more prevalent, and more determinative of our political, legal, spatial, inter-personal, and commercial experiences, a question arises as to whether trying to enforce, through law, a faithful correspondence between internal and external identity is the most meaningful or appropriate approach. The legal programme, visible in privacy and data protection for instance, of attempting to retain control over the interpretive space between person and representation loses its impact when the dominant technical and political narratives accept that such a space has disappeared. Legal narratives around opacity and transparency, for instance, emerged to deal with the potential for misrepresentation, stigmatisation, or inaccuracy produced through technological image-making, data registration, and archiving. However, as techno-political narratives and contexts change, the capacity to insist on a reality or a truth separate and antecedent to the reality generated by technological representations has

[44] Walter Kirn, 'If You're Not Paranoid, You're Crazy' (November 2015) *The Atlantic* www.theatlantic.com/magazine/archive/2015/11/if-youre-not-paranoid-youre-crazy/407833/.
[45] See, e.g., N Katherine Hayles, *How We Became Posthuman: Virtual Bodies in Cybernetics, Literature, and Informatics* (University of Chicago Press, 1999).

weakened. Images, we are told, take us *closer* to the truth. Profilers tell us that the world of infinite possibility now resides in the data rather than in the human spirit. Under those conditions, claims of misrepresentation typically result in *more* surveillance, producing more accurate profiling, creating a cyclical and reiterative techno-politics of perfection. The result is a more accurate, more reliable, more pervasive, less contestable computational empiricism, with a better stake in the epistemological territory of identity.

While maintaining control over one's identity remains a critical exercise, new strategies are needed in contemporary political and technological domains. We live more and more in a paradigm of governance through big data, or 'governance by the numbers'.[46] For Yarden Katz, 'Governance by the numbers works by first defining quantitative metrics and imposing them upon the world, and then using these metrics to "programme" behaviour through rankings and benchmarks.'[47] Under such conditions, we might insist that our identity is who we tell ourselves we are, but that is not the identity connected to our political, legal, administrative reality, and our legal tools need to develop accordingly. Profiles as 'representations' also no longer tell the whole story. The contemporary information-processing terrain engages a very different relationship between technology and human identity than that of the nineteenth or twentieth century. The informational dimension of social and political life has started to go beyond simple representation or documentation, it is now active, real-time, and recursive. In some applications, it is agential. This is to say, in certain examples, our profiles act as decision-making agents, following, to a degree, their own agendas. Data thus plays an *active* and automated role in our lives, guiding our decision-making and the decisions made about us, our privileges and statuses, and our experiences of policing, subjugation, and control. That ongoing feedback guides us through space, time, and activity. Images are similarly no longer simply registrations of a moment, they have become a form of communication between embodied persons and machinic systems.

This book thus describes the existing information law paradigms that address profiling to protect identity, the idea of identity they protect, and the forms of legal subjectivity that are deployed to protect it. The book also presents an argument that these laws are attempting to enforce an idea of individual autonomy that ignores the degree to which our informational existence is part of our contemporary life. Notions of self and identity in the contemporary technological scenario are dramatically different from those implicated by the technologies and practices of the nineteenth and even twentieth century. The way humans are conceptualised by those building and using contemporary profiling technologies challenges the traditional view of liberal humanism, where, building from the enlightenment thinkers,

---

[46] Yarden Katz, 'Manufacturing an Artificial Intelligence Revolution' (2017) available https://papers.ssrn.com/sol3/papers.cfm?abstract_id=3078224, quoting Alan Supiot, *The Spirit of Philadelphia: Social Justice vs. The Total Market* (Verso, 2012) 13.
[47] Ibid.

the mind is posited as the seat of human identity.[48] And while the goal here is *not* to provide an account of the relationship between technology and true selfhood, it has become hard to deny that, as Luciano Floridi has remarked, technology is identity-generating.[49] Rather than lament 'what is left of man when reduced to naked life',[50] or insisting that there is a true internal self that must guide the interpretation of the external image, however, the goal here is to locate a form of legal subjectivity that is meaningful for contemporary experience.

To that end, Chapter 9 suggests a model of legal identity, premised on a composite of embodied and information personhood, that may have greater utility for constraining profiling in its emerging configurations. It is an idea of identity and indeed 'legal personality' intended to constrain the actions of others by providing an account of how certain activities might constitute harms to identity. Developing that idea of legal identity requires thinking about autonomy without re-inscribing the traditional liberal legal subject. It requires thinking about what a legal subject *is* or ought to be in the 'world state'. Barthes may have argued that 'the "private life" is nothing but that zone of space, of time, where I am not an image, an object' and that '[i]t is my *political* right to be a subject which I must protect'.[51] But perhaps, in the context of computation rather than photography, we need to think about how to protect that *subject* when its political and juridical experience is co-constituted by a physical body and a computationally defined pattern of information. To that end, the book tries to answer the question: what kind of legal subject should the law acknowledge or generate in this context? A computational 'law of persons' may require pluralised notions of legal subjectivity that reject the person as a stable juridical subject in favour of a definition based on the capacity to take action and be the abstract bearer of rights in a meaningful way for contemporary computational life.

LEGAL IDENTITY IN THE WORLD STATE

The legal person or legal subject is the bearer of rights and duties.[52] It is an entity with the capacity for legal relations, or rather 'the abstraction of which legal relations are predicated'.[53] Connal Parsley has tracked how, historically, representations and

---

[48] William Fulton, *Cybernetics* (2007) Chicago School of Media Theory https://lucian.uchicago.edu/blogs/mediatheory/keywords/cybernetics.
[49] The terms he uses are egopoieitic and 'informational structural realism' in Luciano Floridi, 'The Informational Nature of Personal Identity' (2011) 21 *Minds and Machines* 549. At 564 he says, 'In a different context (Floridi 2008b, 2011b), I have defended a view of the world as the totality of informational structures dynamically interacting with each other. If this is the case – or at least in order for a philosophy of personal identity to be consistent with such a view – selves too must be interpreted as informational structures.'
[50] Agamben, above n 33.
[51] Barthes, above n 30, 15.
[52] Bryant Smith, 'Legal Personality' (1928) 37(3) *Yale Law Journal* 283.
[53] Ibid 284.

images have actively afforded the very media of legal and political subjectivity.[54] In other words, the way we are addressed by the state has always been informed by representational concepts like *persona*, *dignitas*, and *imago* (each a species of image).[55] Parsley describes how historically the image or mask has constituted the outward site of political identity against which legal or political action is taken, as well as the location at which juridical rights accrue, with the natural or real person behind it remaining in the realm of the private.[56] There is accordingly a complex dynamic between a narrative and categorical identity in which the harm of profiling is defined as the privileging of the image over the subject, and a juridical reality that requires an 'image' of a person – a *persona* – to come to law for remedy. The argument made here is that we need to rethink the legal personality of the profiled subject as a mechanism to address the identity consequences of profiling itself. As Piyel Haldar notes:

> The existence of the legal subject is entirely dependent on its representation. Social, political or civil status ceases to have any standing unless it is channelled into being through the technology of the image ... [I]f there is no concept of the legal person without it being mediated through some form of technological apparatus, then the very format of that representational medium needs to be taken into account more seriously in order to gauge how legal subjectivity undergoes historical transformation. New paradigms of subjectivity emerge depending upon which means of representation, which forms of technological mediation, are assimilated by, and used in, the juridical field.[57]

One of this book's central projects is to investigate the nature of the legal subject under computational conditions, to think about what that type of legal subject might want from law, what kind of legal environment they exist in, what they might be able to obtain from law, and what kind of law that might be.

---

[54] Connal Parsley, 'The Mask and Agamben: The Transitional Juridical Technics of Legal Regulation' (2010) 14 *Law, Text, Culture* 12.

[55] Costas Douzinas, 'The Legality of the Image' (2000) 63(6) *The Modern Law Review* 813. Although photography is examined in Chapter 2 and computer vision in Chapter 8, the significance of 'images' and their relationship to identity in this context goes beyond the pictorial. As Raymond Williams notes, 'image' has long 'referred to mental conceptions, including a quite early sense of seeing what does not exist as well as what is not plainly visible' (Raymond Williams, *Keywords* (Croom Helm, 1976) 158). Even the notion of 'speculation', discussed in Chapter 3, is, according to Costas Douzinas writing in the introduction to Michael Stolleis's book *The Eye of the Law: Two Essays on Legal History* (CRC Press, 2008) at xiv, 'a visual strategy, the Latin cousin of [the Greek] Theoria'. Stolleis himself, at 13, points out that terms like 'speculation' and 'theory' derive from verbs meaning 'to look' or 'to see', suggesting that knowing is a form of (intellectual) seeing, at least of the outer face or shell (rather than of the essence), and that conceptual orientation also applies to broader categories of medium and format.

[56] Parsley, above n 54, 17.

[57] Piyel Haldar, 'Forensic Representations of Identity: The *Imago*, the X-ray and the Evidential Image' (2013) 7(2) *Law and Humanities* 129, 129.

Amongst the vast scholarship, there are distinctive approaches (as well as many sub-approaches) to thinking through 'legal subjectivity'. For instance, Ngaire Naffine describes three broad theorisations of legal person:

> [The first class of] theorists positively reject the claim that legal personality necessarily builds upon a metaphysical conception of the person. [The second class of] theorists seem to assume that humanity, rather than the narrower conception of personhood, is the basis of both moral and legal claims on others and the basis of legal personality. [The third class of] theorists alone invoke metaphysical persons, variously understood, as the basis of their definition of the legal person, but then their definition of the person cannot be said to represent the official legal view of personality.[58]

The idea of legal personality as pure analytical abstraction, described by Naffine as the first type of theory, is likely the oldest, and still most useful, conception. This positivist approach has also been useful in universalist liberal positivism. As John Chipman Gray, a professor at Harvard Law School wrote in 1908:

> Jurisprudence, in my judgment, need not vex itself about the 'abysmal depths of personality'. It can assume that a man is a real indivisible entity with body and soul; it need not busy itself with asking whether a man be anything more than a phenomenon or at best, merely a succession of states of consciousness. It can take him as a reality and work with him, as geometry works with points, lines and planes.[59]

However, others have looked more closely for the political content embedded within the legal person as abstraction. As legal theorist James Boyle points out, legal realists challenged the classical legal subject, and instead offered a vision of the subject that 'was particularized and substantively determined, shaped by the structure of social interaction to such an extent that [the legal subject] popped in and out of existence according to the dictates of public policy'.[60] In other words, the legal subject could be seen as historically, politically, and technologically specific, embodying certain policy ideas or political commitments, but still without referencing the metaphysical person. This understanding of the legal subject was a re-orienting of a Marxist critique towards liberal legal identity, exposing how 'a particular form of subject is brought into existence by capitalist relations of production and that this underpins the form that law gives to its subjects: individual, autonomous, possessive, self-responsible, bearers of rights'.[61] The point is to say that there is political and normative work in how we conceptualise the legal person, and what rights it bears,

---

[58] Ngaire Naffine, 'Who Are Law's Persons? From Cheshire Cats to Responsible Subjects' (2003) 66 *Modern Law Review* 346, 350.
[59] John Chipman Gray, *The Nature and Sources of the Law*, at 29 (1908, 2nd ed 1921) as quoted in James Boyle 'Is Subjectivity Possible? The Post-modern Subject in Legal Theory' 62 *University of Colorado Law Review* 489.
[60] Boyle above n 59, 519.
[61] Nikolas Rose and Mariana Valverde 'Governed by Law?' (1998) 7 *Social Legal Studies* 541, 548.

and that we can see the legal subject as contingent and historical, eschewing its ontological pre-suppositions, instead reflecting a particular political or material reality.

Although the abstraction of legal personality may have begun with the 'persona' in Roman Law as the technology for 'separating the identity of a real living subject from that of a purely artificial, fabricated role that is reserved and instituted at the level of juridical existence',[62] the composition of what those personas refer to has undergone ongoing change. This is because, as Mussawir and Parsley, as well as other authors like Lawrence White and Samir Chopra, argue, both historical and contemporary juridical formations of legal personality serve a 'pragmatic transactional purpose'.[63] That is why, for instance, beyond corporations and nation states, we now also see legal personality for entities like rivers, mountains, and waterfalls.[64] Legal persons are thus the products of interpretive problems of legal order. They are part of the solution to a regulatory puzzle. Throughout this book, the form of legal subject deployed to intermediate between profile and human is explored, and the possibility, utility, and desirability of new forms of legal subjectivity are evaluated.

OUTLINE

The book is divided into two streams that proceed side by side. The first focuses on how the 'world state' has been built, offering accounts of the collection and analysis of biological and behavioural data through various technologies, at various times, and for various purposes. By describing how these processes have emerged, evolved, and reiterated over time, the goal is to acquire insight into the logics, politics, and epistemological programme of the contemporary technological moment that includes behavioural, biological, psychological, and emotional profiling, geared towards different forms of behavioural engineering and optimisation. These chapters provide an account of the theorisations of identity that are put to work in those profiling exercises, and begin the process of trying to figure out what a legal subject in this environment might want from the law.

The second stream explores the emergence of law in the 'world state' with an account of the legal thinking that has evolved in relation to those profiling practices. This is not intended to be an exhaustive legal analysis, but rather a description of the most sophisticated jurisprudence as to how and why law deems certain profiling processes sufficiently objectionable to warrant legal intervention. It also examines the mechanisms by which such legal protection is, or has been, enacted. The goal of

---

[62] Ibid 45.
[63] Ibid 48.
[64] Erin O'Donnell and Julia Talbot-Jones, 'Creating Legal Rights for Rivers: Lessons from Australia, New Zealand, and India' (2018) 23(1) *Ecology and Society* 7; Edward Mussawir and Connal Parsley 'The Law of Persons Today: At the Margins of Jurisprudence' (2017) 11(1) *Law and Humanities* 44.

the analysis is to understand the complex dynamics between surveillance, identity, and law with a view to understanding how and why the legal thinking has evolved, and how and why it might evolve again. What we see as we move through these legal ideas is shifting normative expressions, shifting mechanisms of enforcement, and shifting legal persons that bear the relevant legal rights. This part of the book also investigates what forms of law might be useful for a legal subject, constituted partly by the patterns of information they generate and partly through embodiment, existing and operating simultaneously both in physical and informational space.

To that end, Chapter 2 describes the creation of photographic and biometric identity databases of criminal offenders for the sake of preventing recidivism. Being able to identify individuals through searchable image databases meant judges could accord 'proper' treatment to repeat offenders. Those systems of measurement developed in the context of a political rationality enthralled by the collection of social statistics for the sake of governance, a belief in the machinic objectivity of the photographic apparatus, and an ideology of biological fatalism animated by anthropology and criminology. This socio-technical context facilitated the formation of a social archive, within which undesirable and deviant identities took their place, as well as the first biometrics systems in which identity was reduced to numerical data. That is to say, this was also the beginning of the comprehensive reduction of the individual to numbers that could be recorded, manipulated, and transmitted.

Chapter 3 describes the legal regimes that have since come to address not only the practices of police photography in the context of arrest, but also police identification photography and video in public. It describes how legal rights to private life, particularly as expressed in Article 8 of the European Convention on Human Rights, slowly came to recognise that the building of an institutional identity was a meaningful and potentially objectionable practice. Accordingly, having identity information like images or other biometric data in a police filing system created a risk of stigmatisation for persons who had not been convicted of a crime. The chapter thus describes law's focus, not on photographic observation alone, but rather the use of photography, biometrics, fingerprints, and DNA profiling, as tools for 'systematisation'. That is, how law became concerned with the processing of images into identities and the building of identity databases – a process implicated in the socio-technical systems of contemporary automated facial recognition.

Chapter 4 extends the discussion of biological and anthropometric measurement with an account of the emergence of behavioural measurement and 'mass surveillance'. Behavioural data collection and analysis can be traced back to early intelligence surveillance and political policing. Agents would gather information, salient and trivial, from multiple sources, about individuals with no prior contact with the criminal justice system, in an effort to predict and pre-empt their future behaviour. Often this happened in secret, and was justified by the threat of political violence. This chapter argues that much of the political thinking and technical logics of the contemporary intelligence surveillance environment have their origin in nineteenth-century political policing. It also suggests that because this information gathering and analysis occurred in secret, it produced substantial social anxiety over the potential for inaccuracy.

Chapter 5 describes the legal ideas that emerged on one hand, to address what was perceived as a primary threat from dossiers – inaccuracy of assessment – and on the other hand, that the growth of government data gathering and statistical analysis through the twentieth century could become an 'intelligence' system capable of revealing or generating information about individuals. The chapter describes the relationship between data subject rights, the primary mechanisms for achieving access and rectification of file systems and databases, and the thinking that animates that call for transparency. In particular, it describes the evolution of data protection as a way to ensure that the discursive truth of the data subject – the primacy of self-image – would take precedence over their representation through the concept of informational self-determination. It also describes the somewhat less mainstream theorisation of data protection as serving the functional differentiation of society necessary for modern life.

Chapter 6 explores how the surveillance logics described in Chapters 2 and 4 have been transformed through the use of algorithms, predictive analytics, and artificial intelligence. Law enforcement information systems are extensions of the statistical criminology of the nineteenth century and the turn to individualised treatment that created the actuarial paradigm in twentieth-century penology. Combined with the post-9/11 logics of total data collection, the result is expansive intelligence systems, predictive policing, and risk assessments in criminal justice that recast identity as statistical distributions and logical operations within computational knowledge systems. Whereas early biological measurements were reducible to numbers, but needed supplementation with behavioural descriptions, eventually those behavioural descriptions had to similarly be quantified and reduced to measurements for the sake of computation. Any semantic content was then derived from pattern matching and statistical processes. The chapter also describes the increasing use of commercial proprietary software in government applications, as well as the shift from purposive analysis of targeted data to correlative analyses of disparate data sets to produce knowledge about the criminal propensities of individuals.

Chapter 7 outlines the emergence of algorithmic accountability as a package of legal ideas that, on one hand, attempts to impose administrative law mechanisms such as transparency and due process on automated decision-making systems, and on the other hand, is developing technological approaches to constraining machine learning. In particular, by ensuring the complex computational analysis of individuals occurs more 'fairly', and is more explainable. As well as describing the necessity of computational legal implementations that actively limit how data processing occurs, the chapter also outlines the risks that these mechanisms create of ceding to data science and its corporate stakeholders the epistemological terrain as to what types of calculations are 'fair' and what type of information constitutes an 'explanation'.

Chapter 8 describes the profiling project of computer vision, especially as animated by neural networks. It tracks how systems that use measurements of the physical world as data input operationalise a new form of computational empiricism that automates the process of representation in order to expose or reveal the truth of human identity. The chapter also describes how cybernetic visions of the human subject, that our patterns of information and behaviour are the true stuff of self, are being expressed in the transformation of profiles from representations into 'agents'. Tracking the proposition that our biological and behavioural data function as a type of epigenome operating with purpose and volition, the chapter describes how the processes of behavioural optimisation, premised on leveraging the information flow between profile, platform, and embodied person, work to direct behaviour towards particular goals.

Chapter 9 explores alternative approaches to the regulation of these emerging profiling practices. It describes some of the developing legal narratives in this space, in particular those that challenge human computability, or require the introduction of friction and gaps into information infrastructures as a way of interrupting them as systems of meaning. The chapter also describes the utility of concepts like 'context' for building boundaries and friction into information architectures, not simply in terms of information flow but also as normative principles of design for those architectures that influence and structure behaviour. And it finally suggests the shape of a new 'composite' legal person as a mechanism to constrain profiling behaviour by recognising identity as an 'interface' to the 'world state'. That legal is person is posited as a way to protect individuals from the effects of profiling without resorting to a liberal humanist subject.

The conclusion in Chapter 10 places the strategies discussed in Chapter 9 within the theoretical context of law and automation, and argues that as we build networks of technical relations between persons, objects, and informational infrastructure, we need new thinking about law and the types of protection it can afford. It argues that new systems of control that instrument environments towards certain goals rather than directly enabling or constraining behaviour are increasingly governing our engagement with informational environments, but are under-theorized by law. The chapter argues that we need to transcend the separation between physical and informational, and work on building appropriate techno-legal mechanisms. It suggests that we think about these emerging environments, and the legalities that they embedd, as emerging jurisdictions that do not undermine law, but rather offer law another form of expression.

2

The Image and Institutional Identity

There is a common custom among English sailors, of printing their family and Christian names upon their wrists, in well-formed and indelible characters; they do it that their bodies may be known in case of shipwreck. If it were possible that this practice should become universal, it would be a new spring for morality, a new source of power for the laws, an almost infallible precaution against a multitude of offences, especially against every kind of fraud in which confidence is required for success. Who are you, with whom I have to deal? The answer to this important question would no longer be liable to evasion.[1]

– Jeremy Bentham

The surveillance and profiling systems that form the subject of the following chapters began as systems for both confirming identity, and for tracking and predicting future behaviour. Looking at these surveillance technologies and practices at the time of their emergence offers an insight into the logics, motivations, and politics behind their continued use. It also gives us a starting point to assess how these techniques have changed, how alternative technologies implicate questions of identity in different ways, and how evolving legal narratives relate to these social, political, and technical systems.

The first surveillance system described here is the programme of 'judicial photography' and its transformation into what became the Habitual Criminal Registers. The logics of identity that began with judicial photography are visible on almost every physical identification token we carry with us. These images link an institutional database to a presence or event in the real world. Photography, and the criminal archive it quickly generated, were a large part of law enforcement's transition into an information technology, and are closely linked to contemporary programmes of metrification, quantification and statistical analysis. There are several fantastic histories of the nation state's relationship to statistics, probabilities and governance,[2] but

---

[1] Jeremy Bentham, *Principles of Penal Law* (William Tate, 1843) Part III 'Indirect Means of Preventing Crimes' Chapter IX 'To Facilitate the Recognition and Finding of Individuals'.

[2] See, e.g., Theodore M Porter, *The Rise of Statistical Thinking, 1820–1900* (Princeton University Press, 1986); Stephen M Stigler, *The History of Statistics: The Measurement of Uncertainty Before 1990* (Harvard University Press, 1986); Ian Hacking, *The Taming of Chance* (Cambridge University Press, 1990).

training these knowledge systems at the level of the individual was deeply connected to practices in criminology and criminal justice. In judicial proceedings, the question 'who are you, with whom I have to deal?' was directed at reducing recidivism by preventing migratory criminal classes from representing themselves to police and judges as first-time offenders. Answering that question required new ways to identify criminals remotely, for which the evolution of police and judicial photography was highly suited.[3] That use of photography, however, was already coloured by photography's deployment in the nineteenth-century moral science of social improvement. The criminological imperative of using photography to *improve* society strongly influenced how criminal identification images would be used and interpreted long into the future. The result was a powerful system for keeping track of offenders, and a new way to define the criminal classes. As we shall see, judicial photography was not a stand-alone technology or technique – it required sophisticated interactions with technologies of storage and classification, and also led to new types of bureaucratic filing systems. This amplified the state's relationship to individuals as mediated through technological processes, practices, and artefacts that produced people as sites of information to be interpreted and known.

Judicial and police photography have a history almost as long as the photographic image. Mugshots of Belgian prisoners have been dated as far back as 1843,[4] only a few years after the invention of the daguerreotype process,[5] and the idea that surveillance cameras would sweep city streets was postulated as early as 1869.[6] Technologies like the dry plate and half-tone processes,[7] and instantaneous photographic devices like the Eastman Kodak 'snap' camera facilitated surreptitious photography and the chance to 'catch people in the act'.[8] (These technologies also demonstrate how the story of photography is also a story of automation.[9]) Newspapers enthusiastically adopted those technologies not only to illustrate stories but also expose scandal. It was unsurprising then, that by 1890 legal scholars Warren and Brandeis argued for 'a right to be let alone', reacting

[3] The term 'Judicial Photography' was coined in Alphonse Bertillon, *La Photographie Judiciare* (Gauthier-Villars, 1890). That name reflects the early use of assisting judges in proper sentencing (of repeat offenders).
[4] Andre A Moenssens, 'The Origin of Legal Photography' (1962) 43 *Fingerprint and Identification Magazine*.
[5] Quentin Bajac, *The Invention of Photography: The First Fifty Years* (Ruth Taylor trans, Thames & Hundson, 2002) [trans of *L'Image Révélée L'Invention de la Photographie* (first published 2001)] 17–18, in which it is explained that Daguerre perfected his process in 1837 but did not announce it until 1939.
[6] Note, 'The Legal Purposes of Photography' (1869) 13 *Solicitors' Journal & Reporter* 425, 425.
[7] Bajac, above n 5, 127. This allowed photographs to be taken outside of a studio and images to be developed at the creator's leisure.
[8] Jennifer L Mnookin, 'The Image of Truth: Photographic Evidence and the Power of Analogy' (1998) 10 *Yale Journal of Law & the Humanities* 1, 12.
[9] See, e.g., Daniel Rubinstein, Johnny Golding, and Andy Fisher (eds) *On the Verge of Photography: Imaging Beyond Representation* (ARTicle Press, 2013) 49; Vilém Flusser, *Towards a Philosophy of Photography* (Anthony Mathews trans, Reaktion Books, 2000) [trans of *Für eine Philosophie der Fotografie* (first published 1983)].

to a new reality that 'instantaneous photographs and newspaper enterprise have invaded the sacred precincts of private and domestic life'.[10] In many jurisdictions, including England, the United States, and Australia, privacy law's relationship to the image is, to a large extent, extrapolated from that point – Warren and Brandeis' identification of the conflict between individual freedom and freedom of the press. As the publication of photographs in the press became more widespread after 1890, that idea of privacy was frequently interpreted as preventing the unauthorised *disclosure* of images by media institutions. However, this was not the only privacy-invading character of photography – it also became part of new systems of knowledge about people not necessarily to be disclosed, but to be deployed in new state identity archives. To that end, the 'objective' nature of photographic vision was turned on the criminal body and adopted for prison administration, sentencing, and eventually active policing in order to identify individuals as criminal or deviant. Those identity claims were legitimated by photography's perceived connection to knowledge and truth. Indeed, the objective interpretation of photographic images as artefacts of truth was an early example of technologies (as complexes of objects, practices, and narratives) dissimulating ideology and producing particular meanings about people, according to particular conventions. It also had radical consequences for the identity of photographic subjects.

Another critical feature of the use of photography for those purposes was its connection to the 'measurement' of individuals. Such measurement began with photographic registration, but eventually developed into complex clerical and archival systems that captured other forms of biological data to index photographs as artefacts of identification. The significance of this techno-juridical complex can hardly be overstated. It was the beginning of searchable individual institutional identification systems that included both an 'archival' identification (the linking of a particular criminal body to itself across space and time with the aim of establishing a history of past criminal activities that can be ascribed to a single body), as well as 'diagnostic' identity in terms of character or subjectivity being generated through the interpretation of archival documents.[11] With respect to profiling, that techno-juridical complex is the historical kernel of our contemporary socio-technical configuration.

PHOTOGRAPHIC KNOWLEDGE

As photography developed through the nineteenth century it became a medium of bourgeois self-identity. Collecting *carte de visite* style portraits and having one's

---

[10] Samuel Warren and Louis Brandeis, 'The Right to Privacy' (1890) 4 *Harvard Law Review* 193, 195.
[11] As defined in Simon Cole, *Suspect Identities: A History of Fingerprinting and Criminal Identification* (Harvard University Press, 2002) 305.

picture taken became enlightened gestures. For instance, an edition of *The Quarterly Review* noted in 1864: 'There is scarcely an educated lady, fashionable or unfashionable, whose table is not adorned with the album of *cartes de visite*, containing a full allowance of royalties, half-a-dozen leading statesmen, and a goodly row of particular friends'.[12] The public was also enamoured with photography's new technical domination of time (i.e. its archival character):

> It has forced the sun, which reveals to our senses every object around us, to write down his record in enduring characters, so that those who are far away or those who are yet unborn may read it. It has furnished to mankind a new kind of vision that can penetrate into the distant or the past – a retina as faithful as that of the natural eye, but whose impressions do not perish with the wave of light that gave them birth.[13]

However, alongside this 'social ameliorative' aspect of photography was its deployment as a 'socially repressive instrument'.[14] For example, historians Peter Hargraves and Roger Hamilton argue in *The Beautiful and the Damned* that 'we see a counterpart to the social portraiture of leading (and less exalted) figures of the age in the anthropological, medical, and judicial portraits designed to record, classify and control subject races, degenerate bodies and deviant individuals.'[15] This objective scientific photography co-opted the camera to achieve the type of vision required by empiricism and positivist practices.[16] Diagrammatic representations had been used to illustrate observations in the sciences since the 1500s,[17] but photography gave those enterprises, which had previously been limited to text-based description and illustrative depiction, far greater authority. The photographic image went beyond 'illustrative' to become 'evidentiary'.

The truth-telling character of photography emanated from nineteenth-century beliefs that photographs 'regarded as evidence of that which they represent, differ in essence from any other species of representation that has ever been attempted. They are free, so far as their outlines are concerned, from the deceptive and therefore vitiating element of human agency'.[18] The camera could 'quiet the observer so

[12] 'Photography' (1864) 116 *The Quarterly Review* 482, 483.
[13] Ibid, 483.
[14] Allan Sekula, 'The Body and the Archive' (1986) 39 *October* 3, 8.
[15] Peter Hamilton and Roger Hargraves, *The Beautiful and the Damned* (Lund Humphries, 2001) 63.
[16] Jonathan Crary, *Techniques of the Observer: On Vision and Modernity in the Nineteenth Century* (MIT Press, 1990) 9. Crary comments on the duality of nineteenth century photography in his attempt to locate the ruptures between realism and modernism in the history of visuality. He notes that alongside the objective vision of 'scientific' photography, artistic photographic portraiture at that time invoked a notion of 'subjective vision', linked to Romanticism.
[17] See, e.g., Janice Neri, *Scientific Illustration* (2004) in Gale Encyclopaedia of the Early Modern World www.encyclopedia.com/doc/1G2-3404901017.html, where she discusses how in the late medieval period pictorial techniques designed to convince viewers that an image contained an exact record of the artist's observation were increasingly employed in the illustration of botanical and medical texts, as well as illuminated manuscripts.
[18] 'Photography', above n 12, 483.

nature could be heard', and philosophers of science Lorraine Daston and Peter Galison explain how '"[l]et nature speak for itself" thus became the watchword of the new scientific objectivity',[19] which was exactly what the photograph's 'mechanical objectivity' could achieve. Those authors define 'mechanical objectivity' as 'the insistent drive to repress the wilful intervention of the artist-author, and to put in its stead a set of procedures that would, as it were, move nature to the page through a strict protocol, if not automatically'.[20] That strict protocol sought to control the conditions of image creation such that photographs could be interpreted outside of any specific imagistic convention – in the terms of Roland Barthes, as a form of communication or message without a code.[21] By being analogical with nature, photography was 'able to transmit the (literal) information without forming it by means of discontinuous signs and rules of transformation. The photograph, message without a code, must thus be opposed to the drawing which, even when denoted, is a coded message'.[22] Without this intermediating code, photographic objectivity meant eliminating the distinction between the object (in this case a person), and knowledge of that object.[23]

Other theorists have also commented on the exactness of vision inherent in the technical processes of photography and its extension of renaissance realism and imagistic normativity in the nineteenth century. André Bazin, for instance, points out in 'The Ontology of the Photographic Image' that the photographic lens is named the *'objectif'* in French.[24] Accordingly, Bazin notes how '[f]or the first time, between the originating object and its reproduction there intervenes only the instrumentality of a nonliving agent. For the first time an image of the world is formed automatically, without the creative intervention of man.'[25] Crucially, however, Bazin notes that this interpretation and valorisation of photography's technically flawless reproductions was, in fact, a fantasy and only an effect of the *psychology* of the image:

> Again, the essential factor in the transition from the baroque to photography is not the perfecting of a physical process (photography will long remain the inferior of painting in the reproduction of colour); rather does it lie in a psychological fact, to

---

[19] Lorraine Daston and Peter Galison, *Objectivity* (MIT Press, 2007) 120.
[20] Ibid 121.
[21] Roland Barthes, 'The Photographic Message' (Stephen Heath trans) in Susan Sontag (ed) *A Barthes Reader* (Hill & Wang, 1982).
[22] WTJ Mitchell, *Iconology: Image, Text, Ideology* (University of Chicago Press, 2000) 60, referring to Roland Barthes, 'Rhetoric of the Image' (Stephen Heath trans) in *Image-Music-Text* (Hill & Wang, 1977).
[23] See, e.g., James Boyle, 'The Postmodern Subject in Legal Theory' (1991) 62 *University of Colorado Law Review* 489, 495.
[24] Andre Bazin, 'The Ontology of the Photographic Image' (Hugh Gray trans) (1960) 13(4) *Film Quarterly* 4, 7. Note, this is not directly discussed in the English translation but is mentioned in a note by the translator.
[25] Ibid 7.

wit, in completely satisfying our appetite for illusion by a mechanical reproduction in the making of which man plays no part.[26]

Photography then, followed the same epistemological trajectory as the 'camera obscura' – an early precursor to photographic technology that took advantage of the natural phenomena by which the image of an external object or scene would be projected (and inverted) through a lens onto a surface in a darkened room or box – a technology considered synonymous with empiricism and linear perspective because of its adoption of the 'eye-witness' principle.[27] The camera obscura was used by Locke as a metaphor for understanding in *An Essay Concerning Human Understanding*,[28] and as an instrument for observing empirical phenomena by Newton in *Opticks*.[29] These accounts gave it a privileged position in the generation of knowledge by defining the position of knowing subject to an external world.[30]

In automatically reproducing the captured image, the photographic camera perfected the camera obscura's system by virtue of a particular relation in the 'transference of reality from the thing to its reproduction'.[31] That is, the documentary utility of the photographic image was based on a phenomenological relation between image and referent that could be understood as 'indexical'. CS Peirce describes this relation as one of the 'trichotomy' of signs, along with the symbolic and iconic. The 'symbol' is an arbitrary sign with neither resemblance nor existential relationship to the referent. The 'icon' represents its object mainly through similarity or likeness. The 'index' 'refers to its object ... because it is in dynamical ... connection' with it – it 'has a real connection'.[32] As Peirce notes:

> Photographs, especially instantaneous photographs, are very instructive, because we know that they are in certain respects exactly like the objects they represent. But this resemblance is due to the photographs having been produced under such circumstances that they were physically forced to correspond point by point to nature.[33]

---

[26] Ibid 7.
[27] Mitchell, above n 22, 83 referring to Ernst Gombrich, *Art and Illusion* (Princeton University Press, 1956).
[28] John Locke, *An Essay Concerning Human Understanding* (London, 1690).
[29] Isaac Newton, *Opticks* (London, 1704).
[30] Crary, above n 16, 27.
[31] Bazin, above n 24, 8.
[32] Charles Hartshorne and Paul Weiss (eds) *Collected Papers of Charles Sanders Peirce* (Harland University Press, 1932) Volume 2, 281; See also Jane Caplan, '"This or That Particular Person": Protocols of Identification in 19th Century Europe' in Jane Caplan and John Torpey (eds) *Documenting Individual Identity: The Development of State Practices in the Modern World* (Princeton University Press, 2001) 52; Some, like WJT Mitchell, have noted that photography actually presents a doubly 'natural' sign, both iconic and indexical in Mitchell, above n 22, 60. However it seems the relevant knowledge effects are more a product of the index. Alternatively, Barthes provides his own taxonomy of representations (linguistic, symbolic, and iconic) in which the iconic is taken as the 'literal' or 'non-coded' message in Barthes, above n 21, 120, thus folding the icon and index together.
[33] Peirce in Hartshorne and Weiss, above n 32.

Through this relation, meaning could be located in a singular trace – from the subject of the image. Photography produced images offering 'a fixity in which the signifier is treated as if it were identical with a pre-existent signified and in which the reader's role is purely that of consumer'.[34] That photographic tracing of reality had significant consequences for the interpretation of criminal portraiture. It is why, as argued by Piyel Haldar, such an image 'represents an event, or event identity, as if it were a stable descriptive medium',[35] meaning 'they become the nearest thing to the event itself, or, the closest thing to an identity'.[36] This is also the beginning of the elimination of the subject identified by Antoinette Rouvroy, caused 'a dissipation or an explosion of all forms, objects and persons. What is left are only a set of indexes'.[37]

Of course, objective photographic interpretation was challenged. As Daston and Galison note: 'Far from being the unmoved prime mover in the history of objectivity, the photographic image did not fall whole into the status of objective sight; on the contrary the photograph was also criticised, transformed, cut, pasted, touched up, and enhanced'.[38] Legal thinking also acknowledged those critiques, creating an ambivalent relationship between law and images.[39] As Cornelia Vismann has noted, 'as long as it is not possible to ascribe to images a monosemic pictorial content, they will not be fit to provide a foundation capable of sustaining order'.[40] Good examples of juridical scepticism of imagistic representation can be found in Jennifer Mnookin, Piyel Haldar, and Katherine Biber's various descriptions of the contested acceptance of photographic images as evidence in courtrooms.[41] That said, the law (or perhaps more specifically law enforcement), appears to have dispensed with debates over the credibility of images when the conditions of their creation are firmly under control. This is especially true with respect to images dealing with identity rather than event. Under strictly managed circumstances, photographic realism could still be instrumentalised to chronicle and regulate the growing presence of dangerous classes, and offer a new pathway for the creation of knowledge.[42]

---

[34] John Tagg, *The Burden of Representation: Essays on Photographies and Histories* (MacMillan Education, 1988).
[35] Piyel Haldar, 'Law and the Evidential Image' (2008) 4(2) *Law, Culture and the Humanities* 139, 140.
[36] Ibid 144.
[37] Antoinette Rouvroy and Bernard Stiegler, 'The Digital Regimes of Truth: From the Algorithmic Governmentality to a New Rule of Law' (2016) 3 *La Deleuziana – Online Journal of Philosophy* 6, 9.
[38] Daston and Galison, above n 19, 125.
[39] Note that a great deal of scholarship has been written about 'law and images'. Some of this was noted in Chapter 1. For a general introduction see, e.g., Costas Douzinas and Lynda Need (eds) *Law and the Image: The Authority of Art and the Aesthetics of Law* (University of Chicago Press, 1999).
[40] Cornelia Vismann, 'Image and Law – A Troubled Relationship' (2008) 14(4) *Parallax* 1, 1.
[41] See, e.g., Mnookin above, n 8 discussing a fraud trial in New York against a photographer who claimed to take 'spirit photographs', Haldar, above n 35 discussing the role of the image in the courtroom, and Katherine Biber, *Captive Images: Race, Crime, Photography* (Routledge, 2007) discussing the courts' treatment of identification photographs.
[42] See, e.g., Sekula, above n 14, 5; and Tagg, above n 34, 11.

POLICE PHOTOGRAPHY AND CRIMINOLOGICAL OBJECTIVITY

The objective understanding of photography, and the uses towards which it was oriented, were part of a growing modern belief in the power of measurement and categorisation. The background to photographic deployment in the modern programme was what Ian Hacking called 'an avalanche of printed numbers', through which 'nation-states classified, counted and tabulated their subjects anew'.[43] Statistics had become a prominent means of understanding the world, and governments were increasingly interested in data collection. Through data collection, statistics afforded a method to extrapolate a nation's general status from local accounts.[44] The goal was to ascertain the 'real political state of a country, in its minute details'.[45] And while the term 'statistics' initially meant a 'wholistic' account or general state of affairs, it quickly became a highly quantitative and specific endeavour.

This investigation of general 'states of things' inevitably included crime and criminality. As early as 1830 it was declared that 'innumerable regularities about crime and suicide seemed visible to the naked eye, suggesting the existence of "invariable" laws about their relative frequency by month, by methods, by sex, by region, by nation'.[46] And in 1836 the English Ministry of Justice began gathering data about crimes and suicides.[47] By 1857 there was legislation requiring each police force in Britain to report to the Home Office the number of known thieves and depredators; receivers of stolen goods; prostitutes; suspected persons; and vagrants and tramps in their respective areas.[48] These data collection exercises were instituted according to a prevailing belief that '[t]he moral order falls in the domain of statistics'.[49] Photography's link to knowledge meant it could play a role in divining that moral order through the reduction of nature to statistical essence and as such, these mechanical and statistical ways of knowing moved from understanding the phenomenon of crime, to also understanding the criminal individual.

Indeed, the very nature of the human race was explored photographically, and anthropology was among the first social sciences championing the idea that photographic representations of individuals offered a path to knowledge about both them and society more broadly. Historians like Chris Pinney, Jens Jäger, Daniel Pick, and Hamilton and Hargraves accordingly locate photography's use by prisons, courts, and

---

[43] Hacking, above n 2, 2.
[44] See, e.g., Sir John Sinclair, *Analysis of the Statistical Account of Scotland* (Edinburgh, 1790–1799).
[45] Ibid 225.
[46] Hacking, above n 2, 73.
[47] Ibid 79. This included things like victim's sex, age, state of health, profession or social class, residence, birth place, marital status, children, financial situation, education, religion, history of madness or suicide; as well as a record of the place of crime, the time of the crime, weather, mode of crime, motive, and the items found at the scene or in the victim's pockets.
[48] Chris Williams, 'Police Surveillance and the Emergence of CCTV in the 1960s' (2003) 5 *Crime Prevention and Community Safety: An International Journal* 27, 28.
[49] Hacking, above n 2, 116.

police as a continuation of the social scientific imperative of knowing from photography's use in anthropology.[50] For example, photographic anthropology's connection to the contemporary mugshot is very clear in the 1869 proposal of JH Lamprey, Secretary of the London Ethnographical Society, that anthropologists photograph their subjects against a background grid of approximately 5 cm squares to overcome difficulties in questions of comparison.[51] That was also the beginning of 'anthropometric photography' – an early attempt to systematise portraiture for the sake of an objective relational system for measuring people by reducing the real world to numbers – the images of which provided a stunning historical pre-figuration of contemporary police portraits.

Photography's deployment as a means of knowledge eventually traversed the totality of subordinated classes, from colonised peoples to other groups considered biologically distinct such as the mentally ill, using attributes captured in images, such as 'nigrescence' to evaluate levels of degeneration.[52] Informing the photographic knowledge of these early endeavours were the pseudo-sciences of physiognomy and phrenology – arts supposing that the face, through its representations of the 'four humours', was a sort of *mask* that when read correctly gave true insight into a subject's nature.[53] It was, in other words, a system for reduction of the site of outward identity to a measurable biological morphology. These disciplines afforded further mechanisms of measurement and comparison in which photographic processes could participate. Physiognomic investigation of degeneracy, race, and the lower classes already included the criminal body, and as early as 1846, photography and phrenology had been combined in a book on 'criminal jurisprudence'.[54] Using these tools, criminology sought to 'chart every manifestation, every structure of the pathological'.[55] By recognising features of atavism, backwardness, and deviance within the human face and head, anthropometrics in combination with criminological photography was deployed to justify a positivist biological fatalism.[56]

It is impossible to discuss these developments without acknowledging the contributions of Francis Galton, a cousin of Charles Darwin, and social scientist who enthusiastically adopted the determinist interpretation of photographic images. Galton was

[50] See, e.g., Christopher Pinney, *Photography and Anthropology* (Reaktion Books, 2011); Jens Jäger, 'Photography: A Means of Surveillance? Judicial Photography, 1850 to 1900' (2001) 5 *Crime, Histoire, & Sociétés* 27; Daniel Pick, *Faces of Degeneration: A European Disorder, c 1848–c 1918* (Cambridge University Press, 1989).
[51] Pinney, above n 50, 28.
[52] See, e.g., Hamilton and Hargraves, above n 15, at 93 discussing the British Association for the Advancement of Sciences (BAAS) project on Britain's physical characteristics 1883. Most concerning was the attempt of the BAAS study to measure the 'degeneration' of social groups via an index of 'nigrescence' (the presence of negroid physical attributes).
[53] Sharrona Pearl, *About Faces: Physiognomy in Nineteenth Century Britain* (Harvard University Press, 2010) 102.
[54] MB Sampson and Mathew Brady, *Rationale of Crime, and Its Appropriate Treatment: Being a Treatise on Criminal Jurisprudence Considered in Relation to Cerebral Organisation* (Appleton & Co, 1846) in which Brady accepted a commission to photograph prisoners in NYC's Blackwell's Island Prison.
[55] Pick, above n 50, 138.
[56] Ibid 114, discussing Lambroso's criminal science.

the founder of British eugenics and his overarching project was to construct a programme of social betterment through breeding, which required a 'profoundly ideological'[57] biologisation of class relations, that included constructing a criminal biopathology. He was also a pioneering statistician, credited with inventing the statistical concept of correlation,[58] and psychometrician – exploring mathematical ways to measure and analyse thought processes and content.[59] In 1877 Galton created a crude biometric methodology of re-photographing portraits of criminals on the same plate to create a composite image intended to elucidate a criminal mean or type.[60] Ironically though, after repeated experimentation, he found that the 'special villainous irregularities of the criminal classes' had disappeared to reveal the 'common humanity in all'.[61] Nonetheless, other biological fatalists such as Cesare Lambroso still used the technique to pursue the biological foundation of criminality. Lambroso desperately sought to identify the difference between criminals and the insane,[62] and repeated Galton's process in his famous analysis of criminal skulls.[63] According to historian Daniel Pick, part of Lambroso's motivation was to improve the State's capacity to anticipate dangerousness and delinquency, and thus legitimate the proposed practice of preventative detention.[64] In other words, to statistically predict dangerousness and focus the state's penological resources on those 'dangerous' persons.

Whereas the majority of statistical approaches at the time orbited the notion of 'normal' as a mean or average – a description of how things are – 'normal' (as opposed to pathological) could also describe how things ought to be.[65] Hacking explains, '[t]he magic of the word is that we can use it to do both things at once. The

[57] John Tagg's characterisation in Tagg, above n 34, at 42.
[58] See, e.g., Judea Pearl and Dana Mackenzie, *The Book of Why: The New Science of Cause and Effect* (Basic Books, 2018), where the authors locate statistics' ongoing relationship to the language of correlation (rather than causation) in the work of Galton (amongst others).
[59] See, e.g., Harvey Goldstein, 'Francis Galton, Measurement, Psychometrics and Social Progress' (2012) 19(2) *Assessment in Education: Principles, Policy & Practice* 147.
[60] Francis Galton, 'Composite Portraits, Made by Combining Those of Many Different Persons into a Single Resultant Figure' (1879) 3 *Journal of the Anthropological Institute of Great Britain* 132.
[61] Ibid 135.
[62] Pick, above n 50, 122.
[63] Cesare Lambroso, *Criminal Man* (Mary Gibson and Nichole Hans Rafter trans, Duke, 2004) [trans of *L'Uomo Delinquente* (first published 1876)] xiv–xv, where Lambroso takes photographs of 18 skulls that were combined in order to expose the essential cranial features of the delinquent. A well-known extract from that text reads as follows:

> This was not merely an idea, but a revelation. At the sight of that skull, I seemed to see all of a sudden, lighted up as a vast plain under a flaming sky, the problem of the nature of the criminal – an atavistic being who reproduces in his person the ferocious instincts of primitive humanity and the inferior animals. Thus were explained anatomically the enormous jaws, high cheek bones, prominent superciliary arches, solitary lines in the palms, extreme size of the orbits, handle-shaped ears founding criminals savages and apes, insensibility to pain, extremely acute sight, tattooing, excessive idleness, love of orgies, and the irresponsible craving of evil for its own sake, the desire not only to extinguish life in the victim, but to mutilate the corpse, tear its flesh and drink its blood.

[64] Pick, above n 50, 128.
[65] Hacking, above n 2, 167.

norm may be what is usual or typical, yet our most powerful ethical constraints are also called norms'.[66] That dual use is very clear in the work of Galton and Lambroso, both intent on improving society through anticipating criminality, and for whom there was excellence at one extreme of normality. Identification photography inherited the criminological imperative of knowing through photography, as well as its objective interpretive paradigm and deployment of measurement, and its programme of 'normalisation' through comparison and stratification.

POLICE PHOTOGRAPHY AND IDENTIFICATION

Photographic measurement and comparison required archives of images, and the first comprehensive image datasets were criminal portraits. In the criminal context, it was hoped that archives of identity images would ameliorate insufficiently precise written descriptions of prisoners and convicted persons to help eliminate arguments from individuals, otherwise unknown to officials, that they were first-time offenders who had been temporarily led astray. Photography thus presented an exciting new possibility that recidivism, habitual criminality, and social deviance could be addressed technologically. In the face of a habitual criminal, identifiable and knowable remotely through photography, judges could finally accord 'proper' treatment.

Suggestions for using photography systematically to identify repeat offenders (or at least social undesirables) first emerged around the 1850s. Historian Jens Jäger explains how in 1852 the Swiss Attorney General commissioned a photograph of every vagrant arrested and brought to Bern.[67] In the UK in 1854, the Governor of Bristol Goal, James Gardner, believing that written descriptions of prisoners were insufficiently precise, had begun taking photographs of certain groups of prisoners, such as 'strangers to the city', believing it the most effective means of circulating descriptions of prisoners to governors of other jails. Gardner thought his use of photography so effective that he announced in *The Times* that 'the advantages which I have myself seen derived from the use of photography as an aid to the administration of criminal justice are such that I am induced to make an effort to procure its general adoption throughout the kingdom'.[68] To that end, in 1856 French journalist Ernest Lacan exclaimed:

[66] Ibid 163.
[67] Jäger, above n 50, 31.
[68] James Gardner, 'Photography as an Aid to the Administration of Criminal Justice' *The Times* (London), 29 December 1854, 9; also published in the *Bristol Mercury* (Bristol), 30 December 1854. In his circular he gave the example of one migratory recidivist:

> J.H came to into the Bristol gaol upon commitment for trial, a perfect stranger to me and my officers; he was well attired but very illiterate, the state of his hands convinced me that he had not done any hard work, whilst the superiority of his apparel over his attainments led me to suspect that he was a practiced thief. I forwarded his likeness to several places, and soon received information that he had been convicted in London and Dublin. The London officer who recognised him by his portrait was subpoenaed as a witness, picked him out from amongst thirty or forty other prisoners, and gave evidence on his trial in October last, which led the Recorder to sentence him to six years' penal servitude.

Which outlaw could thus escape the vigilance of the police? Whether he escaped from the walls where he had been confined for punishment, or after being freed, had broken the ban on leaving his place of residence, his portrait would be in the hands of the authorities he would not be able to escape; and would be forced to recognise himself in this accusing image.[69]

Similarly in Australia, an 1860 contribution to the *Launceston Examiner* argued 'photographic apparatus ought to be at the command of the heads of the police in every town, so that, upon the apprehension of an offender, his "counterfeit presentment" might be despatched for recognition to the principle police stations throughout the country'. It further noted, 'we have no doubt that the practice of making every member of the dangerous classes "sit" would result in helping materially forward the ends of justice; while the gallery itself would afford a rich field of study for the anthropologist'.[70]

Despite its potential utility, however, criminal photography remained a marginal practice with little systemic effect on policing, prisons or the administration of justice. One reason was liberal bourgeois reluctance to 'the idea of degrading photography by using it for police purposes'.[71] That attitude is evident in an 1853 contribution to the English periodical *Notes and Queries*, in which the author described applications of photography to judicial means as 'miserable travesties on the lovely uses of portrait painting and photography',[72] arguing '[i]f the French like to carry their portraits about with them on their passports to show to policemen, let them submit to the humiliation'.[73] The French did not actually have photographic passports at the time, but the comment reflects a liberal dismissal of Continental policing (and 'political policing' in particular), discussed in Chapter 4, as improper.

The liberal political milieu, however, had already begun descending from its zenith, and in the end, identifying recidivists and addressing the new migratory character of crime that had emerged since the introduction of railroads and steamers began to shift public opinion. In 1864, the influential *Quarterly Review* argued of identification photography:

> The system has been introduced to some extent into England, but only very partially. It is to be regretted that the adoption of it has not been more general. The cost is quite trivial; and there is no other plan, approaching to it in efficiency, for drawing that clear and certain line between new and old offenders, which is absolutely essential to a sound criminal system. If every prison were armed with its photographic album, containing a pleasing collection of all the physiognomies

---

[69] Ernst Lacan, 'Esquisses photographiques a propos de l'Exposition universel et de la guerre d'Orient' in *Historique de la Photographie* (Grassart, 1856) 39, which was a collection of several of his *La Lumière* reviews as well as articles he had written elsewhere on photography's origins and uses.
[70] See, e.g., *Launceston Examiner* (Launceston), 21 April 1860, 1.
[71] Jäger, above n 50, 33.
[72] *Notes and Queries* (London), 21 May 1853, Vol 186, at 506.
[73] Ibid.

which had ever been shorn of their flowing locks in any gaol in the country, a ruffian out upon his third ticket-of-leave would not be able, as now, by the simple expedient of changing the field of his operations after every fresh conviction, to persuade the magistrates that he was an innocent, accidentally led away by drink.[74]

Throughout the 1860s reports of photography's power to expose those of the professional criminal classes became more frequent and laudatory,[75] and 'rogues' galleries' (a collection of images of known criminals displayed to the public to identify suspects of other crimes) became common law enforcement tools, though not yet the comprehensive archives necessary for preventing recidivism. In fact, the rogues' galleries performed the different task of enlisting the public in locating a known criminal by publishing their appearance. However, there was ongoing resistance to these photographic practices, increasingly channelled through the argument that they might render a person an object of suspicion for the rest of their life.[76] Ultimately, these protests were allayed with the arguments that the photographs are for the police authorities and not the public, and being portraits of wrongdoers, society has a right to be placed on its guard.[77] Slowly, the tide of public opinion began to change, judicial photography became less ad hoc and more systematic, and was more frequently adopted by police forces. This first attempt at photography for institutional identity, in Britain at least, culminated with the passing in 1869, of the *Habitual Criminals Act*,[78] which established a photographic register of the 'dangerous classes'.[79] This was primarily for the service of the courts and prisons, but administered by police through the Habitual Criminals Register.

Although it adopted the most up-to-date technical system available, the Register still had very limited utility. By 1873 more than 43,000 photographs of prisoners had been collected. However, only 156 had been useful in the identification of re-offenders and the total cost of the register was reported at nearly

---

[74] 'Photography' above n 12, 496–497.
[75] See, e.g., *The Times*, 20 October, 1863, 5 which reported when three women arrested for shoplifting refused to provide their real names and addresses to the Court for 'not wishing to bring disgrace on their friends', were in fact found to be convicted felons at large on 'tickets-of-leave' granted three weeks prior.
[76] Ibid 10. Other objections included that it would create a criminal album of most portentous bulk, it would be unfair to photograph a man against his will, and that an ingenious rogue might so effectually distort his features to render identification impossible.
[77] Ibid 11. The issue of possible resistance to being photographed answered through coercive and tricky techniques of subduing the subject. (The article tells of using a decoy photographer and a secondary photographer behind a curtain who could take a photograph when the subject was off guard.)
[78] *Habitual Criminals Act* 1869 (UK) 32 & 33 Vict c 99.
[79] 'Crime: Creating the Criminal' (2009) *The Open University – International Centre for History of Crime, Policing and Justice* www.open.ac.uk/Arts/history-from-police-archives/Met6Kt/Crime/crmCrCrim.html.

3,000 pounds.[80] Although the photographic archive was growing, there was no way of making images retrievable other than names, which could be easily faked. The visual data in the photo galleries had been useful for confirming that the name of a person in physical space matched the institutional identity recorded in the documents. However, the problem of retrieving those identity documents from the archive on the basis of information that could be derived from the body of the person in physical space (in case the name were fake) had not been solved. That meant that while the archive of criminal images was growing, data was not produced in a textual or numerical form that could be easily searched or cross-referenced. As the registers increased in size and cost, they simultaneously diminished in efficacy. Eventually the quantity of criminal images made isolating and identifying particular individuals near impossible. The photographic image alone carried insufficient 'metadata' for the proper functioning of the archive, suggesting the need for new techniques of searching and accessing relevant information. Criminologist Chris Williams describes this problem as a product of the recording of the criminal image as still 'analogue' rather than 'digital' – i.e. not yet properly reduced to manipulable data.[81] The answer for how to know criminals in this context, would again be anthropometric and biometric techniques as systems for reducing individuals to numbers that could be more easily processed.

THE MEASURE OF CRIMINALITY

The first system of comprehensive biological measurement suitable for effectively retrieving archived images is usually attributed to Alphonse Bertillon. However, by 1870 the British had already devised a criminal identification register indexed, not according to names, but by markers on the body.[82] This was the Distinctive Marks

[80] *All the Year Round* (London), 1 November 1873, 8. Despite its meagre statistics and considerable expense, *All the Year Round*, a journal 'conducted' by Charles Dickens, still positively assessed the Register in 1873. Criminal portraiture was described 'not, of course, to gratify the criminals themselves, but to obtain a means of *knowing* them again'. Of particular interest in that article was an outlining of the still lingering 'liberal' objections that found their way into the jurisprudence of constitutional privacy protections in Europe many years later. For instance, that having a photograph in the register would render a person an object of suspicion for the rest of their life. (Another objection was that because criminal faces are almost all of one type any criminal gallery would show so unusually strong a family likeness to be of little practical value in establishing identity.) The article answered those concerns with a reasoning that also persists in the legal decisions limiting the application of privacy to this type of surveillance until later in the twentieth century – that is, the photographs are for the police authorities and not the public, and being portraits of wrongdoers, society has a right to be placed on its guard. The growing bulk of the album was simply something to be dealt with. Apparently the 43,000 photographs cost about one shilling and fourpence each, a large sum at the time, with the author noting, '[t]he rogues are certainly not worthy of this sixteenpence apiece; but then it is bestowed, not for their benefit, but as a safeguard in the hands of justice'.
[81] Williams, above n 48, 29.
[82] Cole, above n 11, 26–27.

Register to be read alongside the Habitual Criminal Register. It divided the body into nine general areas, and each area by type of mark or physical peculiarity. Any individual presenting with a distinctive mark could be cross-checked against the register and have their name confirmed (or at least found amongst a list of convicts with distinctive marks on that area of their body). But it was laborious, too large in scale, and not particularly successful because any 'results obtained were altogether disproportionate to the labour involved'.[83] Further, it relied on criminals carrying distinctive marks in the first place – meaning it could only order human bodies around markers of peculiarity. Bertillon, director of the first official police photography department in France, understood that the essential principle of criminal identification 'consists less in the search for new characteristic elements of individuality than in the discovery of a method of classification'.[84] Bertillon's two-pronged solution improved image retrieval immeasurably. The first element was a formalised and systematised technique for criminal photography using specialised studios and technology. Bertillon believed that systematic criminal photography could be a form of archival memory, and that the superiority of an image therefore came from its documentary accuracy, not its aesthetic quality (to that end, his book *Judicial Photography* reminded practitioners not to retouch the images).[85] According to his instructions, two portraits of every arrested criminal or suspect were to be taken; one from the front and one in profile. The profile (often achieved with a mirror next to the subject) was generally right facing because images taken outside court in the morning before trials began were best lit by the south-eastern sun around 10 am.[86] As Hamilton and Hargrave argue:

> Indeed it is probably due to Bertillon that the full-face 'identity' photograph has become so widespread throughout the world as the standard method for identifying individuals on passports, driving licences, identity cards and credit cards. What began in the mid-nineteenth century as a method of anthropological classification had become the dominant metaphor of photographically supported identity by the twenty-first century.[87]

The second part of Bertillon's solution was the creation of a biometric system for making photographic data readable and classifiable. In its first 10 years, his department had produced a collection of more than 100,000 images.[88] Bertillon then faced the problem that 'the whole range of knowledge that the police had gathered was

---

[83] Ibid 27.
[84] Alphonse Bertillion, 'L'identité des recidivists et la loi de relégation' in *Annales de Démographie Internationale* (1883) 474; See also Alphonse Bertillon, *Signaletic Instructions including the Theory and Practice of Anthropometrical Identification* (Werner Company, 1896) 13.
[85] Alphonse Bertillon, *La Photographie Judiciaire* (Gauthier-Villars, 1890) 9, and 18.
[86] Ibid 11.
[87] Hamilton and Hargrave, above n 15, 106; also see Raymond Williams, 'When Was Modernism?' in *The Politics of Modernism* (Verso, 1989) 50.
[88] *Mercury and Weekly Courier* (Victoria), 19 May 1892, 3.

insufficiently structured and correlated'.[89] By introducing an index system of descriptions, focusing on particular measurements of the adult body, photographic subjects could be classified and described through text and numbers. Judicial photography, combined with systems of measurement, comparison, and biological reduction, had finally become an effective way of identifying individual criminals. The *Mercury Courier* in Victoria (Australia) gave a first-hand account of the system in 1892 after a reporter visited a Paris police department:

> Whilst the Inspector is explaining to us the advantages of measurements as a means of classifying the photographs, and the impossibility of doing so with marks alone, a telegram is placed in his hands from Bordeaux, with the measurements, etc, of a man in that prison who has given the name of Jean Bernard; is anything known of him? A record of Jean Bernard is soon found from the alphabetical index, but his record, and the description given by the telegram, bear only a slight resemblance. What is to be done? Send a detective 390 miles to see if he can identify the man; a long, expensive, and perhaps useless journey. No, the Inspector rapidly runs his eyes over his presses, opens a drawer and produces a card, the measurements, etc., on which exactly tally with those on the telegram, except that the name on the card is not Jean Bernard but Alphonse Dubois, a criminal well-known in Paris, who has been trying fresh pastures.[90]

Across Europe, and indeed the world, policymakers institutionalised Bertillon's techniques. New ideas for identifying criminals spread in line with increased inter-governmental communication provoked by a trans-European effort to deal with increasing anarcho-terrorism. Bertillon's system had already successfully been applied to 'control the heresy of social radicalism' in France when it was used in the apprehension of the anarchist Ravachol after he threw a bomb into the house of a government bureaucrat. However, historian RB Jensen describes how 'at the end of the nineteenth century an alarming number of "undesirable" immigrants, including paupers and Eastern European Jews as well as anarchists, began to come into England'.[91] An international anti-anarchist conference was thus called to promote an agenda of increased direct communication and information exchange between national agencies as well as uniform methods of identifying criminals that could be effectively transmitted across borders. That conference internationalised Bertillon's system, and according the German Anarchist Press in 1899, even resulted in a German police campaign requiring all suspected anarchists to undergo anthropometric measurement.[92] But Bertillonage only remained the dominant method for measuring and indexing criminal persons for a short time. The alternative technological measurement system of fingerprinting (which actually operated in union

[89] Jäger, above n 51, 37.
[90] *Mercury and Weekly Courier*, above n 88, 3.
[91] R B Jensen, 'The International Anti-Anarchist Conference of 1898 and the Origins of Interpol' (1981) 16(2) *Journal of Contemporary History* 323, 326.
[92] Ibid 331–333.

photography), with its own unique and troubled history rooted in colonial governance, was postulated as a new form of criminal identification as early as 1880,[93] and eventually emerged as the successor to Bertillonage at the turn of the century.[94]

Photography and fingerprinting together provided a formidable technical constellation. In fact, it was Francis Galton whose work provided the basis for producing an effective classification scheme for fingerprints (after supplementation by the head of an Argentine police statistics bureau Juan Vucetich, and colonial police official Edward Henry).[95] While initially deployed for similar reasons to photography – identification – fingerprints could be reduced to text and numbers according to far simpler conventions than Bertillon's anthropometric measurements, more accurately, and without needing a complex morphological vocabulary. For instance, those images were easily reduced to numbers for storage, communication, and eventually computational and automated processing. Distance Identification (DI) codes used for fingerprinting, for example '33455 44544 2112 18.5.7.3.9 D 8.21.5–31.64 x 073.92.11 N.B. 7329–5831 73.5 29.4.88'[96] were far more readily parsed by computers than the natural language descriptions of Bertillonage.[97] This made them a very sensible standard for distribution at and across national borders. Fingerprints could also identify criminals at a distance – that is, 'latent' fingerprints could be located at crime scenes, making them useful evidence in court.[98] As described by Simon Cole, fingerprints also better replicated the epistemological claims inherent in the utility of identification photography:

> [Fingerprinting] brought identification back to visual imagery, utilizing an image that, though it bore no topographic resemblance to the body it represented, nonetheless was a relatively unmediated visual image of at least a portion of that body. And Fingerprint records actually touched the body of the criminal, whereas anthropometric records were mediated by a human observer.[99]

Further, capturing fingerprints from live environments in order to identify *suspects*, rather than existing criminal persons, operationalised identity archives for criminal detection as the housing of latent identification data, meaning 'data was collected for its potential use in future law enforcement'.[100] The capture of biology and its

---

[93] Henry Faulds, 'On the Skin-Furrows of the Hand' (1880) 22 *Nature* 605.
[94] Cole, above n 11, 32.
[95] Ibid 81–82, 128; See also Edward Henry, *The Classification and Uses of Fingerprints* (George Routledge and Sons, 1900).
[96] Example taken from Cole, above n 11, 226.
[97] Ibid 251–252, where Cole describes how in 1934, the FBI began using an IBM card-sorter to parse coded fingerprint classifications. However, systems capable of producing candidate matches – that is, systems doing optical recognition of fingerprint images, were not experimented with until the 1960s, and were not broadly implemented until the early 1980s.
[98] Cole, above n 11, 169.
[99] Ibid 167.
[100] Jonathan Finn, *Capturing the Criminal Image: From Mug Shot to Surveillance Society* (University of Minnesota Press, 2009) 81.

reduction to numbers for storage, communication, and processing has only accelerated from that point. The capacity to produce meaningful numbers directly from images, which began with fingerprinting is replicated and amplified in numerous contemporary biometrics like facial recognition and computer vision, which are discussed in later chapters.

POLICE PHOTOGRAPHY AND HUMAN KNOWABILITY

When photography was institutionalised as a technology of identity verification, it brought with it significant epistemological, ideological, and technological baggage. Criminological and anthropological deployments of the technology were linked to technical objectivity, a belief in the 'uncoded' capture and transfer of the real, as well as the knowledge regimes of social statistics that connected identification photography to questions of criminal 'propensity'. As Hacking notes, '"[p]ropensity" was a term of art in phrenology, but the connection with statistical fatalism was closer than that. The French word was *penchant*. Quetelet's statistical expression was identical: *penchant au crime*'.[101] Being the subject of criminal measurement meant being compared to the norm, not simply in terms of who you are, but also what you might do, and who you might be in the future. As the interpretive paradigms for the different types of representational formats used in surveillance have evolved, the forward-looking, predictive (or pre-emptive) orientation has strengthened. But that technical configuration required not only registration and measurement, but also storage. Photographic measurement meant 'traces' of an individual were held in storage, transforming the subject into a piece of information that could be filed away.

Alan Sekula's photographic theory of 'the archive' thus offers useful synthesis of this combination of bureaucratic and optical technologies, the ideological and political commitments that privileged middle-class sensibilities while degrading all forms of otherness, and the criminological and mechanical epistemologies that vectorised these arrangements.[102] For Sekula, the archive was the hierarchical system and bureaucratic complex that established the terrain of 'the other', and defined 'both the *generalised look* – the typology – and the *contingent instance* of deviance and social pathology',[103] through which the more extensive social body was also invented. Sekula describes these processes of recording and categorisation as archival functions in which every portrait took its place within a moral and social hierarchy that both encompassed an entire social terrain as well as located individuals within it. From one's place in the hierarchy it became possible to both look up at one's betters and look down at one's inferiors. Between 1880 and 1910, during the period of systematisation of judicial photography, Sekula argues, the

[101] Hacking, above n 2, 122.
[102] Sekula, above n 14, 6.
[103] Ibid 7.

archive became the dominant institutional basis for photographic meaning. Indeed, this techno-institutional construct emerged as the narrative into and against which many of the subsequent legal protections, particularly liberal constitutional protections of private life, arranged themselves over the following century.

The relationship between these identity practices and the laws that both facilitated and constrained them were complex. Unquestionably, the use of photography and identity archives were oriented towards a new system of social organisation. In that way, photography could be used as an instrument of state coercion and punishment. Limitations to those practices however, particularly those instituted through liberal constitutional instruments, followed class imperatives by constraining, at least at first, the application of that form of state violence to criminals, deviants, and undesirables. As noted by Jäger, 'the ceremony of photographing a criminal became part of the penalty; a part of the symbolic practices used to subject an apprehended person.'[104] Just prior to the invention of photography (or at least, of the Daguerreotype process), criminal branding was reportedly common.[105] The significant distinction with that surveillance procedure, however, was that the criminal mark or measure was recorded on the body rather than being traced off, making it less suitable for efficient archiving and statistical analysis.

As we'll see, privacy jurisprudence as it developed through the twentieth century broadly followed this trajectory. The harmful 'archival' effects of judicial photography, in particular as relevant for privacy law, were understood as related to the storage in police filing cabinets of photographic criminal traces and measurement data where the subject did not deserve that criminal treatment. The legitimate profiling of a convicted person as more likely to commit crime in the future was acceptable in law, that is, once they have degraded themselves out of the scope of protections afforded good citizens. Although specific privacy laws did not address these features of the criminal archive for some time, proto-privacy considerations are visible in the constraints that emerged soon after criminal photography's systematic implementation. For instance, in 1896, Britain introduced regulations under the 1891 *Penal Servitude Act*[106] for the 'Measuring and Photographing of Criminal Prisoners',[107] prohibiting the photographing of untried criminal prisoners except in special circumstances and under application from high-ranking officials.[108] Notably, if such untried (and previously unconvicted) prisoners were photographed and subsequently acquitted, all photographs and measurements including

---

[104] Jäger, above n 50, 41.
[105] Friedrich Kittler, *Optical Media* (Anthony Enns trans, Polity Press, 2010) [trans of *Optische Medien* (first published 1999)] 141.
[106] *Penal Servitude Act 1891*, (UK) 54 & 55 Vict, c 69.
[107] *Regulations for the Measuring and Photographing of Criminal Prisoners 1896* (SR & O 1896/762) made under s 8 of the Act.
[108] Ibid s 4.

fingerprints were to be destroyed.[109] Although those limitations on photography were never directly repealed,[110] their enforcement diminished so as to become irrelevant when police photography eventually moved outside of prisons through the early twentieth century, meaning the regulations were no longer applicable. It took some time for similar constraints to be considered for the more prolific and contemporary application of images taken 'in public'.

CONCLUSION

Oliver Wendell Holmes remarked of photography, 'form is henceforth divorced from matter. In fact, matter as a visible object is of no great use any longer, except as the mould on which form is shaped. Give us a few negatives of a thing worth seeing, taken from different points of view, and that is all we want. Pull it down or burn it up if you please.'[111] The idea that an image or representation stands as a substitution for the thing itself has a long history. The evisceration of substance, including the body, through the capture of form, has been an ongoing and critical theme in work of media studies scholars,[112] and it remains relevant in the context of technology and identity. In the identity discourses emerging after the Second World War, outlined in later chapters, the necessity of materiality and embodiment for identity and the 'self' were rigorously challenged. It is unsurprising then that some theorists link the photographic flash with the material annihilation of a nuclear blast.[113] Indeed, the nuclear bomb also affords a critical historical point of inflection between the image and computation. Paul Edwards, for instance, describes how after the Second World War, the very first 'civilian' tasks given to the early digital computer ENIAC in 1945 was the simulation of thermo-nuclear blasts[114] – i.e. the computational modelling of total material destruction. At the level of profiling, this tension between form and substance translates into the various ways the image and computation have come to marginalise the 'narrative' identity of the individual, and leave as Rouvroy says, only indexes.

[109] Ibid s 5; Around that time, the *Cheshire Observer* even reported of the arrest of eight men for shop stealing, all of whom were photographed for identification, but four of whom were later acquitted. The Chief Constable had indicated 'he was perfectly willing that those four should be taken out of the negative' as they were respectable persons of good character (*Cheshire Observer* [Cheshire], 27 January 1894, 7).

[110] See for example the UK *Prison Act 1952*, (UK) 15 & 16 Geo 6 & 1 Eliz 2 c 52 s 54(3), by virtue of which the regulations appear to remain in force.

[111] Oliver Wendell Holmes, Sr. 'The Stereoscope and the Stereograph' (1859) 3 *The Atlantic Monthly* 738, 747.

[112] Flusser, above n 9; Kittler, above n 105; Paul Virilio, *The Information Bomb* (trans Chris Turner, Verso, 2000) [trans of *La Bombe Informatique* (first published 1998)]; Jean Baudrillard, *Simulacra and Simulation* (trans Sheila Faria Glaser, University of Michigan Press, 1994) [trans of *Simulacres et Simulation* (first published 1981)].

[113] See, e.g., Kittler, above n 105, 41.

[114] Paul Edwards, *The Closed World: Computers and the Politics of Discourse in Cold War America* (MIT Press, 1996).

This chapter presented a story of early 'measurement' of criminal offenders, the subsequent development of an archive of criminality, and outlined the ways in which individuals represented in the archive are interpreted by state entities. Indexable 'measurements', the translation of nature to statistical essence, and the searchable archive, are the pre-conditions for the evolutions in law enforcement and governance information systems that have since consolidated these effects and expanded in scale. This early iteration of the archive depended greatly on the medium of photography, and its particular epistemic function, in order to operate as a system capable of fixing, identifying, and knowing repeat offenders. The criminal archive, however, has been dynamic in both content and form. Evolving governmental and law enforcement imperatives have necessitated new techniques of surveillance, along with new systems of registering and recording individuals and their specific behaviour. When attempting to pre-empt crime, the static nature of the photographic image became too limiting a representational format. Text – words and numbers – in particular descriptions of behaviour (as opposed to measurements of the body) thus facilitated the shift in surveillance focus from identification to intelligence, from biology to behaviour. To that end, Chapter 4 outlines the development of behavioural databases as the second dimension of the early profiling archive, also initially connected with policing and criminal justice, but operating across a far broader domain of people and contexts. Prior to that however, the following chapter describes the slow emergence of legal regimes addressing identification photography and biometric archives.

3

Images and Biometrics – Privacy and Stigmatisation

This chapter explores how the profiling regime initiated through police photography and biometrics has, at least in one way, come to be addressed in law. The legal analyses throughout the book are not presented as the direct regulatory responses to specific surveillance practices, but rather as the legal regimes and legal thinking that are most closely coupled to the techniques, practices, and effects associated with the forms of profiling described. Understanding how these legal mechanisms came to limit profiling instructs us as to why the law determines that a particular information collection, retention, or processing exercise is sufficiently objectionable to warrant legal intervention, and how those legal norms are enacted. We can also derive how law has shaped a legal subject in each of those domains to help draw a line between profile and person.

There are various ways law seeks to protect identity from profiling. For instance, this chapter focuses on rights to private life as a way to resist being installed in the archive, in certain contexts, via highly individualised and vertically applied constitutional rights. In the 'data subject rights' paradigm of data protection discussed in Chapter 5, we see a move to enable individual participation in the production of categorical identity through more diffuse and bureaucratic structures of legal enforcement. In the applications of algorithmic accountability discussed in Chapter 7, we see mechanisms to ensure a fairer calculation of individuals, such that institutional identities are parameterised according to statistical notions, enforced increasingly through computational implementations. The final chapters explore newer proposals that address contemporary practices of human computability more directly, and outline what might be the most useful legal subject, form, and content to limit profiling as those practices become more complex.

PRIVACY AND POLICE PHOTOGRAPHY

Privacy is one information law regime traditionally deployed to protect individuals from inappropriate or incorrect institutional depictions of identity. As surveillance databases developed further, privacy, at least in certain jurisdictions, became an important mechanism for protecting individuals by establishing the boundaries of what material could be retained in institutional archives. Indeed, privacy, for instance as expressed through Article 8 of the ECHR, remains a critical right with respect to the retention of images in police databases and preventing certain types of profiling, as made clear in the 2019 *Catt* decision of the European Court of Human Rights (ECtHR) (or Strasbourg Court).[1] That case, relying on a body of jurisprudence that began developing in the 1970s, concerned the removal of an individual's image and behavioural information from a UK police 'domestic extremism' intelligence database. How Article 8 arrived at this outcome, the way in which it protects identity, and the legal subject it developed to achieve those ends are all described below. It is important to note that along with these cases concerning individuals there have also been several successful Article 8 cases addressing 'mass surveillance' – i.e. the capacity to build archives of personal information through mandatory telecommunications metadata retention,[2] and to access it without reasonable suspicion.[3] Nonetheless, the focus here is the application of Article 8 to profiling specifically. The context

---

[1] *Catt* v. *United Kingdom* (European Court of Human Rights, Application No 43514/15, 24 January 2019).
[2] *Liberty* v. *United Kingdom* (European Court of Human Rights, Application no 58243/00, 1 July 2008); *Big Brother Watch* v. *United Kingdom* (European Court of Human Rights, Grand Chamber, Application nos 58170/13, 62322/14, 24960/15, 13 September 2018); in the United States, *Clapper* v. *Amnesty International*, 568 US 398 (2013); *Carpenter* v. *United States*, 585 US no. 16–402 (2018); *Szabo and Vissy* v. *Hungary* (European Court of Human Rights, Application no 37138/14, 12 January 2016); *Zakharov* v. *Russia* (European court of Human Rights, Grand Chamber, Application no 47143/06, 4 December 2015).
[3] Since the Snowden revelations, a small body of Article 8 (ECHR) case law has emerged addressing issues of mass and automated surveillance. In fact, the 2015 decision of *Zakharov* v. *Russia* and the 2016 decision of *Szabó* v. *Hungary* (*Zakharov* v. *Russia* [2015] ECtHR 1065; *Szabó and Vissy* v. *Hungary* [2016]) have even been interpreted as potentially outlawing 'massive monitoring of communications' in Europe. (See, e.g., Sarah St. Vincent, 'Did the European Court of Human Rights Just Outlaw "Massive Monitoring of Communications" in Europe?' [13 January 2016] Centre for Democracy & Technology https://cdt.org/blog/did-the-european-court-of-human-rights-just-outlaw-massive-monitoring-of-communications-in-europe.) *Zakharov* involved a challenge to the telecommunications interception capabilities of Russian police and security services. The focus of that case was not broad, indiscriminate or 'mass' surveillance, but rather a scenario by which police and security services could commence interception of particular communications with limited institutional obstacles. Of particular interest was the court's recognition that governments should only intercept communications where the body authorising surveillance confirms the existence of a 'reasonable suspicion' of wrongdoing, along with the identification of 'a specific person ... or set of premises' in respect of which the authorisation is ordered. The absence of those features in this case, along with certain other institutional shortcomings, provoked the conclusion that existing Russian legal provisions did not provide adequate safeguards against mismanagement, arbitrariness or abuse, thus breaching Article 8. But the requirement that authorisation for telecommunications interception include a 'reasonable suspicion' could have significant consequences for 'mass' surveillance exercises that use profiling technologies to identify the existence of suspicion at first instance. The opportunity to make that finding came up several months later in the *Szabó* case. However, while deciding that the particular mass surveillance regime in question was in breach of the

in which we see rights to private life develop in this arena is the collection of images, biometrics, and identity information in police files without conviction. Indeed, the gathering, and increasingly analysis, of images from public places for policing purposes continues to grow and include various types of biometric analytics.[4]

Since well before the proliferation of CCTV and automated facial recognition, police photography has been used as a method for identifying individuals who, although not under arrest or accused of criminal behaviour, were objects of suspicion because of activities performed in public. This is ordinarily open, non-surreptitious photography, commonly occurring at public events like protests, by uniformed officers engaged in low-level intelligence work. An example is the collection of images for 'spotter cards',[5] which assist in the identification of activists, and are used for creating simple profiles. It might be asked why this particular surveillance exercise is analysed here as opposed to the more widespread use of CCTV. Indeed, as Alan Westin has argued, the '[k]nowledge or fear that one is under systematic observation in public places destroys the sense of relaxation and freedom that men seek in open spaces and public arenas',[6] and political theorist George Kateb has noted how one is harmed when observed by a surveillance camera 'because one loses all possibility of innocence'.[7] Kateb suggests being exposed to government surveillance cameras means being 'treated as interesting and even as presumptively or potentially guilty, no matter how law-abiding one is'.[8] However, CCTV has received a relatively non-complex treatment in privacy law because it does not necessarily systematise its subjects,[9] and the *far* more pressing contemporary issue of automated biometric facial recognition actually has more in common with the use of image-making to identify and profile individuals than general CCTV

---

right to private life in Article 8, the Fourth Section decision did not impose a requirement of reasonable suspicion on government use of mass surveillance technologies. Unfortunately, these decisions fail to clearly resolve the legal status of mass surveillance by security agencies or police under the right to private life. Further clarification is required by the Grand Chamber, either in the *Szabó* case, for which a request for referral to the Grand Chamber is pending at the time of writing, or possibly in other actions already on foot in the Strasbourg court against the UK for actions taken by its intelligence agency, GCHQ. However, at this stage, the jurisprudence indicates that mass surveillance and large-scale data processing for the purposes of establishing suspicion do not necessarily fall foul of the right to private life as long as there is sufficient supervision and protection against abuse.

[4] See, e.g., George Joseph and Kenneth Lipp, 'IBM Used NYPD Surveillance Footage to Develop Technology that Lets Police Search by Skin Color' *The Intercept* (6 September 2018) https://theintercept.com/2018/09/06/nypd-surveillance-camera-skin-tone-search/.

[5] See, e.g., 'Spotter Cards: What They Look Like and How They Work' *Guardian* (26 October 2009) www.theguardian.com/uk/2009/oct/25/spotter-cards.

[6] Alan Westin, *Privacy and Freedom* (Atheneum, 1967) 31.

[7] George Kateb, 'On Being Watched and Known' (2001) 68 *Social Research* 269, 274.

[8] Ibid.

[9] *Peck v. UK* [2003] I ECtHR 123.

surveillance.[10] Put another way, the general collection of images in public space is a different species of surveillance and a different privacy issue from profiling and the creation of identity archives. The latter practice concerns the creating of, or relating an individual to, an institutional identity, not merely observing people in public. But why did it take so long to be addressed in privacy law?

Following Bertillon's instructions, identification photography gradually moved out of prisons and courthouses and into specialised studios at police stations. Accordingly, the 1896 English Regulations prohibiting the photography of non-convicted persons 'in prisons' became ineffectual.[11] At the turn of the twentieth century then, the photographic databases that had become a common feature of law enforcement agencies around the world faced few, if any, legal constraints. Several reasons are suggested as to why this kind of systematic state surveillance avoided law's purview for nearly a century, despite privacy's centrality in negotiating the liberal contract between citizen and state, and its identification as a unique right as early as 1890. First, as privacy law first developed to deal with press intrusion, the embedded class dimensions of privacy ideas, particularly prior to gaining the status of a universal human right after the Second World War, delimited the scope of its application. As legal scholar Robert Post has argued of Warren and Brandeis' 'right to be let alone':

> Warren and Brandeis wrote their famous article because Warren, a genuine Boston Brahmin, was outraged that common newspapers had had the effrontery to report on his private entertainments. As such the class content of the privacy norms advanced by the article is plain.[12]

---

[10] See, e.g., Monique Mann and Marcus Smith, 'Automated Facial Recognition Technology: Recent Developments and Approaches to Oversight' (2017) 40(1) *UNSW Law Journal* 121 who rely on an article by the author describing some of the case law outlined in this chapter (Jake Goldenfein, 'Police Photography and Privacy: Identity, Stigma, and Reasonable Expectation' (2013) 36(1) *UNSW Law Journal* 256).

[11] *Regulations for the Measuring and Photographing of Criminal Prisoners 1896* (S.R.&O, 1896, No 762).

[12] Robert Post, 'The Social Foundations of Privacy: Community and Self in the Common Law Tort' (1989) 77 *California Law Review* 957, 976; see also Raymond Wacks, *Privacy: A Very Short Introduction* (Oxford University Press, 2010) 53, where he argues Warren wrote the article in response to the presence of the unwelcome 'yellow press' at his daughter's wedding. However, according to Amy Gajda in 'What If Samuel D. Warren Hadn't Married a Senator's Daughter?: Uncovering the Press Coverage that led to "The Right to Privacy"' (2008) 35 *Michigan State Law Review* 37, Wacks' rationale is unlikely considering Warren himself was only married in 1883 and certainly didn't have a daughter of marrying age by 1890. She writes that the article was more likely a response to over 60 news reportages about Warren and his wife (and senator's daughter), Mabel Bayard, and her family, between the years 1882 and 1890 covering topics including their wedding, 'table gossip' about entertainments and art purchases, various deaths in the family, Bayard's friendship with Mrs Grover Cleveland, the scandalous 21-year-old First Lady, and Senator Bayard's marriage to a much younger wife (following the death of Mabel's mother). Gajda adds, at 57, that the irritation may have been increased by these gossip columns being interspersed with advertisements for 'toilet requisites' and fruit juice.

That is, while privacy rights were being formulated to preserve middle-class personality from photographic intrusion, no equivalent was emerging for the lower classes, who were also being surreptitiously documented. For example, Paul Martin, pioneer of concealed London photography (and others), freely engaged in 'middle class social adventurism',[13] intruding on the lives of the downtrodden, the 'abnormal' and the desperate in the name of art. Vagrants and the homeless were relentlessly photographed to satisfy social curiosity, while privacy rights privileged mainly private property and its exemplar, the home, as protected spaces. The liberal commitment to sanctity of the home had even provoked William Blackstone to comment that 'the law has so particular and tender a regard to the immunity of a man's house, that it stiles it his castle'.[14] That distinct class treatment has since been embedded into protections against state interference with individual liberty. For example, a 1962 Australian High Court judgment, concerning the requirement that an individual supply information about his livelihood and means of support in order to answer vagrancy charges,[15] offers another demonstration of privacy's class character continuing into the twentieth century. There, Chief Justice Dixon clarified that the law requiring individuals to answer to the accusation of vagrancy 'was never meant to provide a weapon against the outwardly respectable householder who refuses to divulge his business and declines to discuss his sources of income or subsistence. It has never been regarded as overthrowing the rights to privacy or reticence of the ordinary or outwardly respectable householder.'[16]

The focus on the home in privacy thinking thus initially excluded protections for material produced through interactions with the state. That the people subjected to police photography and biological measurement were criminals, deviants, and undesirables meant privacy was irrelevant. Further, mugshot photos were historically created 'in public', outside the courtroom prior to a trial, in prisons, or at police stations in circumstances of arrest, without intrusion into private spaces. The content of identification images, being representations communicating that an individual had some engagement with the criminal justice system, therefore also revealed nothing private as such. Principles of open justice, by which courts of law should be open to the public, fortified this view. It is not surprising then that privacy law excluded from its contemplation images of the downtrodden collected in public, such as criminal and suspect identification images. As privacy entered the domain of universal human right around the middle of the twentieth century, however, this calculation began to change. Rather than balancing individual privacy rights against

---

[13] Susan Sontag, *On Photography* (Penguin, 1977) 55 referring to the *flâneur*; See also Christa Ludlow, '"The Gentlest of Predations": Photography and Privacy Law' (2006) 10 *Law Text Culture* 135, 138 citing Jacob A Riis, *How the Other Half Lives* (Bedford/St Martin's, 1890), and the work of photographers Paul Martin, Eugene Atget, and Harold Cazneaux.
[14] William Blackstone, *Commentaries on the Laws of England in Four Books* (Oxford, 1765–1769) Book 4, 223.
[15] *Zanetti v. Hill* (1962) 108 CLR 433.
[16] Ibid 7.

freedom of the press or of speech, the law also had to play a role in balancing individual liberty against the requirements of an effective state, something inherent in the political traditions that it emerged from, producing a legal subject entitled to certain 'reasonable expectations'.

CONSTITUTIONAL PRIVACY PROTECTIONS

The law has long played a role in the liberal delimiting of governmental power and thus in intermediating or modulating the relationship between state agencies and individuals. That legal limitation is often framed in terms of 'privacy' and its relationship to the rule of law. Liberal theory, by wrestling 'with the problems of securing governmental legitimacy and authority, political obligation and order',[17] provides an account of the state's legitimate right to resort to force. Privacy, in its connection to the rule of law,[18] plays a role in constraining this legitimate right. Shortly after the English Glorious Revolution of 1688, in which a union of English Parliamentarians overthrew King James II for attempting to make the law 'alterable wholesale by the King', effectively making him 'supreme over Parliament and, in fact, a despot',[19] Locke published his *Two Treatises*.[20] He argued for the separation of executive and legislative powers whereby the legislature has ultimate authority over deploying the force of the Commonwealth, but no power to enforce those laws. This formulation of a limited state suggested that law should be both articulating and restraining of state power at the same time. An early expression of that political exercise is the classic 1765 English case of *Entick* v. *Carrington*,[21] in which officers of the executive searched a man's house for 'seditious libels' without a *judicial* warrant. The judgment is worth quoting at length:

> It now appears that this enormous trespass and violent proceeding has been done upon mere surmise; but the verdict says such warrants have been granted by Secretaries of State ever since the Revolution; if they have, it is high time to put an end to them, for if they are held to be legal the liberty of this country is at an end; it is the publishing of a libel which is the crime, and not the having it locked up in a private drawer in a man's study; but if having it in one's custody was the crime, no power can lawfully break into a man's house and study to search for evidence against him; this would be worse than the Spanish Inquisition for ransacking a man's secret

---

[17] Paul Wilkinson, *Terrorism and the Liberal State* (Macmillan, 2nd ed, 1986) 5.
[18] See, e.g., Lisa Austin, 'Getting Past Privacy? Surveillance, the Charter, and the Rule of Law' (2012) 27(3) *Canadian Journal of Law and Society* 381.
[19] George Macaulay Trevelyan, *The English Revolution, 1688–1689* (Oxford University Press, 1938) 165.
[20] John Locke and John Whiston, *Two Treatises on Government* (6th ed) (London Printed, 1772, first printed 1690). It is believed the book was actually written before the revolution, probably completed around 1680.
[21] *Entick* v. *Carrington* (1765) 19 How St Tr 1029. In that case, the plaintiff brought an action against the clerks of the Secretary of State, the Earl of Halifax, to remedy damage caused in the execution of a search warrant for the plaintiff's premises seeking seditious material he allegedly authored for his as yet unrealised newspaper *The Monitor*.

drawers and boxes to come at some evidence against him, is like racking his body to come at his secret thoughts. The warrant is to seize all the plaintiff's books and papers without exception, and carry them before Lord Halifax; what? has a Secretary of State a right to see all a man's private letters of correspondence, family concerns, trade and business? This would be monstrous indeed; and if it were lawful, no man could endure to live in this country.[22]

Much of the case concerned whether there was due authority for the issuance of the warrant (in that it was ordered by an officer of the executive rather than the judiciary), whether the warrant was properly executed, or whether the plaintiff's case was statute barred. It also began a commentary on how losing control over one's papers and the expression of one's thoughts could be conceptualised as a type of harm compared to unmediated visual perception, which could not.[23] But it also very clearly expressed the role of privacy's liberal legal subject in drawing the boundary around, and protecting, an unknowable inner-self. The proto-privacy ideas expressed in *Entick* also eventually informed the development of the constitutional right to privacy in the United States. *Entick* was first cited in the 1886 case of *Boyd* v. *US*,[24] after which the US courts began to articulate a protected private sphere, with the 'early republican commitment to privacy [eventually] maturing into a much more far-reaching right against state intrusion'. The cases in which this privacy right 'matured' include: *Griswold* v. *Connecticut* (1965),[25] *Eisenstadt* v. *Baird* (1972),[26] *Roe* v. *Wade* (1973),[27] *Pennsylvania* v. *Casey* (1992),[28] and *Lawrence* v. *Texas* (2003).[29] These were all connected to privacy's function in protecting 'liberty' from improper state intrusion.[30] As made clear by Kennedy J in *Lawrence*, 'Liberty presumes an autonomy of self that includes freedom of thought, belief, expression, and certain intimate conduct'.[31]

How privacy law evolved to address the technologies and practices of biological and behavioural archives, however, is better illustrated through the European Constitutional jurisprudence concerning Article 8 of the ECHR – the Right to Private Life.[32] This is, of course, not the only jurisprudence that limits state

[22] *Entick* v. *Carrington* (1765) 19 How St Tr 1029, 812.
[23] Where Camden J noted 'the eye cannot by the laws of England be guilty of a trespass'.
[24] *Boyd* v. *United States*, 116 US 616, 1212 (1886).
[25] *Griswold* v. *Connecticut*, 381 US 479 (1965).
[26] *Eisenstadt* v. *Baird*, 405 US 438 (1972).
[27] *Roe* v. *Wade*, 410 US 113 (1973).
[28] *Pennsylvania* v. *Casey*, 505 US 833 (1992).
[29] *Lawrence* v. *Texas*, 539 US 558 (2003).
[30] For instance, as described in James Q Whitman, 'Two Western Cultures of Privacy: Dignity versus Liberty' (2003–2004) 113 *Yale Law Journal* 1151.
[31] *Lawrence* v. *Texas*, 539 US 558 (2003). Kennedy J notes at 562 just prior to this quote: 'Liberty protects the person from unwarranted government intrusions into a dwelling or other private places. In our tradition the State is not omnipresent in the home. And there are other spheres of our lives and existence, outside the home, where the State should not be a dominant presence. Freedom extends beyond spatial bounds.'
[32] *Convention for the Protection of Human Rights and Fundamental Freedoms*, opened for signature 4 November 1950, 213 UNTS 221 (entered into force 3 September 1953), as amended by *Protocol No*

interference with private lives, the retention of identification images in police databases, or the permissible boundaries of general file-keeping. But the US Fourth Amendment's restrictions on search and seizure, for instance, while representing a significant limitation on governmental capacity to conduct surveillance, never comprehensively extended to preventing the collection, retention, or disclosure of identifiable criminal images, or even to the issue of images taken on arrest remaining available despite no subsequent conviction, as practices like the 'perp walk',[33] commercial companies performing criminal history checks,[34] and the tabloid mugshot publishing industry make clear.[35] For instance, in his text *The Eternal Criminal Record*,[36] legal scholar James Jacobs has comprehensively outlined the discrimination and criminal justice consequences of the US treatment of criminal records as public information, suggesting privacy laws are unlikely to inhibit the collection, retention, processing, or disclosure of identifying information collected by US law enforcement agencies irrespective of a conviction.

The US Fourth Amendment's failure to address these police (and private) practices stems from competing First Amendment protections of speech, and a strong conceptual connection to the protection of private property, the body, and intimate life, rather than identity per se. When *Entick* was adopted by American judges in the Fourth Amendment and 'general right to privacy' jurisprudence,[37] it translated into

---

11 to the Convention for the Protection of Human Rights and Fundamental Freedoms, opened for signature 11 May 1994, ETS No 155 (entered into force 1 November 1998) and by *Protocol No 14 to the Convention for the Protection of Human Rights and Fundamental Freedoms*, opened for signature 13 May 2004, ETS No 194 (entered into force 1 June 2010). This stipulates: *Right to respect for private and family life* – (1) Everyone has the right to respect for his private and family life, his home and his correspondence. (2) There shall be no interference by a public authority with the exercise of this right except such as in accordance with the law and is necessary in a democratic society in the interests of national security, public safety or the economic well-being of the country, for the prevention of disorder or crime, for the protection of health or morals, for the protection of rights and freedoms of others.

[33] Ryan Haggland, 'Constitutional Protections Against the Harms to Suspects in Custody Stemming from Perp Walks' (2012) 81(7) *Mississippi Law Journal* 1757, 1781.

[34] See, e.g., James Jacobs, *The Eternal Criminal Record* (Harvard University Press, 2015), especially Chapter 5. Also note at 10, where he says: 'Strikingly, in the face of the new information technologies, courts have not sought to limit access and dissemination of court records but, to the contrary, have decided to make many records available online and to sell whole criminal record databases to commercial information vendors.'

[35] David Kravets, 'Mugshot-Removal Sites Accused of Extortion', *Wired* (online), 15 July 2013 www.wired.com/2013/07/mugshot-removal-extortion/. This practice involves publishing identification images and arrest information irrespective of conviction, apparently under protection of the US Constitution's 1st Amendment. Under Freedom of Information Laws, publishers can gain access to this material despite the existence of a 'privacy' exemption; See also Haggland, above n 33, and Gregory Nathanial Wolf, 'Smile for the Camera, the World is going to See that Mug: The Dilemma of Privacy Interests in Mug Shots' (2013) 114(8) *Columbia Law Review* 2227.

[36] Jacobs, above n 34.

[37] *Boyd v. United States*, 116 US 616 (1886) which, following *Entick*, held that a search and seizure was equivalent to 'a compulsory production of a man's private papers'. The general right to privacy was derived from a combination of constitutional amendments, this right was expressed in the cases *Griswold v. Connecticut*, 381 US 479 (1965) and *Lawrence v. Texas*, 539 US 558 (2003).

a protection of individuals from governmental intrusion. But even the idea that privacy would 'protect people not places' as expressed in *Katz* and *Griswold* did little to sever privacy's connection to the home (and its attendant categories such as family, communications, sexuality, the body, and other forms of private property). Indeed, it also reified that requirement through contrivance of the 'reasonable expectation of privacy' test[38] – a test that measures the possibility of a privacy violation according to what norm, with respect to disclosure of information or intrusion on seclusion, a reasonable person in that situation might expect. There has, as such, been little conception of privacy in civic, political, commercial, or juridical life.

The US Supreme Court confirmed that interpretation when reconsidering the application of the Fourth Amendment to 'privacy in public' in the 2012 case of *United States v. Jones*, which addressed the question of whether unwarranted surveillance by GPS vehicle tracker attached to a car constituted a search.[39] Privacy's privileging of property was again reiterated in Scalia J's majority. The majority accepted that the vehicle surveillance constituted a 'search' under the Fourth Amendment, but primarily because it constituted a trespass against personal property. The concurring opinion from Sotomayor J did challenge that reasoning, however, claiming such an approach was limited in the context of technologically sophisticated monitoring that, for instance, uses GPS-enabled smartphones to duplicate the monitoring performed by vehicle tracking devices. In particular, she noted that the focus on private property, and thus the organisation of privacy around a 'trespassory' test, provides little guidance in the face of technical advances.[40] And indeed, the more recent *Carpenter* case took this further, suggesting that the third party doctrine as developed in *United States v. Miller* and *Smith v. Maryland* was not absolute,[41] and that cell phone tower location data should be considered a sufficiently sensitive data type to be protected by the need for a warrant showing probable cause.[42] While Justice Roberts described the existence of a reasonable expectation of privacy in cell tower location data premised on the notion that it is reasonable to expect that law enforcement will not maintain records of all persons' movements, especially because those movements become a window into 'familial, political, professional, religious, and sexual associations', that case did not, however, dispense with the idea that the private sphere is defined wholly by the home, property, or the intimacies of life, nor did it deal with impacts on identity in any meaningful way.

---

[38] *Katz v. United States*, 389 US 347 (1967).
[39] *United States v. Jones*, 132 S Ct 945 (2012); See also Daniel Solove, 'United States v. Jones and the Future of Privacy Law: The Potential Far-Reaching Implications of the GPS Surveillance Case' (2012) 11 *Privacy Law and Security Report* 180.
[40] Ibid 2 (Sotomayor J).
[41] *United States v. Miller*, 307 US 174 (1939); *Smith v. Maryland*, 442 US 735 (1979).
[42] *Carpenter v. United States*, 585 US no. 16–402 (2018).

European law has adopted a different interpretation of the 'reasonable expectation of privacy' test in the context of states aggregating information from the public domain, and, in the state surveillance context, looks more closely at the effects of administrative file keeping on individuals. The ECHR, when drafted in 1950 by the Council of Europe and entering into force in 1953, was the pre-eminent human rights system anywhere in the world. Legal historian AWB Simpson points out that while the system drew heavily on the Universal Declaration of Human Rights, it was especially significant for giving individual and group standing to initiate complaints, as well as providing super-national juridical supervision of those actions.[43] It thus produced a largely vertical mechanism for interceding in the relationship between citizen and state, and satisfying individual rights. This post-war push to create a meaningful international human rights regime eventually addressed photographic and file keeping practices by states when institutional identification practices began to enter public space outside the scope of ordinary criminal investigation. In doing so, the case law seems to have eventually abandoned reasonable expectations of privacy as a meaningful determinant of whether Article 8 is enlivened in cases of surveillance by public authorities (in certain situations), although retaining the standard in the context of press intrusion.[44] Abandoning that test is precisely what has rendered privacy useful in the profiling context. This also reflects recognition that file-keeping by media organisations and law enforcement agencies may require the application of different legal standards, as well as an understanding of the private–public distinction as irrelevant for determining the appropriate scope of legal protection. Article 8 of the ECHR addressed those practices by focusing on identity as the site of protection and producing a legal subject that was entitled not to be burdened by the mark or stigma of a particular type of institutional representation.

PRIVACY, IDENTIFICATION, STIGMATISATION

As noted above, the 2019 ECHR decision of *Catt v. United Kingdom* clarified that retention of identity information in certain types of policing databases may infringe on rights to private life with absolutely no reference to a reasonable expectation of privacy. This particular decision concerned the degree to which the data and images stored in a domestic intelligence policing database attracted adequate oversight considering their sensitivity, and whether there was a 'pressing social need' to retain that data (in the absence of rules establishing a maximum retention period). The

---

[43] A W B Simpson, *Human Rights and the End of Empire: Britain and the Genesis of the European Convention* (Oxford University Press, 2004).
[44] See, e.g., Eric Barendt, '"A Reasonable Expectation of Privacy": A Coherent or Redundant Concept?' in Andrew Kenyon (ed) *Comparative Defamation and Privacy Law* (Cambridge University Press, 2016), where he argues for abandoning the standard in both contexts.

judgment also demonstrated a lack of sympathy for the tacit common law powers relied on by UK police to compile a 'domestic extremism database', as well as the police's cynical use of the language of 'domestic extremism'. But as we will see, the turning point in the Article 8 jurisprudence, and the touchstone upon which the *Catt* court constantly referred, concerned recognition that being identified in a police information system has the potential to stigmatise those represented.[45] The language of stigmatisation is telling, as it refers etymologically to the process of being branded with hot iron,[46] the practice for criminal identification that was directly usurped by police photography in the nineteenth century.[47] The specificity of harm is an important dimension to these privacy actions as identification of citizens has long been a critical state function – sometimes called the traditional 'regulatory power' – that was part of the liberal contract necessary to make private transacting juridically possible.[48] Privacy thus becomes an issue only in the context of identity mechanisms that are objectionable in some way – typically those exercises in policing or criminal justice that give content to a representation beyond simple identification. These are often exercises that follow historian Jane Caplan's recognition that the question of 'who is that person?' is usually accompanied by the question 'what type of person is that?'[49] A question that is inevitably raised in the context of police identification images.

That identification photography could interfere with Article 8 for problematically archiving identity in police files was argued for the first time in the 1973 case of X v. *United Kingdom*.[50] While demonstrating against apartheid at a rugby match between Britain and South Africa, a protestor was arrested, forcibly restrained, and photographed against her will. Police informed her the images would be retained for future reference in case she caused trouble at other Springbok matches. After her release, X complained that retention of those images violated her Article 8 rights. The Commission found the application inadmissible for three reasons. First, the issues raised were not those ordinarily dealt with by privacy, in that 'there was no invasion of the applicant's privacy in the sense that the authorities entered her home and took photographs of her there'. There was thus no physical invasion of the

---

[45] S v. *United Kingdom* [2008] Eur Court HR 1581.
[46] See, e.g., entry in Samuel Johnson's *A Dictionary of the English Language* (W Strahan, 1755).
[47] In the lower court *Catt* decision, Lord Sumption of the UK Supreme Court did not believe that being listed in the 'National Domestic Extremism Database', a computerised and searchable police database storing intelligence about public protests and their attendees, carried any stigma or suspicion of guilt. However, this position was implicitly rejected by the Court, which insisted that the Article 8 jurisprudence was very much interested in the restrictions of processing of (especially sensitive categories of) data imposed by the GDPR and *Law Enforcement Directive*.
[48] See, e.g., Markus Dirk Dubber, *The Police Power: Patriarchy and the Foundations of American Government* (Columbia University Press, 2005).
[49] Jane Caplan, '"This or That Particular Person": Protocols of Identification in 19th Century Europe' in Jane Caplan and John Torpey (eds) *Documenting Individual Identity: The Development of State Practices in the Modern World* (Princeton University Press, 2001).
[50] X v. *United Kingdom* (European Court of Human Rights, Commission, Application No 5877/72, 12 December 1973).

private sphere. Second, 'the photographs related to a public incident in which she was voluntarily taking part'. There was thus nothing 'private' about the content of the images or what they communicated. And third, 'they were taken solely for the purpose of her future identification on similar public occasions and there is no suggestion that they have been made available to the general public or used for any other purpose'.[51] There was thus no improper disclosure of private information – an integral element of the right of privacy as it applied to press institutions.

These arguments represent the starting point of privacy law's application to identification photography. The Commission had no concept of how images revealing nothing private nor intimate, taken in public, and not made publicly available, could interfere with the protected realm. The fact that X was identified, with her personal details being recorded along with her image for storage in police files, was of no consequence. The focus remained on the location in which the images were collected (outside the home), the quality of the information captured (in this case nothing sensitive nor intimate – simply the fact that she had been at a protest and was confronted by authorities), and the absence of disclosure. Retention was irrelevant because the information was prima facie public. The decision represents an understanding of the photographic archive as defensible in liberal thinking when the photographed subjects were deserving of such treatment. But this photographic practice was not in a prison, courthouse, or police station – it was in public. The photographed subject was not a deviant, criminal, or vagabond, but a protester expressing a political position, and her image remained in the archive representing that she was 'known' to police.

Related practices came to the courts again in the 1992 case of *Lupker and Others v. The Netherlands*,[52] concerning the police's use of images that were initially created by other government agencies. There, police were showing passport and driver's licence photographs to witnesses for suspect identification in a criminal investigation. Complainants argued that an ordinance requiring administratively collected images (i.e. licence and passport photos) to be copied and stored in police archives, which gave the police the ability to perform that type of investigation, constituted an Article 8 violation.[53] It is worth noting the aggregation of administrative images into centralised databases managed by security and intelligence

[51] Ibid at [2].
[52] *Lupker v. The Netherlands* (European Court of Human Rights, Commission, Decision No. 18395/91, 7 December 1992).
[53] Elizabeth Lupker was one of a group of demonstrators occupying an office building to protest against new anti-squatting laws. According to police, within that group a more radical core had escalated the protest by starting a fire. Police had used wire-tapping and informants to ascertain the participants' identities and motives, but they also exhibited a book of suspects' photographs, aggregated from other administrative agencies, to anyone who may have known them in an effort to confirm the occupants' identities. When that activity was challenged under Article 8, the Dutch government submitted to the Commission that while there was some disclosure of the photographs it was only to witnesses who stated they recognised the persons possibly involved, and that any criminal investigation inevitably entails intrusion upon the privacy of potential suspects.

policing agencies is precisely the process necessary for building national facial recognition databases and capabilities.[54] With respect to the police archiving of administration images in the early 1990s, however, the Commission did not believe the gathering of identification information in that way, particularly when subsequently used in the context of criminal investigation, had sufficient impact on the individual to violate privacy. That is, because the photographs were not *taken* in a way that intruded on the applicants' privacy (as they had been gathered in police archives only after they were voluntarily provided with passport or licence applications), the Commission followed the precedent from X. There was not yet any understanding that the aggregation of otherwise 'public' images or information into a police file itself could have privacy implications, especially where those images were initially produced outside of a police context.

It was only a few years later, however, that the court began to acknowledge that the creation of a permanent identified record within a criminal information system could constitute a violation of private life.[55] The relevant question became the degree to which this information was entered into a *data processing* system for the sake of identification. That case was *Friedl* v. *Austria*, which also concerned police photography of protestors in public places for the sake of identification.[56] Initially, the Commission found no breach of Article 8, as there had been no intrusion into the 'inner circle' of Friedl's private life, and the prevention of crime and disorder were seen as legitimate aims of the state and necessary in democratic society. But in so finding, neither the location the images were taken (i.e. whether in private or public), the quality of information recorded, nor the absence of any disclosure were of particular influence. Rather, the reasoning placed greater (and arguably more sophisticated) emphasis on the fact that Friedl's image had neither been 'processed' nor 'identified':

> In this context, the Commission attaches weight to the assurances given by the respondent Government according to which the individual persons on the photographs taken remained anonymous in that no names were noted down, the personal data recorded and photographs taken were not entered into a data processing

---

[54] Jake Goldenfein, 'Close Up: The Government's Facial Recognition Plan Could Reveal More than Just Your Identity' *The Conversation* (online), 5 March 2018, https://theconversation.com/close-up-the-governments-facial-recognition-plan-could-reveal-more-than-just-your-identity-92261.

[55] Ludwig Friedl was one of a number of participants protesting in an underground walkway to draw attention to the situation of homeless persons in Austria. Pedestrians routinely complained about these demonstrators, who slept and cooked in situ, thus creating a public inconvenience. Eventually police instructed the demonstrators to vacate, citing the need for statutory authorisation to occupy that location. Police took photographs of protesters while removing them for use in case of prosecution, and the entire process was recorded on video. Although the applicant claimed he was photographed individually and identified under coercion, the Government argued no personal information was recorded, nor were photographs entered into any 'data-processing system'.

[56] *Friedl* v. *Austria* (European Court of Human Rights, Application No 15225/89, Chamber, 31 January 1995).

system, and no action was taken to identify the persons photographed on that occasion by means of data processing.[57]

After the Commission's decision, the issue was referred to the Strasbourg Court but settled in favour of the complainant before being heard, resulting in compensation and the images being destroyed. But even the Commission decision still refocused the question of what constituted a reasonable expectation of privacy away from a simple assessment of an image taken in public, and towards an understanding of those images in their archival context – that is, how those images would be put to use – for creating an institutional identity. Similar practices and legal thinking eventually resulted in a finding that Article 8 had been violated in the 2003 case of *Perry v. The United Kingdom*,[58] where police surreptitiously used surveillance cameras to link an image to an individual and facilitate witness identification (i.e. non-automated facial recognition). In bringing identification and data processing into privacy law's purview, the court here did not entirely abandon the reasonable expectation of privacy test, but rather refocused it away from the traditional preoccupation on the character of the information captured, and towards its use by public authorities.

Around the same time, the Strasbourg Court was also considering privacy's application to the creation of administrative and intelligence profiles about individuals in the absence of conviction. Although not in a photographic or biometric context, the cases of *Amman v. Switzerland*,[59] *Rotaru v. Romania*,[60] *PG v. The United Kingdom*,[61] and *Segerstedt-Wiberg v. Sweden*[62] dramatically suggested that private life considerations arise once any systematic or permanent record of material from the public domain comes into existence and is held by the state. Underpinning those cases was the idea that individuals not having committed crimes should not necessarily be the subjects of ongoing police observation (although some judges still struggled to see how 'non-private' information could affect private life).[63] These cases did not suggest that such surveillance was always unjustifiable and rights-offending, but rather clarified that the quality of information recorded was not the only determinant of whether the surveillance affected privacy (something that the *Carpenter* case clarifies is still the preoccupation of privacy in the United States). From here, the reasonable expectation of privacy test that had prevented (and in certain jurisdictions continues to prevent) privacy jurisprudence from addressing

---

[57] Ibid at [50].
[58] *Perry v. The United Kingdom* [2003] VI Eur Court HR 141.
[59] *Amann v. Switzerland* [2000] II Eur Court HR 245.
[60] *Rotaru v. Romania* [2000] V Eur Court HR 109.
[61] *PG v. The United Kingdom* [2001] XI Eur Court HR 195.
[62] *Segerstedt-Wiberg v. Sweden* [2006] VII Eur Court HR 87.
[63] See, e.g., the partially dissenting opinion of Bonello J in *Rotaru v. Romania*, who asked, at [6] how the storage of records of an individual's public pursuits violates privacy, reiterating that the protection of Article 8 had until that point only protected confidential matters such as medical, sexual, family, and possibly professional information, being intimate areas in which 'public intrusion would be an warranted encroachment on the natural barriers of self'.

the collection of non-convicted persons in police filing systems, began to accommodate recognition of 'archival harms', especially with respect to photography and biometrics. The clearest expression can be found in the 2008 decision of *S and Marper v. United Kingdom*, which effectively abandoned the language of 'reasonable expectations' altogether in the context of identification information retained in police databases.[64] S had been charged with attempted robbery at age 11, and had his fingerprints, images, and DNA samples taken by police, but he was later acquitted. Marper was arrested for harassment of his partner, but they reconciled and the charge was not pressed. Both applicants requested that police destroy their images, DNA samples, and fingerprints after the investigations were resolved, but police refused. At that time, the collection and retention of evidence in the UK was governed by legislation stipulating that data need not be destroyed unless the person is no longer suspected of having committed the offence.[65] If a person was convicted, had been previously convicted, or suspicion remained after an investigation had concluded, retention was permitted.

The applicants argued that retention of fingerprints and DNA constituted a violation of their Article 8 rights because it created ongoing suspicion about them, despite not having being convicted. They submitted that the information retained was critically linked to their individual (physical and social) identity, being a type of personal information they were entitled to keep within their control. Counsel for the Home Secretary argued that retention was for the purpose of future investigation of offences, meaning the applicants would only be affected if their profiles matched those found at future crime scenes. It was thus submitted that retaining this information did not interfere with privacy because without further data, a person is not identifiable from fingerprints or DNA samples. Several instances were cited wherein retained DNA profiles from persons who had been suspected but not convicted of offences matched crime-scene stains from rape victims several years later. But the Court objected to that argument, noting, 'notwithstanding the advantages provided by comprehensive extension of the DNA database, other Contracting States have chosen to set limits on the retention and use of such data with a view to achieving a proper balance with the competing interests of preserving respect for private life'.[66] It was thus unimpressed by the 'blanket and indiscriminate nature of the power of retention' under the UK domestic laws in this case.[67] There was also a wholesale rejection of the argument that retention had no significant effects on applicants unless matches implicated them in a subsequent offence, and the Court recognised that of 'particular concern' was the risk of '*stigmatisation*, stemming from the fact that persons in the position of the

---

[64] S v. *United Kingdom* [2008] Eur Court HR 1581.
[65] The *Police and Criminal Evidence Act 1984* (UK) (C.60) and the *Criminal Justice and Police Act 2001* (UK) (C.16).
[66] S v. *United Kingdom* [2008] Eur Court HR 1581, at [112].
[67] Ibid at [89].

applicants, who have not been convicted of any offence and are entitled to the presumption of innocence, are treated in the same way as convicted persons'.[68] The 'reasonable expectation of privacy' test was not used to determine whether the retention offended private life, with the Court preferring to base its decision on 'the specific context in which the information at issue has been recorded and retained, the nature of the records, the way in which these records are used and processed and the results that may be obtained'.[69]

This reflected a very significant change in how privacy was to be conceptualised with respect to government records and the specificities of law enforcement archiving and information processing. However, the new privacy envelope was yet to include images and information not collected on arrest – i.e. collected in public, often in the context of intelligence work, without any pursuit of a charge or conviction. That ultimately took some time, with recalcitrant judges insisting that neither 'data processing', the creation of profiles, nor the risk of stigmatisation sufficed to enliven Article 8. Rather, in the 2009 case of R (on the application of Wood) v. Metropolitan Police Commissioner,[70] where a police unit was taking photographs of anti-arms trade protestors to make identified 'spotter cards', the focus remained on how, where, and for what purpose the images were collected, with judges insisting on the reasonable expectations standard. That insistence is also what led to the rejection of Article 8 violations in the lower court Catt decisions.[71] But the tide was changing. The 2013 MK v. France case,[72] concerning the construction and use of a biometric fingerprint database including non-convicted persons, 'the automated fingerprint identification system', echoed the risk of stigmatisation associated with retained data giving the impression that persons represented are not being treated as innocent, while also avoiding the language of 'reasonable expectations'. The question of reasonable expectations in these cases become precisely the question of whether the 'social' mask and the 'institutional' mask could be thought through in similar terms, with the courts unsure whether the law should see a difference in the observations and reports compiled by members of the public such as journalists, and observations and reports prepared by the police.[73]

The 2019 Catt decision appears to have finally resolved the issue. As the case law unfolded, there was an acknowledgment of harm to identity and recognition of Article 8's interest in the relationship between identification photography, archives and databases, and the capabilities of law enforcement information processing. However, the limitations of this constitutional privacy mechanism also became clear. For instance, in the penultimate Catt appeal, the court held that Article 8(1)

---

[68] Ibid at [122] (emphasis added).
[69] Ibid at [67].
[70] R (Wood) v. Metropolitan Police Commissioner [2009] 4 All ER 951.
[71] R (Catt) v. The Commissioner of Police of the Metropolis [2012] EWHC 1471 (Admin); R (Catt) v. Commissioner of Police for the Metropolis [2013] EWCA Civ 192; R (Catt) v. Commissioner of Police for the Metropolis [2015] UKSC 9.
[72] MK v. France (European Court of Human Rights, Application No 19522/09, 18 April 2013).
[73] Ibid at [4].

was engaged by the intelligence activities of police, but that the interference was justified under Article 8(2),[74] and ultimately deferred to the more bureaucratic and procedural laws of data protection (discussed further in Chapter 5) to establish the boundaries of legality. That court expressed concern as to whether constitutional privacy rights were still the appropriate mechanism for addressing the realities of state information gathering. The final appeal overturned the decision, however, with the Grand Chamber showing some territorial muscle in claiming that data protection was a sub-species of privacy law and not necessarily a contiguous right.

FACIAL RECOGNITION

In dealing with a set of technological practices that drew information from the body, stored it in filing systems, and created institutional identities, legal protections associated with constitutional privacy rights, in Europe at least, came a long way. The shifting boundary between permissible and impermissible photographic observation and measurement in this context appears to be linked to a judicial understanding of the significance and form of the police archive – specifically, the growing relationship between identification through photography and biometrics, data processing, and systematic profile creation. That is, privacy law evolved to address the harms associated with the 'bureaucratic-clerical system' that included photography and the filing cabinet, along with the technical capacity to cross-reference and identify individuals. Privacy law, in the form of a constitutional human right, reacted to photography's capacity to betray identity,[75] hold on to that identity in the law enforcement information systems that comprise the state's memory, assign categorical identity,[76] and read that information in a way that produces its subjects as criminally suspect.[77] The potential stigmatisation caused by having identification material in police files was understood as a product of the state's assignment of categorical identity. It was not merely the recording of a name and likeness, it was the recording of a name and likeness in a situation which could prompt a calculation as to criminal propensity. It is not necessarily about protection from error, but rather protection from the potential for error in judgment about individuals caused by what the representation of an individual in a police information system communicates. The solution was to privilege the unknowable dimensions of self by removing the representation from the archives and making the person again unknown.

This jurisprudence concerned a particularly narrow form of information gathering and profiling, however. A critical question is its applicability to automated facial recognition of images collected in public, particularly when using portraits

---

[74] Ibid at [6].
[75] *Friedl* v. *Austria* (European Court of Human Rights, Application No 15225/89, Chamber, 31 January 1995).
[76] *Perry* v. *The United Kingdom* [2003] VI Eur Court HR 141.
[77] *S* v. *United Kingdom* [2008] Eur Court HR 1581.

generated outside the policing context. Indeed, it is unclear that privacy law will *prevent* the deployment of such systems in the United States or Europe, especially as enrolment in biometric databases typically occurs outside of the policing context. That said, there are now actions challenging police use of facial recognition technologies in lower courts that may ultimately, if appealed, become tests of whether Article 8 will govern or prohibit these practices.[78] There is also movement on these issues outside of Europe. For instance, a national biometric identification regime was struck down on privacy grounds by constitutional courts in Jamaica for making the recording of biometric information compulsory.[79] Explicitly noting the risk of using biometric data for profiling, the Jamaican court followed the dissent from the Indian *Aadhaar* case, where the majority limited but ultimately upheld the validity of a national biometric identification system in that jurisdiction, partly because it did not violate a reasonable expectation of privacy.[80] Critically, the privacy issue in both these cases was the building of centralised, systematic institutional citizen identity systems that relied on biometrics, (even in the context of certain government agencies having that information already), rather than the *use* of biometric technologies by particular agencies.

Regulating the technology by regulating particular applications has gained some traction in places like London, where a police ethics committee deemed facial recognition technology did not sufficiently improve policing capabilities for its potential to undermine the idea of policing by consent. Although the panel also offered a set of guidelines for how facial recognition might be used more ethically by police in the future. They noted this required: ensuring the benefit to public safety was not outweighed by public distrust of the technology; that the technology did not generate gender or racial bias in policing; that each deployment was assessed and authorised as necessary and proportionate; that operators are adequately trained; and that further guidelines are developed.[81]

In the United States, some privacy advocates have proposed banning facial recognition technology wholesale, but not necessarily through preventing the creation of biometric databases.[82] To that end, multiple jurisdictions are addressing facial recognition at the *application* level by implementing (or considering) bans or moratoriums on the use of facial recognition by state entities. For instance, the city of San Francisco made it unlawful for government departments to obtain, access, or

---

[78] See, e.g., Steven Morris, 'Office Worker launches UK's first facial recognition legal action' *Guardian*, 21 May 2019, www.theguardian.com/technology/2019/may/21/office-worker-launches-uks-first-police-facial-recognition-legal-action.

[79] *Julian J Robinson v. The Attorney General of Jamaica* [2019] JMFC Full 04.

[80] *Justice K.S. Puttaswamy (Retd.) v. Union of India and Others* [2018] Writ Petition (Civil) No. 494 of 2012 & Connected Matters.

[81] See e.g., 'Ethics Panel sets out future framework for facial recognition software' (29 May 2019) www.london.gov.uk/press-releases/mayoral/future-framework-for-facial-recognition-software.

[82] See, e.g., Evan Selinger and Woodrow Hartzog, 'Opinion: It's Time for an About-Face on Facial Recognition' *Christian Science Monitor* (online), 22 June 2015 www.csmonitor.com/World/Passcode/Passcode-Voices/2015/0622/Opinion-It-s-time-for-an-about-face-on-facial-recognition.

use 'face recognition technology' or any information obtained from face recognition technology where face recognition means an automated or semi-automated process that assists in identifying or verifying an individual based on an individual's face.[83] In reality, this may be a symbolic but ultimately meaningless exercise (or in the worst case, a calculated distraction), as the law only addresses facial recognition, not other types of similarly effective remote biometrics such as gait or voice recognition, nor the use of video analytics for other types of profiling (as discussed in Chapter 8). Other US jurisdictions like Massachusetts have adopted a more meaningful approach, for instance a Bill establishing a moratorium on state entities from acquiring, possessing, accessing or using *any* remote biometric surveillance system.[84] This would extend to other recognition processes including, gait, voice or other immutable characteristic, and include systems that infer emotion, associations, activities, or locations of individuals. It does not, however, address the building of biometric databases. That said, the US approach of regulating particular uses may be more practical in the context of a large proportion of the population already enrolled in biometric databases, and that enrolment already reflecting racial disparities.[85] Accordingly, the US regulatory trajectory seems to be animated by the discriminatory effects and uses of the technology rather than its more structural consequences.

One high-profile example of potential discrimination in application includes New York City Police using IBM software for analytics on software footage from select cameras around the city.[86] That system allowed officers to search camera footage by skin tone, facial hair, and hair colour, with other systems enabling 'ethnicity tags' like Asian, Black, and White. While this might enable certain types of racial profiling, it is unclear whether this searchability introduces new considerations into the strict privacy analysis. It is also unclear whether engaging in information processing (identification) alone, when data has been voluntarily submitted to the government, would offend these rights outside the policing context. That reading also accounts for why CCTV surveillance generally fails to offend privacy laws.

Meaningful regulation requires recognition of privacy interests in 'public images' like passports and drivers' licences, alongside police portraits. Further, it requires contending with the reality that, in the context of intelligence work, there is no data 'outside' of the policing context. In Europe, the collection and archiving of biometric templates are permitted under data protection law, though protected as

---

[83] Stop Secret Surveillance Ordinance (6 May 2019).
[84] An Act Establishing a Moratorium on Face Recognition and Other Remote Biometric Surveillance Systems Commonwealth of Massachusetts Bill S.1385.
[85] Clare Garvie, Alvaro Bedoya, and Jonathan Frankle 'The Perpetual Line-Up: Unregulated Police Face Recognition in America' (18 October 2016) www.perpetuallineup.org/.
[86] Joseph and Lipp, above n 4.

a special category of personal data,[87] and with less protection in the law enforcement context where processing need only be authorised by law,[88] an approach reflected in US states like Illinois.[89] And while those regimes place procedural limitations on the use of biometric data (although very few in the context of law enforcement) they are not limitations that address building biometric identity databases for the sake of policing. They are instead procedural limitations about the conditions of use. To that end, it is unclear the line of Article 8 jurisprudence discussed above would *prevent* identity matching from CCTV footage of public places (although it would have to be authorised by law) unless that data was used to generate a systematic profile about a person's location, behaviour, associates, or anything else, in a police information system, or used specifically for the purpose of categorisation or segregation.[90] The case law will clarify this in due course.

Another limitation to this jurisprudence is the type of criminal justice profiling to which it applies. The community has become aware that the scale and reach of *intelligence* data collection, analysis, and profiling has never been greater. While perhaps useful in the context of ordinary police forces, including some of their more high-level, political, or intelligence-driven applications, Article 8 has typically not interfered with the practices of intelligence agencies, instead leaving them a wide 'margin of appreciation'.[91] To that end, the privacy jurisprudence focuses on supranational supervision and oversight of states especially with respect to arbitrary interference with individuals, but does not prescribe specific rules for managing information. As Gutwirth and De Hert argue, because 'Article 8 of the Convention is no place for procedural questions ... The transformation of Article 8 into a source of procedural rights and procedural conditions takes it away from the job it was designed for, viz. to prohibit unreasonable exercises of power and to create zones

---

[87] Governed by Article 9 of the GDPR under the rules for processing of special categories of personal data. Here, biometrics is defined in Article 4(14) as data resulting from processing of physical, physiological or behavioural characteristics that allow identity confirmation. Those rules require clear consent.

[88] *Directive (EU) 2016/680 of the European Parliament and of the Council of 27 April 2016 on the protection of natural persons with regard to the processing of personal data by competent authorities for the purposes of the prevention, investigation, detection or prosecution of criminal offences or the execution of criminal penalties, and on the free movement of such data, and repealing Council Framework Decision 2008/977/JHA* (Law Enforcement Directive) [2016] OJ L 119/89, Article 10, suggests when processed by a competent authority for the purposes of preventing, investigating, detecting, or prosecuting criminal offences, it can be processed when provided for by law.

[89] *Illinois Statute Biometric Information Privacy Act* (740 ILCS 14/1 et seq) (West 2016) although this only applies to private entities; House Bill 1493 (2017 Wash Rev Code) (2017).

[90] See Article 29 Data Protection Working Party, 'Opinion 3/2012 on Developments in Biometric Technologies' (Working Paper No WP193) European Commission, 27 April 2012.

[91] See, e.g., *Klass v. Germany* [1978] Eur Court HR 4 concerning 'notification' whether information were held in a filing system; *Leander v. Sweden* (1987) 9 EHRR 433 which gave states the wide margin of appreciation on the article 8 analysis; and *Segerstedt-Wiberg v. Sweden* [2006] VII Eur Court HR 87 in which access to an intelligence archive was again flatly refused.

of opacity.'[92] In the post-9/11 'security' context, the idea of being removed from or not being included in the massive information analytics ecosystem of intelligence work at all strikes as almost absurd. To that end, legal regimes that manage rather than limit the archive, and *focus* on 'access', such as data protection, have ascended in relevance.

CONCLUSION

It is worth breaking down the form of the legal subject developed through this jurisprudence. The structure of Article 8 is useful in this regard as we can read 8(1) as establishing when the right to private life is enlivened, i.e. the conditions by which a person is addressed by the law, and 8(2) as addressing the contingent content of those rights.[93] In the earlier cases, the right was not enlivened by police activities occurring in public, that did not interfere with private spaces or with unauthorised disclosures of classically private (or intimate) information. This then slowly shifted away from concerning only an intimate or spatial dimension of self to also concerning the institutional informational dimensions of self. As was made clear in the *Rotaru* and *Amann* cases in 2000, the collection of information from the public domain into a systematic profile to create a form of institutional identity did more than merely 'identify', it brought that physical person under the purview of privacy. It was a recognition that the institutional mask had replaced the social mask as an important determinant of self. Privacy's subject thus became the inner self of the entity whose outer self was a form of institutional identity that enabled some sort of evaluation or action, whether or not the creation of that categorical or archival identity was objectionable or justified. The jurisprudence made this move in recognition that this institutional identity could *mark* or burden the person through misrepresentation, and therefore had to be justified in the circumstances, because any such representation carried the significance of interaction with the state's criminal justice or security apparatus.

Abandoning the reasonable expectation of privacy test thus redrew the rights-bearing subject of privacy law. The vertical structure implemented by the ECHR's granting to individuals the right to participate in supra-national supervision of states

---

[92] Paul de Hert and Serge Gutwirth, 'Privacy, Data Protection and Law Enforcement: Opacity of the Individual and Transparency of Power' in E Claes, A Duff, and S Gutwirth (eds) *Privacy and the Criminal Law* (Oxford/Intersentia, 2006) 61, 84.

[93] *Convention for the Protection of Human Rights and Fundamental Freedoms*, Article 8 – Right to respect for private and family life:

1. Everyone has the right to respect for his private and family life, his home and his correspondence.
2. There shall be no interference by a public authority with the exercise of this right except such as is in accordance with the law and is necessary in a democratic society in the interests of national security, public safety or the economic well-being of the country, for the prevention of disorder or crime, for the protection of health or morals, or for the protection of the rights and freedoms of others.

also situated this legal subject as the dividing line between the knowable juridical or political role, and the unknowable human subject in a very traditional liberal, citizen–state relation. The legal subject thus privileged the discursive account of the unknowable human.

The case law above outlines a slow evolution in privacy doctrine in line with increased judicial understanding of the ways in which surveillance by law enforcement agencies may be harmful for individuals. Beginning with the question of reasonable expectation of privacy in the contents of the information collected, the test measuring interference with privacy subsequently transformed by interrogating the reasonable expectation of privacy in how that information might be used, and then again by looking at 'the specific context in which the information at issue has been recorded and retained, the nature of the records, the way in which these records are used and processed and the results that may be obtained'.[94] The latter test clearly takes greater account of the surveillance assemblage of the camera (or inkpad or DNA profiler) and the database together, wherein harm is perpetuated through the processing and systematisation of data, rather than the collection or disclosure of sensitive content. But even within that expansion and opening of doctrine, privacy still held defined contours. Indeed, photographic and biometric identity data are not the only data collected by law enforcement or state agencies. And the next chapter describes the practices and political imperatives of behavioural data collection, applied at mass scale, as a mechanism for speculating about how individuals might act in the future.

---

[94] *S and Marper v. UK* [2008] Eur Court HR 1581 at [67].

4

Dossiers, Behavioural Data, and Secret Speculation

The second dimension of the surveillance archive that, complimented biological identity registers, was the recording of behavioural information. Behavioural monitoring emerged with its own technical constellation, its own political rationality, its own capacity to interpret and produce identities, and its own resulting set of social anxieties. It has also received its own treatment in information law. General behavioural data collection, like biological data collection, also began in the realm of policing and criminal justice, specifically intelligence surveillance. Whereas the photograph was the central identifying technique of the criminal register, the 'dossier' – the individuated compilation of highly detailed yet often highly trivial information, covertly amalgamated from multiple sources – is, historically, the central medium of intelligence surveillance.

The knowledge regime of identification photography allowed a single image to answer the questions: 'who is this person?' and to a certain extent 'what kind of person is this?'[1] As Jane Caplan argues: 'Here the juridical identification of the individual actor meets the categorical identification of a type or class: in virtually any systematics of identification, everyone is not only "himself" but also potentially the embodiment of a type, and in an important respect the history of identification is a history not so much of individuality as of categories and their indicators.'[2] In this schema, questions of criminal propensity were directed less at the prediction of specific future criminal behaviours and more at the social distribution of criminality as a particular characteristic or trait. The categorical identity associated with judicial photography arose through the combination of the technical features of the photographic format as well as the 'system of signs and recognitions'[3] that produced the conventions for reading those images. That system of signs and recognitions was originally premised on 'mechanical objectivity' and its perceived purchase on

---
[1] Jane Caplan and John Torpey, 'Introduction' in Jane Caplan and John Torpey (eds) *Documenting Individual Identity: The Development of State Practices in the Modern World* (Princeton University Press, 2001) 3.
[2] Jane Caplan, '"This or That Particular Person": Protocols of Identification in 19th Century Europe' in Jane Caplan and John Torpey (eds) *Documenting Individual Identity: The Development of State Practices in the Modern World* (Princeton University Press, 2001) 51.
[3] Ibid.

natural and 'true' representations. The capture of behavioural data outside of the criminal context required different media, however. Intelligence surveillance and the dossier were thus directed at the question of criminal propensity in a very different way, using text and language (along with images) to narrate the behaviours of surveillance subjects, and assess their implications.

Intelligence surveillance also extended the technology of the archive to the general population, commencing the first programmes of 'mass surveillance' with surreptitious techniques. In addressing populations at large, this expression of state power expanded the institutional and administrative reality of law enforcement data systems to include everyday life, not only interactions with governance or criminal justice. Data was collected from the world 'out there' rather than in a specific context like prison administration, through different technological systems that eschewed the objectivity of the image in favour of a future-oriented speculation, description and assessment. What emerged in response was a massive general anxiety about the inaccuracy and inaccessibility of those speculations.

Many elements that originated with the intelligence and political policing accounts presented below, have over time been incorporated into broader criminal justice,[4] administrative governance processes, and general commercial practice. In other words, the logics, rationales, motivations, secrecy, and speculative assessments of large populations that began in this historical intelligence arena, clearly continue in contemporary surveillance arrangements.

The emergence of these surveillance practices is described in this chapter through an account of the English 'Metropolitan Special Branch' in the second half of the nineteenth century. That was the beginning of 'detective work', 'political policing', and mass surveillance for intelligence purposes in the UK. The compilation of intelligence dossiers did not, of course, commence with the English Special Branch. Continental Europe had been utilising 'spy police' and dossiers in at least the early nineteenth century, with some sources claiming they 'date[d] back ... to the days of the Empire under Napoleon II, when the secret police employed by the heads of the Government carried out the most extensive and elaborate system of espionage ever known in Europe'.[5] Other sources locate the practice even earlier, noting of dossiers, '[i]t pleased Louis XVI ... to know what roysterers were abroad yesternight, and that the monarch's curiosity might be satisfied, a method of discovery was devised'.[6] Nevertheless, the focus here remains in the UK, which, with its intellectual and political relationship with liberalism, and perhaps, the common law tradition, developed political policing and the dossier system substantially later than continental Europe. This should be qualified, however, as various 'espionage' or 'secret policing' techniques were operating in England well before the emergence of

[4] See, e.g., Jenny Hocking, 'Charting Political Space: Surveillance and the Rule of Law' (1994) 21(4) *Social Justice* 66, 67.
[5] 'A French Custom', *The Singleton Argus (NSW)* (26 September 1899), 2.
[6] 'The Spy System in France', *Daily News (Perth)*, (20 June 1899, 1).

the Special Branch. For instance, mail interception had been performed on behalf of the English Home Department since at least 1663,[7] but this did not include a dedicated political policing force with a comprehensive surveillance system, of which the Special Branch was the first English incarnation.

DETECTIVES AND DOSSIERS

Paul Wilkinson, scholar of terrorism and political violence, argues that 'by the mid-nineteenth century, despite revolutions in Europe and civil war in America, English liberalism had become remarkably complacent about the problem of maintaining internal peace'.[8] As an example he notes that John Stuart Mill hardly touched on the matter of internal security in his lengthy essay 'Considerations on Representative Government'.[9] By this time, a metropolitan police system had been introduced in England,[10] but its focus was on deterring crime through uniformed officers on 'the beat'.[11] The *Peelian Principles* – a police code emphasising that the test of police efficiency was the absence of crime and disorder,[12] not the visible evidence of police action in dealing with it – meant the 'bobbies', though still perceived as an infringement on liberal existence, were tolerable as they in no way constituted a political policing system that could undermine social ideals. Nevertheless, even in its liberal zenith, in 1842 England established a plain-clothes detective force, taking its first tentative steps towards a state apparatus capable of drastically altering the political milieu. That force was strictly constrained, however, being

---

[7] 'Interception of Communication in the United Kingdom: A consultation paper' (June 1999) *Presented to Parliament by the Secretary of State for the Home Department by Command of Her Majesty* referring to a 'proclamation' on 25 May 1663 authorizing the opening of letters. For more information concerning the history of interception see Kate Lawson, 'Personal Privacy, Letter Mail, and the Post Office Espionage Scandal, 1844' in *Branch: Britain Representation and Nineteenth-Century History*, Dino Franco Felluga (ed) Extension of Romanticism and Victorianism on the Net. www.branchcollective.org/?ps_articles=kate-lawson-personal-privacy-letter-mail-and-the-post-office-espionage-scandal-1844.
[8] Paul Wilkinson, *Terrorism and the Liberal State* (Macmillan, 2nd ed, 1986) 5, 18.
[9] John Stuart Mill, 'Considerations on Representative Government' (1861) in J M Robson (ed) *Collected Works of John Stuart Mill* (University of Toronto Press, 1977) 572 (first published 1861).
[10] T A Critchley, *A History of Police in England and Wales 1900–1966* (Constable, 1967). The metropolitan police were introduced in 1829. Also see J L Lyman, 'The Metropolitan Police Act of 1829' (1964) 55(1) *Journal of Criminal Law and Criminology* 141, where he describes the introduction of this force as revolution in traditional methods of law enforcement, whereas previously, 'the historical English concept of liberty was embodied in the accepted theory of community responsibility for keeping the King's peace' at 141.
[11] See, e.g., Susan A Lentz and Robert H Chaires, 'The Invention of Peel's Principles: A Study of Policing "Textbook" History' (2007) 35(1) *Journal of Criminal Justice* 69.
[12] *Metropolitan Police Act 1829* (UK) (10 Geo.4, C.44).

staffed by only two inspectors and six sergeants with severe admonitions for any notion of trickery such as disguises or clandestine surveillance.[13]

By comparison, fewer such reservations were experienced in colonial governance. For instance, in Australia, where in 1844, 'in contrast to the tentative beginnings of English detectives,' the Victoria Police 'readily embarked upon an active detective system' with over 40 men.[14] Each detective was encouraged to form a 'police circle' of their own 'comprised of himself and informers to keep track of crime and criminal movements'.[15] Naturally, the Australian frontier was manifestly distinct from civilised England, meaning the enthusiasm for detective and plain-clothes officers marked the striking difference between the English domestic system and the exercise of colonial power. Nevertheless, even in Australia, an 1862 Select Committee on Police heard that compared to the 'idyllic images of uniformed London Bobbies pounding a beat', 'no doubt the whole system of detective police [in Australia] is utterly repugnant to English feelings'.[16]

Those English feelings are clearly expressed in various mid-nineteenth-century writings about policing and the liberal state. For example, an 1850 piece in *Household Words* (a periodical edited by Charles Dickens) expressed pride in the absence of political police in England and powerful disdain for the repugnant criminal and political policing in France and Continental Europe. The author notes of England: 'We have no political police, no police over opinion. The most rabid demagogue can say in this free country what he chooses provided it does not tend to incite others ... He speaks not under the terror of an organised spy system.'[17] The tyranny of the spy system and its instrument the dossier was vividly communicated in this text with hyperbolic comments like 'woe be to you if you have been betrayed into any thoughtless expression of opinion; for every word is registered'.[18] However, the belief that such surveillance was incommensurable with liberal life was also expressed by the political classes. For instance, parliamentarian and constitutional theorist Thomas Erskine May wrote of political surveillance in 1861:

> Next to importance to personal freedom is immunity from suspicions and jealous observation. Men may be without restraints on their liberty; they may pass to and fro as they please: but if their steps are tracked by spies and informers, their words noted down for crimination, their associates watched as conspirators – who shall say that they are free? Nothing is more revolting to Englishmen than the espionage which

---

[13] Bernard Porter, *The Origins of the Vigilante State: The London Metropolitan Police Special Branch before the First World War* (Weidenfeld and Nicolson, 1987) 5. Porter tells of a constable who was reprimanded in 1845 for disguising himself as a cobbler in order to observe a counterfeiter, and in 1851 another constable was similarly censured for hiding behind a tree to watch an indecent offence.
[14] The Victoria Police Management Services Bureau, *Police in Victoria: 1836–1980* (Victoria Police Force, 1980) 37.
[15] Ibid 42.
[16] Ibid.
[17] 'Spy Police' (1850) 1 *Household Words* 611.
[18] Ibid 613.

forms part of the administrative system of continental despotisms. It haunts men like an evil genius, chills their gaiety, restrains their wit, casts a shadow over their friendships, and blights their domestic hearth. The freedom of this country may be measured by its immunity from this baleful agency.[19]

Such statements reflected the prevailing belief that 'stability grew best in a free soil'.[20] Political subversion and violence (like assassinations) were seen as the stuff of repressed nations. Only tyrannical governments engendered revolutions. Spy or political police, because of their capacity to undermine confidence in government, were thus figured as the cause of subversion rather than its cure. All that began to change however, when in the 1880s a fierce bombing campaign by the Irish Republican Brotherhood (the Fenians) ushered 'terrorism' into the British political experience,[21] with its most powerful and fearsome incarnation – the dynamiter.

Tracking the evolution of early English political policing, historian Bernard Porter argues that the invention of dynamite, first perfected and developed commercially in 1867, powerfully affected the possible scale of political violence. He notes 'it made two important differences. One was that it was less discriminate in its impact than knives or pistols, and consequently posed more of a threat to "innocents" ... The second important difference arose from its efficiency. Revolutionaries had used bombs before, but generally unsuccessfully'.[22] In the later parts of the nineteenth century, dynamite had taken its place in the arsenal of social agitators, particularly anarchists, all over continental Europe, Russia, and the United States. Historian Barbara Tuchman describes how for certain anarchist groups, '[t]he bomb was to be the messiah'.[23] A good example of its political significance is in the song 'La Ravachole', chanted in the streets after the execution of the anarchist Ravachol in 1892 (after being captured and identified through Bertillonage):

[19] Thomas Erskine May, *The Constitutional History of England since the Accession of George the Third by the Right Hon. Sir Thomas Erskine May (Lord Farnborough)* (Longmans, Green, ed, and continued to 1911 by Francis Holland ed, 1912) (first printed in 1861).
[20] Porter, above n 13, 3.
[21] For a thorough description of Irish political violence at that time see Niall Whelehan, *The Dynamiters: Irish Nationalism and Political Violence in the Wider World, 1867–1900* (Cambridge University Press, 2012). This campaign included bombs at: (1881) the military barracks in Salford, Greater Manchester; Mansion House, London (defused); the military barracks in Chester; Hatton Garden police station; (1882) Mansion House, London; (1883) the gasworks, coaling shed and canal viaduct in Glasgow; government buildings, Whitehall; Offices of *The Times* newspaper; Paddington Station and Westminster Bridge Station, London Underground; (1884) Victoria Station, London; Charing Cross Station, Ludgate Hill Station and Paddington Station, London (all defused); headquarters of the Criminal Investigation Department, London; the Metropolitan Police Service's Special Irish Branch, London; the Carlton Club (a gentlemen's club for members of the Conservative Party), London; the home of Conservative MP Sir Watkin Williams-Wynn, London; Nelson's Column, London (failed); London Bridge (failed); (1885) Gower Street Station, London; the House of Commons chamber (Westminster Hall), London; the Banqueting Room of the Tower of London.
[22] Porter, above n 13, 24.
[23] Barbara W Tuchman, *The Proud Tower: A Portrait of the World before the War, 1890–1914* (Random House LLC, 2011) 66.

It will come, it will come,
Every bourgeois will have his bomb.[24]

The anarchist programme, dynamite, and the fear they provoked were well entrenched in the mainstream imagination by the 1880s, with authors like Henry James offering convincing accounts of the radical political reality at the time.[25] This growing public consciousness of terror, especially in the context of Fenian violence, meant English liberal convictions began to falter. Even *The Times* suggested, perhaps in response to being the target of a Fenian bomb, that the time had come for a qualification of liberal political opinion. In 1883 it commented that: 'The notion that the highest wisdom consists simply in standing aside and letting every unregulated impulse and movement have its way, becomes questionable when the movement happens to be one for abolishing things in general by means of dynamite.'[26] The political reaction to Fenian terror was the formation of the first English political police force – the Metropolitan Police Special Branch. Novel features of this force included the first covert political surveillance (of anarchist and socialist groups) whether or not any of them was suspected of plotting or committing crimes,[27] and the associated deployment of covert agents, meaning a police force operating under a cloak of secrecy for gathering information.

Porter offers some explanations for the use of secrecy in political policing. First, there was residual popular and political disdain for secret policing and covert surveillance, which meant that in reaction to the methods used by the dynamiters, '[g]uile had to be met with guile; and if the public would not swallow guileful methods then those methods would have to be hidden from them'. Second, the 'Home Secretary was responsible for internal state security, but he was also supposed to be responsible in another way to Parliament, and the two seemed to conflict,' suggesting there was impropriety in the potential for the Home Secretary to not be frank with Parliament. And third, 'it provided the government with an excuse, if things went – as they often did go – wrong. If Britain's political policing was not known about, then it followed that it could not be blamed if it failed'.[28] Some further peripheral benefits of secrecy noted by Porter included that

> it made its quarry nervous and confused. It protected agents. It provided an alibi. It enabled activities, necessary ones in the government's eyes, which might not have been sanctioned in the clear light of day. It enabled quick and resolute executive action. And it could be justified on grounds of national security, without any details needing to be scrutinized. The negatives, of course, were that the absence of

---

[24] Ibid 80.
[25] Henry James, *The Princess Casamassima* (Penguin Classics, 1987) (first published 1886); See also G K Chesterman, *The Man Who Was Thursday* (J W Arrowsmith, 1908).
[26] *The Times*, (20 January, 1883), 9.
[27] Porter, above n 13, 42.
[28] Ibid 64–67.

accountability acceded the possibility of wrongdoing, such as breaking laws with impunity.[29]

There were also some fundamental disagreements within the Special Branch as to how surveillance would be carried out. Those still influenced by traditional English policing methods suggested a technique called 'picketing' whereby agents would maintain visible surveillance of all subjects to deter them from committing crimes. The alternative, and eventually adopted technique, was the deployment of covert agents to develop informers, infiltrate groups, and uncover the plans of conspirators. Surveillance techniques included obtaining intelligence from spies, reading the anarchist press, interviewing people who knew anarchists, shadowing, and infiltrating (and occasionally raiding) anarchist meetings. The recording medium for the information gathered by agents was the intelligence dossier, with a considerable number being produced on (especially foreign) anarchists by the 1890s.[30] This text-based system introduced a new way of capturing surveillance targets. Agents gathered and described what they saw, heard, and were told, with the actions of surveillance subjects mediated through the detective's own perception and assessment as a way to pre-empt and prevent future bombings and attacks. All that information was recorded and aggregated in a dossier, assigned to each surveillance target.

Although beginning in response to Irish terrorism, dossier production in England increased rapidly around the end of the nineteenth century. In reaction to the perceived German spy threat, in 1909 a Secret Service Bureau was formed that eventually became MI5, and an Aliens Register was implemented in 1911 that remained unofficial.[31] This became the first English register and dossier system for non-suspect persons, albeit applied exclusively to foreigners. As AWB Simpson argued of this growing trend in espionage activity, '[h]and in hand with this increase in the numbers of persons engaged in counter-subversion was the development of a monstrous secret archive' which 'like some obscene fungal growth which flourishes in darkness, continued to swell'.[32] Simpson cites a US embassy memorandum from 1940 indicating the central index of suspicious persons in London held over 4,500,000 names (although he also challenges the reliability of that assessment).[33] Nevertheless, the expansion to an archive of that size has been characterised as 'the beginning of an end of the age of liberal innocence, of which there is scarcely any trace left today'.[34]

---

[29] Ibid.
[30] Ibid 123.
[31] Ibid 168.
[32] A W B Simpson, 'The Judges and the Vigilant State' (1989) 4 *Denning Law Journal* 145, 150.
[33] Ibid 151.
[34] Porter, above n 13, 192.

THE OFFENCE OF DOSSIERS

Either the secrecy by which intelligence surveillance was performed in England, or the dominant focus on foreigners, meant that even at the turn of the twentieth century, the practice of political policing was still considered exclusive to Continental Europe. International press discussing the 'Dreyfus affair' in France reinforced that belief, but also clearly exposed the depth and nature of social anxiety around the practices of dossier surveillance. Dreyfus, a Jewish French army officer, had been accused of treason for selling military secrets to Germany. He was tried and convicted in 1894 based on the contents of a secret dossier assembled by the military that had been provided to the Court but not the defence. After the conviction, it emerged that much of the material in the dossier may have been fabricated or improperly attributed to Dreyfus, provoking a furore lasting several years over whether or not to re-open the case.[35]

In response to the massive media coverage and growing global fascination with Dreyfus, there was a slew of newspaper and periodical articles in the late 1890s with titles like 'The Police of Paris',[36] 'The Spy System in France',[37] and 'A French Custom',[38] that amplified the fear the dossier system impressed on liberal sensibilities. For instance, the *Liverpool Herald* noted of political policing, '[t]his system produced the dossier, the small portfolio or cover, one of which appertained to each individual, high and low, innocent or criminal, and was carefully preserved in the archives of the prefecture'.[39] That article went on to describe the colour coding system for dossiers (which seemed to persist well into the twentieth century): 'There are three classes of dossiers: the yellow for the criminal classes; white for foolish, but not guilty people; blue, by far the largest number of all, of public and political personages – all those, in fact, who make any figure in the world.' Similarly, the *West Australian Daily News* reported that: 'The police in France is organised less with a view to the detection of the guilty than to the observation of the innocent.'[40] The mechanism of that observation being that '[e]very man, has his dossier, to which is added the smallest fragment of information which assiduity can gather'.[41]

How intelligence surveillance and the dossier so deeply offended the liberal political outlook is clearly visible in these articles (which also explains why these practices were hidden from view in England). First, the 'smallest fragments' – the most anodyne or trivial pieces of information – from public to private and highly embarrassing – were recorded. Second, the surveillance technique was applied

---

[35] For a good general analysis of the Dreyfus affair, see Hannah Arendt, *The Origins of Totalitarianism* (G. Allen & Unwin, 3rd ed, 1967) or Tuchman, above n 23, especially Chapter 4.
[36] *Liverpool Herald* (NSW) (2 December 1899), 5.
[37] *The Daily News* (WA) (20 June 1899), 1.
[38] *The Singleton Argus* (NSW) (26 September 1899), 2.
[39] 'The Police of Paris', *Liverpool Herald* (NSW) (2 December 1899), 5.
[40] Spy System, above n 6, 1.
[41] Ibid.

universally – to the good and the bad, the guilty and the innocent – an early iteration of mass, or at least untargeted, surveillance. An article published in the *Daily News* expressed that concern by describing the difference of 'spy' practices from criminal records extant at the time:

> In Great Britain and the United States ... no man figures in what is popularly known as the 'Rogues' Gallery' unless he has been duly convicted of some felony or misdemeanour. In Continental Europe, especially France, Belgium, Italy, Germany, or Russia, there is no person of any degree of social eminence and of political and professional or administrative prominence whose record is not on the file at police quarters, either of the metropolis of his native land or else at those of the chief city of the province in which his residence is situated.[42]

Third, there was a new politics of surreptitious law enforcement, guileful and secret, that could only be legitimised by fear of terrorism, anarchy, and the indiscriminate destructive power of dynamite. The law enforcement archive and the technologies that animated it have become part of an ideological 'security' apparatus that insists on recording the present in order to assess the future, running over any liberal objection.

INACCURACY, SECRECY, INACCESSIBILITY

In the end, Dreyfus returned from exile to France, exonerated from accusations of treason. The secret dossier used to convict him was found to be too inaccurate, with many inculpatory elements having been fabricated.[43] The fear of inaccurate recording and assessment had also penetrated the public, with, for example, the *Singleton Argus* reporting of dossiers:

> These papers contained the confidential reports written about the individuals concerned by the spies, in which they related every little circumstance they could pick up in the streets respecting him, especially if it happened to be damaging to his character. They were mostly written without any regard to truth; and often with so little foundation in actual fact that perfectly innocent men were frequently reported as traitor or conspirators in disguise.[44]

Similar anxieties over the accuracy of representations in dossiers have re-emerged again and again over time. For instance, an investigation into political policing in the Australian State of South Australia in the 1970s, the *White Report*, contended that in addition to the irrelevance and illegitimate scope of the Special Branch records, much of the material kept in Special Branch files was 'scandalously

---

[42] 'The Spy System on the Continent: An Army of Sneaks and Informers Employed', *Daily News (WA)*, (26 June 1899) 4.
[43] See Arendt above n 35, and Tuchman above n 23.
[44] 'A French Custom', *The Singleton Argus (NSW)*, (26 September 1899), 2.

inaccurate'.[45] White found a real risk of 'malicious accusation' associated with 'erroneous recording practices' and 'false information being kept on persons',[46] which had been deployed against their interests. To that end, Reginald Victor Jones, military intelligence expert and philosopher, wrote in his 1989 book *Reflections on Intelligence*: 'I for one would have little objection to any authority having any information it wished about my actions – or even my thoughts – provided that I could be sure that it would not misinterpret the information to come to false conclusions about me.'[47] In the context of a law enforcement archive inscribed with text and narrative, and a political environment that demands constant surveillance universally applied, irrelevance or inaccuracy in both intelligence documentation and/or assessment exemplified the line between objectionable and acceptable profiling. And it is this issue of inaccuracy that highlights the greatest distinction between factual, administrative identity records and a potentially harmful feature of behavioural data gathering. As already discussed, various theories of the state describe citizen identification as a basic and essential function.[48] It is accordingly the recording of identity information in the context of police filing systems without deserving it, or presentation in another false context, that produces identity harms. A discursive file, however, has the potential to include manifestly irrelevant or false information, gathered, assessed, and applied in an entirely covert and unreviewable manner. The danger of that inaccuracy is a product of the 'subjective' assessment of either irrelevant or inaccurate information that can both present individuals in a false light or colour the context of how they are assessed. As we will see in later chapters, with few limitations on what data can be gathered and retained, the question of 'access' – of accessing the archive to expose and potentially correct its contents – accordingly became the identity-protecting mechanism articulated in the law.

IMAGES AND TEXT: BIOLOGY AND BEHAVIOUR

'Will captions not become the essential component of pictures?'[49]

Administrative criminal records evolved out of the Habitual Criminal Registers and prison administration files described in Chapter 2. Modern examples of

---

[45] South Australia, Special Branch Security Records: Initial Report to the Honourable Donald Allan Dunstan by the Honourable Mr Acting Justice White, Parl Paper No 145 (1978) 32; South Australia, *Report on the Dismissal of Harold Hubert Salisbury/Royal Commission 1978* (Government Printer, 1978).
[46] Peter N Grabosky, *Wayward Governance : Illegality and Its Control in the Public Sector* (Australian Institute of Criminology, 1989) 118.
[47] Reginald Victor Jones, *Reflections on Intelligence* (Heinemann London, 1989) 52.
[48] See, e.g., Malcolm Thorburn 'Identification, Surveillance, Profiling: On the Use and Abuse of Citizen Data' in Dennis Sullivan (ed) *Preempting Criminal Harms* (Hart 2012); Markus Dirk Dubber, *The Police Power: Patriarchy and the Foundations of American Government* (Columbia University Press, 2005).
[49] Walter Benjamin, 'A Short History of Photography' in Alan Tractchtenberg (ed) *Classic Essays on Photography* (Leete Island Books, 1980) 199 [trans of *Kleine Geschichte der Photographie* (first published 1931)].

administrative law enforcement information systems include the police 'rap-sheet', but also court documents and case-files, prison files, and various other identity databases that might include images, fingerprints, cell samples, DNA profiles, or biometric templates. In the policing context, that information is often collected on arrest, in quasi-public circumstances, with its retention generally dependent on authorities securing a conviction (depending on the jurisdiction in which the record lies). The way that information was recorded in, and interpreted from, *intelligence* dossiers however, was drastically distinct from photographic images or other biological measurements. Dossiers privilege text over images, 'predict' rather than 'document' crime, and register temporally ranging events rather than administrative moments. Rather than an indexical reading of images, the reception of behavioural information has a more subjective character, facilitating novel mechanisms for identity distortion or stigmatisation associated with the distance from and mediation of the subject. In his study of police files, sociologist James Rule notes that while factual records are generally terse and condensed, intelligence records are 'stubbornly discursive and unstructured'.[50] Intelligence filing systems also emerged in the context of a very different political terrain to photographic and biological surveillance. Rather than focusing on the past or present for the according of 'proper treatment' and deterring recidivism, they look to the future in an effort to pre-empt criminal behaviours.

As the temporal range of surveillance systems expanded (i.e. from including information about what a person has done to also including what they are doing and what they might do), behavioural description became imperative. For identification purposes, the indexical imprint of a photographic instant – the 'singular'[51] – was considered sufficient to 'know' the subject. However, whether human experience could be properly understood through segmental isolation, or whether an isolated moment could exist in the real world without temporal extension was eventually contested.[52] If perception only operated within the context of memory, knowledge required a 'certain depth of duration'.[53] Even Bertillon, whose project was generally limited to identification, believed the photograph became obsolete the moment the shutter snapped.[54] To that end, historian Michael Roth argues that it was 'photography's episodic intensity [that]

---

[50] James Rule, *Private Lives & Public Surveillance* (Schocken, 1974) 284.
[51] Michael S Roth, 'Photographic Ambivalence and Historical Consciousness' (2009) (Theme Issue 48) *History and Theory* 82, 93 citing Mary Ann Doane, *The Emergence of Cinematic Time: Modernity, Contingency, the Archive* (Harvard University Press, 2002) at 208.
[52] Ibid 83–84.
[53] Henri Bergson, *Time and Free Will: An Essay on the Immediate Data of Consciousness* (Dover Publications, 2001) 76.
[54] Simon Cole, *Suspect Identities: A History of Fingerprinting and Criminal Identification* (Harvard University Press, 2002) 48.

dialectically seems to call forth a variety of framing devices to provide a content of meaning'.⁵⁵ The employment of textual narrative was one such media system capable of providing the necessary temporal framing for deeper knowledge of surveillance subjects.

As the objective understanding of photography was increasingly marginalised, WTJ Mitchell claims images were themselves eventually 'understood as a kind of language; instead of providing a transparent window on the world ... [they were] regarded as the sort of sign that presents a deceptive appearance of naturalness and transparency concealing an opaque, distorting, arbitrary mechanism of representation, a process of ideological mystification'.⁵⁶ That interpretation emerged in the context of a 'protracted struggle for dominance between pictorial and linguistic signs, each claiming for itself certain proprietary rights on a "nature" to which only it has access'.⁵⁷ Irrespective of semiotic dominance, Mitchell suggests that the determinative feature for interpretation is not so much convention but rather ideology:

> What are we to make of this contest between the interests of verbal and pictorial representation? I propose that we historicize it, and treat it, not as a matter for peaceful settlement under the terms of some all embracing theory of signs, but as a struggle that carries the fundamental contradictions of our culture into the heart of theoretical discourse itself. The point then, is not to heal the split between words and images, but to see what interests and powers it serves.⁵⁸

The institutional archive that collected biological information implicated identity in one way, the collection of behavioural information – in another way. The knowledge paradigms of photography reflected a specific political imperative to know certain segments of the population, whereas the remote recording and analysis of behaviour reflected the knowledge regime necessary for the political context in which it emerged. The capacity to determine the legitimacy and utility of a format, especially with respect to recording data about people, accordingly becomes the capacity to define the institutional or political identity of an individual. But this has never been an absolute capacity, and the law is one modality by which that institutional identity can be contested or constrained. Similarly, the degree to which particular technologies and formats shape meaning remains critically important and cannot be reduced wholesale to ideology.

---

55 Roth, above n 51, 93.
56 W T J Mitchell, *Iconology: Image, Text, Ideology* (University of Chicago Press, 2000) 8.
57 Ibid 43.
58 Ibid 44.

CONCLUSION

This and previous chapters have given an account of the early building of identity databases, the purposes and politics they served, the technologies they employed, and the impacts (or harms) they generated. The biological and behavioural monitoring that began with states and intelligence surveillance, and the anxieties they elicited, has, however, continued into more modern formations. It is not difficult to point out analogues between the political rationalities attendant on Fenian violence, and those of post-9/11 terrorism. The 'politics of secrecy and guile' seem to antedate the politics of Total Information Awareness that notoriously emerged in 2002, and arguably never disappeared. In the same way that all behaviour became fodder for the archive, we are presently experiencing the translation of all-of-life into behavioural data.[59] The intelligence archive as it began then strikes as a similar construct to the massive stores of telecommunications data produced through mandatory data retention policies. The subjective and unchallengeable analysis of the political police echoes the black boxes of contemporary algorithmic decision-making. The use of images as the biological data of identity is now augmented by automated biometric facial recognition. The translation of biology and behaviour into data collected in registers and filing systems described in the past few chapters now proceeds according to the logics and capacities of computation.

Similarly, the harms and anxieties identified in the previous chapters remain the critical issues that contemporary law addresses. The profilers, the builders and operators of these sites of external institutional identity, understood their subjects in a particular way, informed by the politics, purposes, and technological affordances of their surveillance systems. Identity databases and the capture of biological information enabled the state to 'know' a person, to connect an institutional record to a person in physical space, and to address them in a way that recognised the history of their interactions. But it also risked 'identity harms'. The creation of that archive, coupled with the epistemological paradigm of the camera, introduced a notion of objectivity into the interpretation of persons, the idea that the image could stand for the thing itself, with no interpretive distance between a person and their representation.

The general anxiety these systems caused, what can be understood in relation to their potential for harm, was very much connected to liberal sensibilities about the proper domains of government in private life. That such records were constructed for innocent citizens of good standing was difficult to stomach. Considering that the photographic record was used to keep track of criminals, deviants, and the mentally ill, there was fear that such records might render a person an object of

---

[59] See, e.g., Nick Couldrey and Ulises A Meijas, *The Costs of Connection: How Data Is Colonizing Human Life and Appropriating It for Capitalism* (Stanford University Press, 2019).

suspicion in improper circumstances.[60] Behavioural databases introduced another set of circumstances and concerns. The recording of behaviour meant a translation of real life into the documentary register of the dossier. Behavioural information was also recorded for the sake of pre-emption, and applied to non-suspicious persons under the impenetrable political logics of security that seemed to conflict with liberal political institutional design. It resulted in the production of speculative assessments of behavioural information, produced in secret, without knowledge or access of their subjects. Its mass character threatened intellectual freedom, and beyond the liberal objections noted above, there was fear that such a translation was crude, remote, subjective, ideologically motivated, and entirely inaccurate.

Both these surveillance systems participated in a programme of building an institutional identity that was significant for political and juridical life. Both these surveillance programmes used technological systems that produced knowledge about their subjects in a way that undermined control over the subjects' 'personas', the masks through which political and juridical life proceeded. These were interpreted as harms to identity because, on one hand, the external site of identity was captured in an institutional context, with the person reduced to an image and biological record, ready for judgment or comparison with a norm. On the other hand, harms stemmed from a system that enabled that external or outward site of identity to be constructed in secret, become total and indiscriminate, and result in opaque and unchallengeable assessments that may distort or misrepresent.

Through the twentieth century, the technologies, practices, and intellectual foundations of profiling evolved further through their encounter with computation. The consequences of these new computational profiling practices have not been a mere loss of control over the representations and images used to generate institutional identity, but to eliminate the space between experience and representation altogether. While writing could extend the temporal range of the episodic image, it remained a static technology. What was written in a dossier could not self-amend in relation to its environment (i.e. more or new information). Computation made representation *dynamic*, an ongoing capture of experience, capable of continuous tracking, meaning a representation or profile capable of assuming a coterminous temporal reality with its subject, and thus instigating a new regime of objectivity.

---

[60] See, e.g., Peter Galsion and Martha Minow in 'Our Privacy, Ourselves in the Age of Technological Intrusions' in R A Wilson (ed) *Human Rights in the War on Terror* (Cambridge University Press, 2005) 258, discussing the effects of twenty-first-century law enforcement surveillance:

> This e-interpellation goes farther than the information separately considered – by the very act of naming you as a suspect (or 'person of interest') you have changed status in the eyes of others who know about this, and if you come to know or fear, in your eyes as well. Correlating state databases (including taxes, criminal records, social security, voting registration) with private databases (purchases, travel, on-line clicks) does more than merely assemble a tad more information here or there. It undermines the very concept of a private life.

5

Data Subject Rights and the Importance of Access

The secret archive does not simply create a 'data double', wherein individuals are replicated through mediated representations, stored in files, and subjected to unknowable assessments or manipulations. Rather, the anxieties around granular surveillance, filing systems, and impenetrable assessments and evaluations might be better framed as the production of a 'data triple'[1] – an institutionally distorted dissemblance. With respect to profiling and the production of knowledge about people, the concern historically is not only that we are watched, but also how we are seen. It is not only that we are inscribed in the 'monstrous secret archive', but that from the archive we are badly read or interpreted.[2] Even in the nineteenth century, it had become clear that there was a real risk of inaccurate interpretation of individuals on the basis of irrelevant or factually inaccurate information, or poorly executed speculative evaluation. Many have argued this risk is replicated and augmented through the profiling logics of statistical pattern analysis, data mining, and machine learning. As we will see, the information law regime considered in this chapter is directed at these concerns, and focuses on achieving access to the archives as a mechanism to protect identity. Its goal is to give individuals the opportunity to not only challenge the claims, categorisations, and conclusions deployed by states and other profiling entities, but to actively shape them.

Some have claimed 'Access' has become 'the keyword of the twenty-first century',[3] and that conditions of access define the materiality of power dynamics in an informational world. Access in the context of data subject rights discussed here offers a way to ensure that the documentary reality of a filing system accords with an

---

[1] See, e.g., Jacques Rancière, *The Future of the Image* (Gregory Elliott trans, Verso London, 2007) 8.
[2] The relationship between privacy and being 'read' is discussed briefly in Mireille Hildebrandt, 'Legal Protection by Design: Objections and Refutations' (2011) 5(2) *Legisprudence* 223, 230 where she follows Niklas Luhmann to say that 'A large part of our inner life and interactions is co-constituted by unconscious processes, and by the process of anticipating how others will "read" our actions. Luhmann has qualified this as the double contingency of social interaction.' She goes on at 232–233 to make arguments that identity (and consequently privacy) are affected by 'the fact that we are being "read" whereas we don't know how and by whom'.
[3] Cornelia Vismann and Martin Krajewski, 'Computer Juridisms' (2007) 29 *Grey Room* 101.

individual's own sense of narrative identity. It operationalises an individual's own sense of truth, accuracy, and relevance. In the second half of the twentieth century, as computerised information technologies began influencing state administrative processes, data protection emerged as a right with a more genetic connection to access than rights to private life. 'Data subject rights' designed to give access to the archive are only one element of data protection law however. The 'algorithmic accountability' dimensions of data protection, which overlap with data subject rights in many ways, also implement more structured transparency mechanisms. However, that latter dimension of data protection, discussed further in Chapter 7, has only more recently come into focus, whereas transparency as effected through rights of access, rectification, and erasure has been part of the DNA of data protection (or information privacy) since its inception in the 1960s and 1970s. Those mechanisms are inherent to data protection law and target profiling by ensuring, to an extent, that data held about a person is accurate and relevant. By ensuring the quality of information held, the goal is to enhance the legitimacy of its processing, and make decisions more fair or reasonable. But while these provisions are relatively well used and understood, the relevance they have to contemporary profiling by states and other entities, and the information processing environment generally, may ultimately be limited. In particular, there are significant derogations from the rights afforded by data protection in the context of law enforcement. And when access is possible, it may not be to the categories of information necessary to protect identity. Despite the many innovations of data protection, especially as implemented in the GDPR, data subject rights fail to adequately address profiling, as the data to which access is given is treated as merely a record or representation, without taking into account the complexities of data in contemporary processing environments. In other words, the protections of identity that the legal subject (as data subject) obtains through data subject rights are inextricably connected to a four-decade old notion of 'informational self-determination' that may have since become an inept way of framing what a desirable relationship between an individual and data about them should look like.

The origins, politics, and implementation of data subject rights are outlined below, and their application to law enforcement information systems is assessed. That analysis demonstrates an engagement with the actual *procedures* determining how law enforcement files and records are administered. It also shows a dramatic shift in the technologies and format of legal compliance and enforcement. As data protection law has evolved, it is increasingly enacted through a rich bureaucratic structure, with multiple entities dealing with compliance, monitoring, and complaints. In describing the connection between data subject rights and identity, this chapter also provides an account of the data subject as a type of legal person that mediates between a profiler and a physical person. The chapter then questions the degree to which a legal subject, defined this way, overly privileges the liberal, autonomous subject in a way that ignores material and technological reality.

PRIVACY'S ACCESS FAILURE

Before going further with access rights in data protection, it is worth noting that Article 8 of the ECHR has also been used for accessing government filing systems. However, Article 8's limitations in this context have been clear for some time. The Strasbourg Court has recognised that states do not enjoy unlimited discretion to engage in secret surveillance because of the 'danger such a law poses of undermining or even destroying democracy on the ground of defending it'.[4] However, intelligence-gathering and dossier-building have typically been deemed as sufficiently proportionate and necessary in democratic society.[5] The case law has established that states have a 'margin of appreciation' when it comes to building secret file systems, confining the relevance of Article 8 to ensuring adequate oversight of public authorities.[6] Article 8 *has* facilitated access more readily outside the law enforcement context however, particularly in situations where identity is somehow implicated in stored information.[7] However, these cases represent a different relationship to identity, and do not concern institutional identity-building or file-making generally. For instance, those cases clarify that basic family life matters about childhood and formative years (*Gaskin* v. *UK*;[8] *MG* v. *UK*),[9] tracing one's origins and the identity of natural parents (*Odièvre* v. *France*),[10] or information about possible exposure to health risks (*Guerra and Others* v. *Italy*)[11] relate to information about private life to which applicants should have access. The provision of access is thus to facilitate physical and social identity formation by enabling individuals themselves to interpret information held by administrative agencies about those private categories.[12] Access in these cases is not, however, a means of preventing or shaping the interpretation of that information by other parties that engage in profiling.

Other Article 8 cases have addressed government profiling capabilities by governments in their application to mass surveillance. However, these outcomes have also

---

[4] *Klass* v. *Germany* (1978) A28 Eur Court HR (ser A), [49].
[5] Ibid at [50].
[6] *Leander* v. *Sweden* (1987) 9 EHRR 433; *Segerstedt-Wiberg* v. *Sweden* [2006] VII Eur Court HR 87.
[7] For more detail see Yutaka Arai, *The Margin of Appreciation Doctrine and the Principle of Proportionality in the Jurisprudence of the ECHR* (Intersentia, 2002).
[8] *Gaskin* v. *United Kingdom* (1989) 12 EHRR 36, which required establishing a procedure for accessing 'care files' containing information about an individual while a foster child.
[9] *MG* v. *United Kingdom* (2003) 36 EHRR 3, which also required establishing a procedure for accessing 'care files' about the complainant's formative years (being information relating to private and family life).
[10] *Odievre* v. *France* (2004) 28 EHRR 43, in which Article 8 was enlivened but not breached when the applicant was unable to access information about their birth mother, who had requested anonymity.
[11] *Guerra* v. *Italy* (1998) 26 EHRR 357 considered a chemical factory where the effects of exposure to pollution had the possibility of affecting private and family life of nearby inhabitants.
[12] Paul de Hert, *A Right to Identity to Face the Internet of Things* (2008) UNESCO https://pure.uvt.nl/ws/portalfiles/portal/1069135/de_Hert-Paul.pdf, 1.

had limited effects. For instance, the 2018 *Big Brother Watch* decision,[13] while clarifying that the UK telecommunications data retention regime may have violated Article 8, did not specify that mass data retention was *necessarily* contrary to Article 8 or categorically disproportionate. In fact, the judgment likely contributed to normalising that form of indiscriminate and mandatory data collection, retention, and archive-building, while also clarifying that bulk retention *can* occur without judicial authorisation, or even reasonable suspicion, as long as there is some sort of oversight mechanism. Focusing on high-level oversight rather than interrogating the logics and mechanisms of filing systems, however, is insufficient to curb inaccuracy or improper assessments. Mechanisms for obtaining access to filing systems in order to protect identity require different normative commitments, different engagements and processes, different relationships to data, and a different conceptual organisation than that of Article 8. In other words, the filing system as a critical site for negotiating the relationship between citizen and state has become too complex a technical, social, and political system to address with such a blunt tool focused on removing individuals from filing systems. Instead, the logic of data subject rights is better expressed along the lines of 'show me how you see me' – a movement from opacity to transparency.

Serge Gutwirth and Paul De Hert have famously claimed that, whereas privacy (in the sense of Article 8) is about setting normative limits to power, data protection is about channelling a normatively accepted exercise of power.[14] That is, data protection is not about prohibition – it is about defining permissible conditions for action. Of course, these mechanisms for inflecting power overlap, but data protection is less a liberal delineation of the state's right to interfere with the individual, and more an attempt to modulate the exercise of an accepted right to do so through specifying certain procedural obligations for information systems. On Gutwirth and De Hert's analysis, data protection therefore 'does a lot more than echoing a privacy right with regard to personal data' because it operates both more widely and more narrowly than ideas like the right to private life. It is wider because the category of information protected ('personal information') is broader than what has classically been understood as 'private information' – information from within the private sphere. It is narrower because it *facilitates* the processing of this information rather than prohibits its collection, retention or disclosure. The widening speaks to the realities of information collection by state entities, the sophistication of contemporary information systems, and an anchoring of the concept around identity (or 'identifiability'). The narrowing speaks to the inability to normatively delineate

[13] *Big Brother Watch* v. *United Kingdom* (European Court of Human Rights, Grand Chamber, Application nos 58170/13, 62322/14, 24960/15, 13 September 2018).
[14] Paul de Hert and Serge Gutwirth, 'Data Protection in the Case Law of Strasburg and Luxenburg: Constitutionalisation in Action' in Serge Gutwirth et al (eds) *Reinventing Data Protection* (Springer, 2009); Serge Gutwirth and Paul de Hert 'Regulating Profiling in a Democratic Constitutional State' in Mireille Hildebrandt and Serge Gutwirth (eds) *Profiling the European Citizen* (Springer, 2008) 271, 275.

permissible and impermissible practices absolutely. For those reasons, Gutwirth and De Hert describe privacy as an 'opacity tool', and data protection as a 'transparency tool'. Stefano Rodotà clarifies this distinction:

> The right to respect one's private and family life mirrors, first and foremost, an individualistic component: this power basically consists in preventing others from interfering with one's private and family life. In other words, it is a static, negative kind of protection. Conversely, data protection sets out rules on the mechanisms to process data and empowers one to take steps – i.e., it is a dynamic kind of protection which follows data in all its movements.[15]

Data protection also has the status of constitutional right. The European Union Charter of Human Rights, ratified through Article 16 of the Treaty on the Functioning of the European Union, states: 'Everyone has the right of access to data which has been collected concerning him or her, and the right to have it rectified.'[16] Nonetheless, the vertical dimension of data protection is likely its least meaningful enforcement modality. In many ways, data protection's triumph is its impact on nuts-and-bolts regulatory compliance. Scholars like Chris Hoofnagle, for instance, see the primary mechanisms of the GDPR as encouraging firms to produce internal data governance frameworks.[17] From that perspective, the GDPR requires consideration of data lifecycles (including data breach requirements), and 'elevates privacy officials within companies, giving them a tenure-like right but also responsibilities that transcend loyalty to the firm'.[18] That said, much of the GDPR, like other data protection frameworks, still operates through the category of the data subject as the relevant rights-bearing entity.

WHAT IS A DATA SUBJECT?

Cornelia Vismann has discussed the relationship between secret files and democracy, noting '[t]he political demands for access to records turned them into objects of political, legal and sociological discourse and into an indicator for the transparency of politics and administration'.[19] State file-keeping has existed since biblical times,[20] but file-keeping in 'modern' governance likely has its origins in the French

---

[15] Stefano Rodota, 'Data Protection as a Fundamental Right' in Serge Gutwirth et al (eds) *Reinventing Data Protection?* (Springer, 2009) 77, 79.
[16] European Union, *Charter of Fundamental Rights of the European Union*, 26 October 2012, 2012/C 326/02. Note that this constitutional document also includes a right to private life mirroring Article 8 of the ECHR.
[17] Chris J Hoofnagle, Bart van der Sloot, and Frederik Z Borgesius, 'The European Union General Data Protection Regulation: What It Is and What It Means' (UC Berkeley Public Law Research Paper, October 2018) https://papers.ssrn.com/sol3/papers.cfm?abstract_id=3254511.
[18] Ibid.
[19] Cornelia Vismann, *Files: Law and Media Technology* (Geoffrey Winthrop-Young trans, Stanford University Press, 2008) 112 [trans of *Akten, Medientechnik und Recht* (first published 2000)] 12.
[20] For example, the Census of Quirinius in approximately 6 CE.

Revolution.[21] There were material constraints at that time, however, limiting the efficacy of bureaucratic information systems. For instance, 'a considerable number of ordinary people had not yet mastered the elementary rules of written communication' and the papers used were sometimes of 'the very worst quality, gray in color, rough and heavy grained' such that 'when one uses it, it will not take the impressions of the pen'.[22] One can imagine then the significance of technical improvements like general literacy and reliable stationery, let alone the 'development of computers and their marriage with telecommunications'.[23] The latter not only made file-keeping easier, but also profoundly altered techniques of administration and processes of governance. The special insight in Vismann's equating the development of files with the development of law in her book *Files: Law and Media Technology* is that she sees, as an important part of the history of law, a history of access points into the otherwise protected inner workings of an administration:[24]

> Ever since the publication of records could create a public, that is, ever since the historian August Ludwig von Schlözer (1735–1809) called for an end to state secrecy (and followed up on his demands by founding a journal dedicated exclusively to publishing records), files have been the medium instrumentally involved in the differentiation processes that pit the state against society and administration against citizenry. The state compiles records, society demands their disclosure.[25]

Disclosure of files has thus had a rich political character, as demonstrated for instance by remarkable stories concerning access to, and destruction of, Stasi files.[26] In cases like the Stasi, access to files was more an exercise in lustration than democratic accountability. However, within functioning states, access, at least when it comes to personal information, serves different or additional purposes. As noted in the previous chapter, access is, on one level, about accuracy and relevance. Accuracy and relevance are, however, also deeply connected to issues of informational asymmetry and institutional accountability, especially in the context of digital computing.[27] In fact, data protection laws emerged to deal with

---

[21] Gerard Noiriel, 'The Identification of the Citizen: The Birth of Republican Civil Status in France' in Jane Caplan and John Torpey (eds) *Documenting Individual Identity: The Development of State Practices in the Modern World* (Princeton University Press, 2001) 28.
[22] Ibid 40, referencing a communication from the prefect of the Côte D'or in 1812.
[23] James B Rule, *Privacy in Peril: How We Are Sacrificing a Fundamental Right in Exchange for Security and Convenience* (Oxford University Press, 2007) 20.
[24] Ibid.
[25] Ibid 175.
[26] See, e.g., John Miller, 'Settling Accounts with the Secret Police: The German Law on the Stasi Records' (1998) 50(2) *Europe-Asia Studies* 305; Eric Ketelaar, 'Access, The Democratic Imperative' (2006) 34(2) *Archives and Manuscripts* 62.
[27] For instance, the 1978 Lindop Committee Report in the UK considered these issues specifically from the perspective of 'data privacy' and argued that 'the time has come when those who use computers to handle personal information, however responsible they are, can no longer remain the sole judges of

multiple concerns, including the possibilities of producing statistical intelligence about individuals.

From around the 1960s, there was significant growth in the amount of, and appetite for, personal data held by various types of organisations. For some, this produced a concern that, as the 'data subject's role in organisational decision-making processes [was] diminishing, the role of their registered data-images [was] growing'.[28] But it was not only the creation of, and potential usurpation by, a data double that worried publics and regulators. For instance, a critical institutional transformation that provoked the discussions leading to global data protection laws was the proposal for a US National Data Centre (NDC) in the mid-1960s. The NDC was primarily promoted as facilitating the application of statistics to public policy and the management of public affairs. The NDC was not, however, merely a repository of government data and records for the sake of efficiency, it also enabled novel statistical interrogation of populations with questions like: 'What proportion of the residents of Appalachia have incomes under $3000 a year and how do their age, race, sex and educational character-istics differ from those with higher incomes both within and outside Appalachia.'[29] The capacity to ask that type of question was entirely new, and only made possible through increasing availability of data and computational power.

Integral to the privacy debate in this context, even before the evolution and application of automated pattern matching, was the risk that statistical knowl-edge systems could also be used as 'intelligence systems'. That is, that computa-tional statistical systems could be used for 'finding out' information about individuals, particularly as those filing systems grew to include categories like criminal records, medical records, or psychological tests.[30] Privacy advocates were worried that as filing systems expanded it would be impossible for them to not become systems for deeper knowledge of individuals. And indeed, the 'intelligence data bank', even in 1965, appeared to be already under construction.[31] From here, we can read the concern embedded in data protec-tion law that data pertaining to individuals rather than populations needed stricter protection, especially from statistical analyses able to draw information about a person from different dimensions of their life. Hence data protection's organising principle of personal information – data that can be generally con-nected to a specific individual.

whether their own systems, adequately safeguard privacy'. See *Report of the Committee on Data Protection* (1978) (Lindop Committee Report) at 30.

[28] Lee Bygrave, *Data Protection Law: Approaching its Rationale, Logic, and Limits* (Kluwer Law International, 2002) 96.
[29] Edgar S Dunn Jr, 'The Idea of National Data Center and the Issue of Personal Privacy' (1967) 21(1) *The American Statistician* 21, 22.
[30] Ibid.
[31] Ibid 24, referring to comments from employees of the RAND Corporation.

Those concerns eventually evolved into regulatory intervention in the form of data protection laws passed in multiple jurisdictions. The language used varies, but as Bygrave notes, '[r]egardless of the terminological differences, all of the instruments ... are specifically aimed at regulating the processing of data relating to, and facilitating identification of, persons (i.e. personal data) in order to safeguard, at least partly, the privacy and related interests of those persons'.[32] Multiple jurisdictions, including the United States, passed laws through the 1970s.[33] Data protection moved towards global standardisation with the 1980 OECD *Guidelines on the Protection of Privacy and Transborder Flows of Personal Data*, which introduced the Fair Information Principles,[34] and the European Convention of 1981,[35] which required European nations to begin implementing domestic data protection regimes directly. For the sake of harmonising those various regimes in the context of the 'single market', the European Commission (EC) *Directive on the Protection of Individuals with Regard to the Processing of Personal Data and on the Free Movement of Such Data* was adopted in 1995, and became the primary guiding instrument for the application of data protection laws in Europe.[36] That was replaced with the General Data Protection Regulation (GDPR) in 2018,[37] and complimented with

---

[32] Lee Bygrave, 'Privacy and Data Protection in an International Perspective' (2010) 56(8) *Scandinavian Studies in Law* 165.
[33] This included the West German State of Hesse in 1970, Sweden in 1973, West Germany in 1977, France in 1978 (and Australia in 1988 – although Sir Zelman Cowan, who was later Australia's Governor General, gave a Boyer Lecture on the need for privacy laws as early as 1969). There were private members bills suggested in the UK as early as 1961 and 1967, and government reports (from which no further action was taken until a data protection law was passed in 1998) issued in 1972 (Younger Report) and 1978 (Lindop Committee Report). Some of these regimes expressly reference privacy as the fundamental principle from which data protection is reasoned. Others fail to mention privacy and note that the aim of the law is to protect personality, identity or personal integrity.
[34] *OECD Guidelines on the Protection of Privacy and Transborder Flows of Personal Data*, 1980 (online) www.oecd.org/internet/ieconomy/oecdguidelinesontheprotectionofprivacyandtransborderflowsofpersonaldata.htm.
[35] *Convention for the Protection of Individuals with Regard to Automatic Processing of Personal Data*, opened for signature 28 January 1981, ETS 108 (entered into force 1 October 1985).
[36] *EC Directive on the Protection of Individuals with Regard to the Processing of Personal Data and on the Free Movement of Such Data* (1995). More recently, documents like the European Commission's E-Privacy Directive have aimed at 'adapting and updating the existing provisions to new and foreseeable developments in electronic communications services and technologies'. See, e.g., Peter Carey, *Data Protection: A Practical Guide to UK and EU Law* (Oxford University Press, 2009) 12. The intention was that data protection regimes would apply to transactional data produced through internet use and audio and visual material in the same way as older technology. Although this Directive arguably still trails behind technological developments, with some claiming 'it has become abundantly clear that although the original Directive might be fairly successful at responding to the issues caused by large-scale databanks, it is much less appropriate for application to the more diffuse use of personal data on global computer networks', in Diane Rowland, Uta Kohl, and Andrew Charlesworth, *Information Technology Law* (Routledge Cavendish, 4th ed, 2011) 184.
[37] *Regulation (EU) 2016/679 of the European Parliament and of the Council of 27 April 2016 on the Protection of Natural Persons with Regard to the Processing of Personal Data and on the Free Movement of Such Data, and Repealing Directive 95/46/EC (General Data Protection Regulation)* [2016] OJ L 119/1.

a fundamental right to data protection in the EU Charter of Human Rights,[38] which together have prompted renewed global fascination with data protection law as a regulatory construct.

Beyond accountability in bureaucracy, data protection's relationship to individual identity, and the connection between identity and statistically inferred profiles, are best located in the foundational concept of 'informational self-determination'. This *personality*-based concept emerged from the German Constitutional Court's decision in the *Census Act Case*[39] and became the legal anchor for German Data Protection,[40] but is widely accepted as a basic premise of 'data subject rights'. Although that decision was based on German idealist philosophies underpinning the rights to 'personality' and 'dignity' found in the post-war constitution rather than any explicit constitutional 'privacy' right, the connection to identity is clear. Earlier decisions of the Constitutional Court had set the stage for this new informational right. For instance, the *Microcensus Case* had dealt with the privacy implications of the state's use of statistical surveys,[41] and the *Eppler*,[42] *Tape Recording*,[43] and *Soraya* cases[44] espoused the idea that even if there were no invasion of the private sphere, an individual's right to privacy could be implicated if 'words were put into their mouth, which they did not utter, and which adversely

---

[38] *Charter of Fundamental Rights of the European Union*, 26 October 2012, 2012/C 326/02.
[39] *Census Act Case*, Bundesverfassungsgericht [German Constitutional Court], 1 BvL 209, 269, 362, 420, 440 and 484/83, 15 December 1983 reported in (1983) 65 BVerfGE 1.
[40] Gerrit Hornung and Christoph Schnabel, 'Data Protection in Germany I: The Population Census Decision and the Right to Informational Self Determination' (2009) 25(1) *Computer Law & Security Report* 84.
[41] *Microcensus Case*, Bundesverfassungsgericht [German Constitutional Court], 1 BvL 19/63, 16 July 1969 reported in (1969) 27 BVerfGE 1; this case considered the validity of a census requiring information on vacation and recreational trips taken by household residents. In that decision, relying on the dignitarian clause in Article 1 of the constitution, it was stated: 'The state violates human dignity when it treats persons as mere objects. It would thus be inconsistent with the principle of human dignity to require a person to record and register all aspects of his personality, even though such an effort is carried out anonymously in the form of a statistical survey; [the state] may not treat a person as an object subject to an inventory of any kind. The state has no right to pierce the sphere of privacy by thoroughly checking into the personal matters of its citizens' (Donald Komers, *The Constitutional Jurisprudence of the Federal Republic of Germany* [Duke Press, 3rd ed, 2012] 299). However, the primacy of the 'protected sphere' is still evident in this reasoning. To that end, it was accepted by the court that not every statistical survey impinges upon the right to self-determination, which would only occur when the questionnaire intruded 'into that intimate realm of personal life which by its very nature is confidential in character' (at 300). Consequently, 'administrative depersonalisation' did not occur merely by answering questions about the relation of the person to the world around him or her, as that did not implicate the private sphere (at 300).
[42] *Eppler*, Bundesverfassungsgericht [German Constitutional Court], 1 BvR 185/77, 3 June 1980 reported (1980) 54 BVerfGE 148.
[43] *Tape Recording II Case*, Bundesverfassungsgericht [German Constitutional Court], 2 BvR 454/71, 31 January 1973 reported (1973) 34 BVerfGE 238.
[44] *Soraya*, Bundesverfassungsgericht [German Constitutional Court], 1 BvR 112/65, 14 February 1973 reported (1973) 34 BVerfGE 269.

affect their self-image'.[45] Constitutional legal scholar Donald Kommers interpreted that jurisprudence as indicating 'the individual should have the freedom to decide for himself – without any limitation of his private sphere – how he wishes to portray himself to third parties or to the public ... Thus the content of the general right to personality is largely determined by the self-image of its bearer'.[46] This critical point was elaborated in the *Census Act Case* itself, which assessed the validity of a general population census, to be processed by computers, for statistical purposes and correcting resident registers. The court initially found the census unconstitutional on the basis that the human person is more than the sum of his parts and 'a spiritual-moral being', and that 'the state therefore cannot inventory the individual with respect to every aspect of his being without threatening his personal autonomy'.[47] That an individual should participate in the creation of their own self-image, especially in the context of large-scale data collection, and that this self-image should be the dominant account of identity and personality, was thus an important rhetorical impetus in data protection's evolution.

Alongside the personality-based account of data protection in the form of informational self-determination, however, was the systems theoretical account of law, human rights, and ultimately privacy, developed by Niklas Luhmann.[48] A brief summary of Luhmann's theory of functional differentiation suggests that social systems differentiate themselves from an 'environment' according to the function they perform in modernity. Within Luhmann's formulation, the horizon of possible meaning of any communication is always broader than any particular communicative action. Accordingly, social spheres guide processes of self-selection and boundary formation that, at the same time, separate any particular social sphere from the general environment. The codes of communication for each social sphere thus become self-referential, and inattentive to alternative spheres, except through webs of loose 'structural coupling'. The function of sub-system self-selection is to render the complexity of the real world more manageable. This 'autopoietic' account of sub-systemic *self*-making and *self*-referential closure was an extension into sociology of similar ideas in biology developed by Humberto Maturana and Francisco Varela.[49] Those authors are considered the pioneers of second wave cybernetics, and dismissed the idea of entirely permeable system boundaries, instead defining the identity and autonomy of a system as dependent on closure and observation by an observer.

[45] Kommers, above n 41, 322.
[46] Ibid.
[47] Ibid 323. Note that the census did eventually still occur in 1985 after the process was adjusted to ensure anonymity of respondents.
[48] See, e.g., Hugh Baxter, 'Niklas Luhmann's Theory of Autopoietic Legal Systems' (2013) 9 *Annual Review of Law and Social Science* 167.
[49] Huberto Maturana and Francisco Varela, *Autopoiesis and Cognition: The Realization of the Living* (Boston Studies in the Philosophy of Science, 1991).

Some commentators have argued that Luhmann's sociology was highly influential on data protection's relationship to individual identity, though more focused on general communications and social structures than on individual rights. For Luhmann, the basis of fundamental rights was to serve the necessary differentiation of society into various sub-systems.[50] The structural role of privacy and data protection was thus to ensure that information that is part of the communicative world of one context or social sub-system does not migrate to others.[51] In other words, rights to privacy facilitate the maintenance of separate identities for people within each social sub-system for the sake of living our complex and segmented modern lives. If individuals express identity differently or perform different roles within different social systems and sub-systems, the capacity to coalesce these roles into a single identity or profile becomes a threat to autonomy and an interference with personality, but also a structural threat to society's (self-) organisation. A similar normative rationale for limiting the flow of information between societal sub-systems, or contexts, is found in Helen Nissenbaum's seminal concept of 'contextual integrity'. That account argues for addressing normative parameters of an information flow as dependent on context because each context contains its own normative communicative dynamic, the separation of which is critical as individuals move 'about, into, and out of a plurality of distinct realms'.[52]

For some privacy theorists, then, privacy violations occur when information communicated, or an event occurring, in one social system becomes relevant to the selection of communication in another social system.[53] On this account, the premise of data subject rights is thus less informational self-determination and more a limitation on 'information power' expressed by social actors, such as profilers, with the capacity to transcend the separation of social personas and identities embedded in specific communicative realms and systemic information flows.

WHAT ARE DATA SUBJECT RIGHTS?

These multiple influences are why some characterise data protection as an attempt to balance informational power,[54] whereas others, like Rule, have argued it is not

[50] See, e.g., Jörg Pohle, 'Social Networks, Functional Differentiation of Society, and Data Protection' (online), 14 June 2012 https://arxiv.org/abs/1206.3027.
[51] Malcolm Thorburn, 'Identification, Surveillance, Profiling: On the Use and Abuse of Citizen Data' in Dennis Sullivan (ed) *Preempting Criminal Harms* (Hart, 2012).
[52] Helen Nissenbaum, 'Privacy as Contextual Integrity' (2004) 79 *Washington Law Review* 100, 119; Helen Nissenbaum, *Privacy in Context: Technology, Policy, and the Integrity of Social Life* (Stanford University Press, 2010).
[53] Katayoun Baghai, 'Privacy as a Human Right: A Sociological Theory' (2012) 45(5) *Sociology* 951.
[54] Antoinette Rouvroy and Yves Poullet, 'The Right to Informational Self Determination and the Value of Self Development' in Serge Gutwirth et al (eds) *Reinventing Data Protection* (Springer, 2009) 69.

'aimed at arresting the trend towards wider use of and reliance upon personal information' but rather with 'whether information practices are fair'.[55] Nissenbaum similarly writes with respect to a 1973 US Governmental Report on the impacts of computerised record keeping that there was a 'concern for balancing power, and for limiting the power of state and large institutions over individuals by warning that the net effect of computerisation is that it is becoming much easier for record-keeping systems to affect people than for people to affect record-keeping systems'.[56] Others, like Roger Clarke, argue that commercial considerations, rather than the protection of individuals or fairness, were likely the most significant drivers.[57] Clarke claims that early data protection ideals (for instance, as set out in the OECD Fair Information Principles) relied heavily on the work of Alan Westin, which primarily deployed free market thinking to protect privacy against information technologies. He argues that use of those ideologies (including a privileging of consent) meant that the protection of individual rights through privacy was marginalised, and that the regulations were shaped to minimise any detrimental effects on business and government. Indeed, the GDPR was likely shaped by corporate lobbying more than any other piece of law in Europe's history.[58] Nonetheless, 'access' has always played a role in data protection thinking.

In *Files*, Vismann notes that 'files alone pave the legally acceptable way to reality'.[59] It thus becomes 'up to the world to prove that something which is not on file indeed exists'. Data subject rights represent a recognition that files, though excluding the world not described, do not necessarily reject the world outside as meaningful or a source of truth. The inclusion of access rights in data protection law thus acknowledges the role that individuals play in data management through reconciling personal and documentary realities. For Rule, this means, for data protection, the right of record-keepers to compile records 'carries with it the obligation to maintain them fairly', suggesting the 'individual must normally have ready access to his record to ensure that this obligation is being upheld'.[60]

This leads us to the question of how access and the contiguous right of rectification protect identity precisely? Bygrave gives the best account in describing how these rights give content to certain sub-principles of data protection such as 'validity'

---

[55] James Rule, *The Politics of Privacy: Planning for Personal Data Systems as Powerful Technologies* (Elsevier, 1980) 40.
[56] Referencing the *Hew Report: Report of the Secretary's Advisory Committee on Automated Personal Data Systems* (July, 1973).
[57] Roger Clarke, *Beyond the OECD Guidelines: Privacy Protection for the 21st Century* (4 January 2000) 6 www.rogerclarke.com/DV/PP21C.html.
[58] Carole Cadwalladr and Duncan Campbell, 'Revealed: Facebook's Global Lobbying Against Data Privacy Laws', *Guardian* (online), 2 March 2019 www.theguardian.com/technology/2019/mar/02/facebook-global-lobbying-campaign-against-data-privacy-laws-investment.
[59] Vismann, above n 19, 52.
[60] Rule, above n 55, 39.

and 'quality', which mean 'personal data should be valid with respect to what they are intended to describe, and relevant and complete with respect to the purposes for which they are intended to be processed'.[61] Bygrave notes that in this way, data protection regimes 'attempt to maintain "borderlines of meaning" in the face of the technological possibility for cross-contextual processing of data'.[62] In other words, an inherent and fundamental characteristic of data protection is an attempt to preserve the resonance, unity, and semantic link between document and event, especially for persons. As Vismann notes:

> This goal indicates a closure. This genealogy of the subject from records returns to its point of origin: after census technologies have for centuries provided information that turned humans into an object of knowledge, this very same knowledge is returned to them as their personal data, of which they may dispose of as they wish. In the eyes of the law, the census object becomes the sovereign of its data.[63]

Sovereignty over one's own data is the animating principle of data subject rights as expressed in the GDPR as well as, to a lesser extent, in the European Directive aimed at harmonising data protection in the context of law enforcement processes, the Law Enforcement Directive (LED).[64] Indeed, Article 8 of the *EU Charter of Fundamental Rights*, which specifies the protection of personal data as a fundamental right, includes in paragraph 2 that 'everyone has the right of access to data which has been collected concerning him or her, and the right to have it rectified',[65] clarifying the centrality of 'access' to data protection as a whole.[66] To be specific, in the GDPR, Article 5(1)(d) requires personal data to be 'accurate and, where necessary, kept up to date; every reasonable step must be taken to ensure that personal data are accurate, having regard to the purposes for which they are processed, are erased or rectified without delay',[67] and 5(1)(c) requires data be

---

[61] Bygrave, above n 32.
[62] Ibid 136–137.
[63] Vismann, above n 19, 149–150, quoting Spiros Simitis, 'Bundesdatenschutzgesetz – Ende der Diskussion oder Neubeginn' (1977) 30 *Neue Juristische Wochenschrift* 731.
[64] Directive (EU) 2016/680 of the European Parliament and of the Council of 27 April 2016 on the protection of natural persons with regard to the processing of personal data by competent authorities for the purposes of the prevention, investigation, detection or prosecution of criminal offences or the execution of criminal penalties, and on the free movement of such data, and repealing Council Framework Decision 2008/977/JHA (Law Enforcement Directive) [2016] OJ L 119/89.
[65] Charter of Fundamental Rights of the European Union, 26 October 2012, 2012/C 326/02, Article 8 – Protection of personal data: 1. Everyone has the right to the protection of personal data concerning him or her.
   2. Such data must be processed fairly for specified purposes and on the basis of the consent of the person concerned or some other legitimate basis laid down by law. Everyone has the right of access to data which has been collected concerning him or her, and the right to have it rectified.
   3. Compliance with these rules shall be subject to control by an independent authority.
[66] Charter of Fundamental Rights of the European Union, 26 October 2012, 2012/C 326/02.
[67] General Data Protection Regulation [2016] OJ L 119/1.

'relevant and limited to what is necessary in relation to the purposes for which they are processed'.[68] Article 15 spells out those access rights that require the data controller to inform the data subject about the purpose of processing, the categories of data stored, recipients to whom the data has been disclosed, storage periods, rectification rights, and procedures for lodging complaints, as well as provide a copy of the personal data undergoing processing. Article 16 outlines rights of rectification, and, following the *Google Spain v. AEPD and Mario Costeja González* decision,[69] Article 17 specifies rights of erasure, or the 'right to be forgotten'.[70] Whereas Article 16 only offers rectification in cases of inaccuracy, Article 17(1)(a) facilitates erasure (not rectification) of information no longer necessary in relation to the purposes for which it was collected. However, these rights are all limited by Article 23, which stipulates that member states may restrict the scope of rights by legislative measures when necessary and proportionate in a democratic society to safeguard both national security, and the prevention, investigation, detection or prosecution of a criminal offence.[71] In fact, Article 2(2)(d) entirely excludes the application of the regulation to the processing of personal data 'by competent authorities for the purposes of the prevention, investigation, detection or prosecution of criminal offences, the execution of criminal penalties, including the safeguarding against and the prevention of threats to public security', directing us to the importance of data subject rights within the LED.

Although managing law enforcement databases was not a primary data protection function when initially conceptualised, some argue that data protection has, especially since 2001, evolved to include preserving privacy in criminal justice systems.[72] Indeed, separating law enforcement databases from general government databases is becoming more difficult, with growing examples of 'collaborative' approaches of integrating databases from health, education, social welfare, geography, and social media into corrections and police information systems for the sake of producing *risk* scores for individuals (something explored further in Chapter 6).[73] Whether or not this is through the GDPR or LED, data protection does indeed seem to have become the forthright mechanism for defining data management procedures in law enforcement agencies.[74] The LED provides derivatives of GDPR data subject rights, with

[68] Ibid.
[69] *Google Spain v. AEPD and Mario Costeja González* (C-131/12) [2014].
[70] General Data Protection Regulation [2016] OJ L 119/1.
[71] Ibid.
[72] Francesca Bignami, 'Privacy and Law Enforcement in the European Union' (2007) 8(1) *Chicago Journal of International Law* 233.
[73] Nathan Munn, 'Police in Canada are Tracking People's "Negative" Behavior in a "Risk" Database', *Motherboard* (online), 27 February 2019 https://motherboard.vice.com/en_us/article/kzdp5v/police-in-canada-are-tracking-peoples-negative-behavior-in-a-risk-database.
[74] See, e.g., Article 10 in the General Data Protection Regulation which states:

> Processing of personal data relating to criminal convictions and offences or related security measures based on Article 6(1) may only be carried out either under the control of official authority or when the processing is authorised by Union law or Member State law providing for

'specific rules relating to the protection of natural persons with regard to the processing of personal data by competent authorities for the purposes of the prevention, investigation, detection or prosecution of criminal offences or the execution of criminal penalties, including the safeguarding against and the prevention of threats to public security, respecting the specific nature of those activities'.[75] This excludes however 'national security' practices which are typically dealt with under another pillar of European Law (Chapter 2 of Title V of the Treaty of the European Union). Data subject rights in the LED include the right to know the identity and contact details of the relevant controller and data protection officer, the intended purposes of the processing, the right to lodge a complaint, and the right to request access, rectification, or erasure, as well as potentially the legal basis for processing, the retention period for the data, and who might receive the data.[76] However, Articles 13–18 also enable member states to legislate limitations on providing that information to prevent obstructing legal investigations or procedures, criminal investigation or prevention, the protection of public security and national security, and to protect the rights and freedoms of others. A right to restrict processing is provided in Article 16(3) as an alternative to erasure where the accuracy of the data is contested or cannot be ascertained, or where the data must be maintained for the purpose of evidence. The Directive also acknowledges in Article 6 that different categories of information should be distinguished in accordance with their degree of accuracy and reliability, and that personal data based on facts are therefore different from personal data based on assessments (without going further as to the significance of that distinction), which affects the degree to which data might be considered inaccurate.[77] That means rectification rights are only relevant to data supplied directly by the data subject.[78]

Article 16 of the LED also facilitates a right to erasure, with one criterion being where processing of data fails to comply with the requirement of 'relevance' in Article 4, or when files include 'special categories' of data such as 'race, ethnic origin, political opinion, religion or belief, trade-union membership, genetic data or data concerning health or sex life'.[79] The LED also requires time-limits on data storage,[80] as well as that controllers make a distinction between different categories of data subjects. This is a meaningful specificity for the otherwise generic data subject.

adequate safeguards for the rights and freedoms of data subjects. Any comprehensive register of criminal convictions may be kept only under the control of official authority.
[75] *Law Enforcement Directive* [2016] OJ L 119/89, Recital 11; See also Recital 40.
[76] Ibid Article 13.
[77] Ibid Article 6(1) and 6(2). Recital 30 reiterates the goal of 'accuracy', noting that sometimes statements containing personal data are based on subjective perceptions and are not always verifiable. So accuracy does not mean accuracy of a statement but that it was made (i.e. no making stuff up).
[78] Ibid Recital 47.
[79] Ibid Article 16(1); Article 4(c); Article 8(1). There is also a derogation in Articles 8(2)(a) and 8(2)(b) from the restrictions on processing types of data listed in Article 8(1) if that processing is authorised by law, or necessary to protect the vital interests of the data subject or another person.
[80] Ibid Article 5.

Here, data subjects are addressed as: individuals suspected of committing or being about to commit a criminal offence, convicted persons, victims and potential victims of crime, and other parties to offences including witnesses or informants.[81] The LED thus embodies a tension between access and permissible limitations on access that are necessary and proportionate in a democratic society. This likely excludes access to the data itself, and according to the distinction between facts and assessments recognised in Article 6, almost certainly any assessments made on the basis of that data.

Profiling in the LED is governed by Article 11, where fully automated processing requires an authorising law governing the conduct of the data controller, which provides appropriate safeguards including, at least, the right to obtain human intervention. But such systems cannot use 'special' categories of data without suitable measures in place to safeguard data subjects' rights, freedoms and legitimate interests. Recital 57 suggests the keeping of logs for all automated data-processing activities. Member states have two years from when the Directive comes into force to transpose it into national law, and seven years to build logging mechanisms for automated processing (including profiling) systems. There are also requirements for when data processing is performed by a 'processor', which would include a commercial provider of analytics software and services.[82] General transparency of processing is promoted by Article 24 and 25, which requires controllers to maintain a record of all categories of processing activities that describe, including other things, the use of profiling, and that controllers keep logs for various operations performed by automated processing systems (for the purpose of verifying the lawfulness of processing).

Also interesting are the 'infrastructural' dimensions of compliance and enforcement in the LED. Rather than the individual invoking supra-national supervision as with the ECHR, Article 19 of the LED specifies obligations on the controller (i.e. competent authority or policing agency) to implement appropriate technical and organisational measures to ensure (and to be able to demonstrate) that processing is performed in accordance with the directive – including, in Article 20, the implementation of the vague requirements of data protection by design and default. Another infrastructural dimension is the instalment of a 'data protection officer' to inform controllers of their obligations and monitor compliance,[83] as well as an appropriate 'supervisory authority', being an *independent* public authority responsible for monitoring the application of the Directive, and dealing with (including investigating) complaints lodged by a data subject,[84] and capable of ordering controllers to bring processing operations into compliance or entirely banning or

---

[81] Ibid Article 6.
[82] Ibid Article 22.
[83] Ibid Article 34.
[84] Ibid Article 41.

limiting processing.[85] Member states must also afford data subjects a right to a judicial remedy against the binding decisions of a supervisory authority.[86]

The LED has been characterised as unsatisfactory because of its focus on cross-border data transfers, its unenforceability,[87] the inclusion of exemptions for almost every principle, its failure to account for various mandatory data retention regimes around Europe,[88] and thus ultimately for its failure 'to update the regulatory framework into the new Internet reality'.[89] Further, there is still no useful clarification on the relation between access rights and derogations from access rights in law enforcement files. The idiosyncrasies of law enforcement data collection, retention, and processing methods clearly require different constraints than administrative or commercial entities. For instance, as De Hert and Papakonstantinou say, 'law enforcement agencies thrive on "hearsay", and thus not in data quality-certified personal information', and 'they may need to keep data for very long periods, if possible for ever, and correlate them incessantly in relation to crimes which appeared irrelevant when the data first appeared'. There is also the argument that profiling in the policing context, while risky, can produce effective results, meaning any regulation needs to find a way of facilitating the exercise while still excluding impermissible uses of data. The possibility of providing access to non-factual or intelligence information is therefore particularly fraught. Even informing individuals that they are the subjects of police scrutiny is problematic, as this may undermine law enforcement exercises. The law enforcement specific rules thus inflect data protection more towards ensuring accountability than the protection of identity. The information provided may be sufficient to ensure police are not acting illegally, but insufficient to ensure the accuracy or relevance of that data itself. There is little in the regime, then, that would facilitate accessing the rationale or reasoning behind such a decision, in order to contest its validity, potentially for bias, for use of irrelevant information, or to challenge the quality of logic used, even if doing so would not adversely prejudice law enforcement activities in any way.

Ultimately, these mechanisms are not equipped to deal with the reality that web-browsing histories and telecommunications traffic data, for instance, are unlikely to be inherently factually inaccurate. Those data points record the occurrence of an interaction between information systems and the mere fact that the interaction occurred is rarely wrongly recorded (although there remains difficulty in correlating internet protocol addresses used in transactions with specific users in cases where there might be multiple users of a device). The issue of relevance encounters similar

---

[85] Ibid Article 47.
[86] Ibid Article 53.
[87] See, e.g., Maria Eduarda Gonçalves and Inês Andrade Jesus, 'Security and Personal Data Protection in the European Union: Challenging Trends from a Human Rights Perspective' (2012) 1 *Human Security Perspectives* 117.
[88] Ibid 118.
[89] Paul de Hert and Vagelis Papakonstantinou, 'The Police and Criminal Justice Data Protection Directive: Comment and Analysis' (2012) 22(6) *Computers & Law Magazine of SCL* 1.

obstacles. If relevance in law enforcement intelligence means data that enables the selection of a surveillance target, how do you distinguish what type of information might or might not be relevant when attempting to identify suspicion at first instance?

CONSENT

Another important dimension of data subject rights for understanding the nature of the legal subject in data protection, the trajectory of data subject rights under the GDPR, and its relationship to institutional identities, is the way in which consent operates in data protection frameworks.[90] Without rehearsing the insightful commentary on the utility and failures of the notice and consent paradigm, its limitations in this context cannot be ignored. For instance, Barocas and Nissenbaum, in a 2009 paper, describe the hegemonic nature of opt-out/opt-in approaches that have ironically become the preferred mechanism of both profiling critics and practitioners.[91] They describe how the complexity of information flows makes consent a difficult paradigm, and how the bogus use of privacy policies to describe information processing practices undermines real privacy protection. Ultimately, they argue when it comes to cases like online behavioural advertising, users 'literally cannot know what they are consenting to', and thus challenge the moral legitimacy of this method. But while consent is clearly relevant to practices like behavioural advertising, its relationship to government and law enforcement profiling and assessment is less clear. Indeed Recital 35 of the LED clarifies that consent ought not be the lawful basis for data profiling in the law enforcement context. To that end, an interesting tension around consent arises.

One critical element of the update from the 1995 EU Data Protection Directive to the GDPR was enhancing the content of consent. This focus on consent is premised on the idea that the data subject can better express their autonomy and self-determination when given the capacity to make properly informed decisions. We are now starting to learn what the higher-level 'meaningful' consent requirements of the GDPR might require in practice. In France, for instance, the French Supervisory Authority, the CNIL (the National Commission for Informatics and Liberties) heard GDPR complaints against Google concerning the requirement that Android users accept Google's privacy policy and general terms of service which permit behavioural and targeted advertising.[92] The CNIL found that the privacy policy did not satisfy the requirements of Articles 12 and 13 of the GDPR by not

---

[90] See, e.g., Eleni Kosta, *Consent in European Data Protection Law* (Martinus Nijhoff, 2013).
[91] Solon Barocas and Helen Nissenbaum, 'On Notice: The Trouble with Notice and Consent' (Presented at the First International Forum on the Application and Management of Personal Electronic Information, October 2009).
[92] *Commission Nationale de l'Informatique et des Libertes*, 21 January 2019, Deliberation No SAN-2019–001, pronouncing a financial penalty against the company Google LLC.

providing sufficient information to users, thus failing in its transparency obligations. The information provided in the privacy policy did not properly account for the ways in which Google combines and processes data retrieved from external sources, data produced by the person, data generated by the person's activity, and data derived or inferred from data provided or activity data. In other words, the user was not able to measure the primary effects of that processing on their private life. Similarly, a German anti-trust (competition) decision, though based on the data protection principles in the GDPR, has prohibited Facebook from making the use of its social network conditional on the collection and combination of user and device-related data from other Facebook owned services *WhatsApp, Oculus, Masquerade,* and *Instagram.* That decision determined the combination of those datasets through user consent as an abuse of market power, a violation of the GDPR's goals of countering informational asymmetries, and a violation of informational self-determination under Article 6(1)(a).[93] The decision did not address the collection or amalgamation of data after users had signed up to Facebook, but rather focused on the lack of meaningful consent for user and device data associated with those secondary services to be combined with their Facebook user data when initially signing up to the service. This hybrid of data protection and competition law has become critical in the context of large data processing companies being able to acquire smaller companies and datasets, rather than use them as a third party for data collection. It will of course be interesting to see how these decisions play out in appeal in the CJEU. There is also discussion of augmenting the value of consent by making Do Not Track expressions legally enforceable in the coming update to the EU e-Privacy Directive.[94]

Some have suggested marginalising and challenging the third-party data market is a primary goal of the GDPR, while at the same time privileging first-party data collection and processing for not requiring consent as its legal basis (instead being permitted by the legitimate interests of the processing party).[95] Achieving that change on a structural level would be a very meaningful outcome for the GDPR. Prohibiting the processing of data as it moves across social sub-systems would be a radical shift in the contemporary data ecology, but to what degree this might be applied to government and law enforcement decision-making is yet to be seen. While this line of regulation might tackle the data broking and 'ad tech' business models of obtaining data from third parties in order to profile a user, it is unclear what value it will have for profiling operating on the register of governance, or as we will see in Chapter 8, for types of profiling that do not require the amalgamation of giant data sets from third parties.

---

[93] Bundeskartellamt, B6-22/16, 6 February 2019.
[94] Lukasz Olejnik, 'A Second Life for the "Do Not Track" Setting – With Teeth', *Wired* (online), 28 February 2019 www.wired.com/story/a-second-life-for-the-do-not-track-setting/.
[95] Hoofnagle et al, above n 17.

DATA SUBJECT AS LEGAL SUBJECT

As far-reaching as these regulations are, and as structural as their enforcement procedures might be, they retain a relatively basic understanding of the relationship between a person and the data through which that person can be profiled. As Spiros Simitis said, data protection operates on the risk of individuals being treated as objects of knowledge. Data is thus understood as a static representation of a person and little more. While data protection legislation might be effective in dealing with personal data, it fails to adequately address the far more important issue of dealing with '*patterns of correlated data*' through which statistical analysis yields intelligence and insights. In other words, data protection fails to think about profiles as 'knowledge' rather than data.[96] It thus fails to address what were some of the very first and most pressing privacy concerns around the power of statistical analysis, and its capacity to know people. Nor does it address the contemporary information reality of data within dynamic, constantly updating systems that operate on individuals recursively through time.

Access and rectification rights in data protection were described earlier as an attempt to return control of data to individuals, as a way of ensuring fidelity between data and its semantic source. 'Informational self-determination' as affected by access and rectification rights was thus presented as potentially more useful than traditional privacy ideas for alleviating the harms of profiles and dossiers. And while the new regulatory environment may be meaningful in many ways, when it comes to automated profiling, data protection laws, or data subject rights at least, still, as Mireille Hildebrandt suggests, 'seem to miss the point'.[97] Some have thus argued there is a need to refocus attention away from access and rectification of data inputs, and towards transparency in the decision-making process.[98] This is becoming the domain of 'algorithmic accountability', a collection of legal and technical ideas that also address profiling, discussed further in Chapter 7.

Whereas the privacy jurisprudence created a private person capable of remaining unknowable behind a legal subject, the legal subject of data protection changes the relationship between the physical person and the profile by affording a right to insist on seeing the data on which a profile is built (to a certain degree) rather than eliminating the profile. At the same time, the discursive output of the human subject is privileged, with the capacity to rectify and occasionally erase factual data about a person controlled by others. And while the individualism of constitutional privacy rights is replicated to a certain extent in the requirement that data subjects protect

---

[96] Mireille Hildebrandt and Serge Gutwirth, 'General Introduction and Overview' in Mireille Hildebrant and Serge Gutwirth (eds) *Profiling the European Citizen* (Springer, 2008) 2.
[97] Mireille Hildebrandt and Bert-Jaap Koops, 'The Challenges of Ambient Law and Legal Protection in the Profiling Era' (2010) 73(3) *Modern Law Review* 428, at 442.
[98] For authors other than Hildebrandt writing about this, see, e.g., Ronald Leenes, 'Addressing the Obscurity of Data Clouds' (2009) *TILT Law & Technology Working Paper No 012/2009*, 98.

themselves, the GDPR also entirely re-shapes the enforcement technology and environment by delegating enforcement to a bureaucratic architecture of supervisory authorities, data protection authorities, and internal and independent data protection officers within firms (i.e. data controllers) each tasked with monitoring, record keeping, and compliance.

Nonetheless, the data subject remains a deeply liberal contrivance, with the electronic body or data double understood primarily as a static representation. Data protection is thus about returning 'control' to physical individuals tasked with exercising autonomous and self-determining decision-making over their informational representation. Stefano Rodotà's vision that data protection may constitute an equivalent of habeas corpus for the electronic body,[99] a way to expose or produce the contours of the electronic self, may go a certain way toward constraining certain pernicious activities, but it still insists on treating that electronic body as little more than an image. It is argued in the following chapters that this may not be enough, and that we need law to reflect a more complex reality of information and identity in contemporary life.

CONCLUSION

Information processing techniques of contemporary governance have increased in scale and complexity, and generated new narratives about the people and the world. The notion of identity that privacy and data protection seek to protect or privilege may no longer be the appropriate site of legal intervention. In other words, Kommers's account of informational self-determination, that 'the content of the general right to personality is largely determined by the self-image of its bearer', may be losing its significance in the contemporary information processing regime. Whereas arguments about identity that operationalised a duality between 'narrative' and 'categorical' identity frame the risk to the individual as a usurpation of that external site of identity, newer surveillance systems seem to be operationalising a very different understanding of human identity. To that end, the following chapter begins the exploration of some of those more contemporary exercises of automated information processing, their changing logics and politics, and the new models of identity they put to work.

---

[99] Stefano Rodotà in Serge Gutwirth et al (eds) *Reinventing Data Protection* (Springer 2009).

6

Automation, Actuarial Identity, and Law Enforcement Informatics

What happens when we bring the practices, political rationalities, and technological approaches that we have discussed so far into the world of computation and automation? From the creation of biological and behavioural archives in the nineteenth century, the automation of profiling represents a categorical shift in surveillance capacity. The speculative knowledge logics behind intelligence dossiers take on new dimensions when refracted through massive telecommunications databases and computational pattern matching that elevate correlation and association as processes for understanding the subjects of surveillance. At the same time, the political rationalities that animated responses to Fenian terror become visible in the post-9/11 expansion of surveillance capability associated with the logics of Total Information Awareness[1] and the USA PATRIOT Act. The types of data collected for pattern matching systems that developed after September 11 were vast, crossing private and public repositories, and covering both biology and behaviour. As Peter Galison and Martha Minow describe:

> An early description of the [Total Information Awareness] initiative explained how it would 'detect, classify, identify, track, understand, and preempt,' using biometric data, such as images of faces, fingerprints, iris scans, and transactional data, such as 'communications, financial, education, travel, medical, veterinary, country entry, place/event entry, transportation, housing, critical resources, and government'. The Lawyers Committee for Human Rights described the data sources to be examined more vividly as encompassing: 'religious and political contributions; driving records, high school transcripts; book purchases; medical records; passport applications; car rentals; phone, e-mail and internet search logs'. Subject to such searches would be public records held by local, state, and federal government agencies, and databases purchased by the government from commercial vendors, such as credit card companies and retail stores. The project 'would make available to government employees vast amounts of personal information about American citizens who are

---

[1] See, e.g., Gina Marie Stevens, 'Privacy: Total Information Awareness Programs and Related Information Access, Collection, and Protection Laws' (2003). Report for Congress; Laura K Donohue, 'Anglo-American Privacy and Surveillance' (2006) 96 *Journal of Criminal Law and Criminology* 1059.

not suspected of any criminal conduct,' according to lawyer Floyd Abrams, who served on the Technology and Privacy Advisory Committee ultimately created by Donald Rumsfeld, Secretary of the Department of Defense, to review TIA in response to public outcry.[2]

Biological information in this early paradigm of automated profiling had a relatively limited, or at least quite coarse, impact on the generation of profiles, with the majority of techniques focusing on various forms of behavioural data. The richest source of that data were the vast records created by interaction with telecommunications systems. Accessing those records required coordination, cooperation, and active participation from the private telecommunications and logistics industries. But the tools for analysing all that data have their own history, and of course, their own idiosyncratic effects on the types of institutional identities produced through profiling and surveillance. This broad family of techniques associated with big data and data mining, as well as the automation of actuarial approaches in criminal justice and administrative governance.

The logic of data mining and 'knowledge discovery in databases' for profiling has been described as generating new types of knowledge by making visible previously 'unknown structures of reality in flux'.[3] The scholarly research from the first decade of the twenty-first century broadly defined profiling in this context as 'the use of predictive data mining to establish recurrent patterns or "profiles" permitting the classification of individuals into different categories'.[4] That broad category includes a variety of techniques.[5]

This chapter briefly traces the origins of the 'pattern identification' thinking that animates these processes from its military and commercial origins. It interrogates the degree to which the harms generated by these practices are reproductions of the problems of inaccuracy and misrepresentation, and the elimination of the

---

[2] Peter Galison and Martha Minow, 'Our Privacy, Ourselves in the Age of Technological Intrusions' in R A Wilson (ed) *Human Rights in the War on Terror* (Cambridge University Press, 2005) 258.
[3] Mireille Hildebrandt, 'Who Is Profiling Who? Invisible Visibility' in Serge Gutwirth et al (eds) *Reinventing Data Protection?* (Springer 2009) 241; Mireille Hildebrandt, 'Defining Profiling: A New Type of Knowledge?' in Mireille Hildebrandt and Serge Gutwirth (eds) *Profiling the European Citizen: Cross-Disciplinary Perspectives* (Springer 2008) 17.
[4] Gloria Gonzalez-Fuster, Serge Gutwirth and Erika Ellyne, 'Profiling in the European Union: A high-risk practice' (2010) *INEZ Policy Brief No 10, Centre for European Policy Studies*, 2.
[5] A general description of profiling in this area: First, a group profile or category is created through data mining, sometimes described as 'descriptive', 'bottom-up', or 'unsupervised' processes. This targets the discovery of novel unknown relations between data objects in (or across) databases. An individual's data is then measured against that 'group profile', or category for the sake of classification. That comparative exercise is 'predictive', 'top-down', or 'supervised' data mining, which is used to make predictions based on patterns of known information. Another set of terms used to describe automated profiling is 'distributive' and 'non-distributive' profiles. Distributive profiles indicate that the characteristics which together constitute the profile are applied to all members of the group. Alternatively, non-distributive profiles, like criminal profiles, signify that members of a profiled group may not demonstrate all the characteristics of a particular profile. Bart Schermer, 'The Limits of Privacy in Automated Profiling and Data Mining' (2011) 27(1) *Computer Law & Security Review* 45, 46.

interpretive space between individual and representation already discussed, and what might be novel to these systems.

FROM COMMERCE TO CRIME

Louise Amoore's history of algorithmic information processing in *The Politics of Possibility* traces the origins of 'pattern identification' thinking to the UK government's engagement of Price Waterhouse accountants to devise and administer restrictions on supplies and rations during the Second World War.[6] These accountants were tasked with providing the state with 'actionable data to deal with an uncertain future'[7] by identifying population-level behaviours and formulating techniques for governing production and consumption. Other scholars locate the origins of pattern identification thinking in different facets of military practice, in particular the evolution of Operations Research as a discipline for analysing the data generated throughout the Second World War. Paul Edwards, for instance, describes how the analysis of U-Boat dive patterns for targeting ultimately became a metaphor for 'pattern analysis' thinking about humans. Edwards argues that the scaling up of these techniques during the Vietnam War reflected a belief that the path to victory was the capacity to measure and calculate.[8] For Amoore, however, the use of correlation in *modern* data mining, first appeared in the work of an IBM research fellow Rakesh Agrawal, 'widely considered to have pioneered the techniques of identifying usable patters in large volumes of data'.[9] In 1992, his data mining research was presented to supermarket executives as a demonstration of how data could be used, not only to extrapolate historical data into future predictions, but to make inferences about the probability relationships between purchased items for the sake of identifying patterns 'within and between transactions'.[10] In the supermarket context, this meant algorithms capable of enquiring into, for example, '[w]hat pattern of items has to be sold with sausages in order for it to be likely that mustard will also be sold?'[11] Amoore, following Brian Masumi, characterises this as a change from 'the effort to predict future trends on the basis of fixed statistical data to a means of pre-empting the future, drawing probable futures into imminent and immediate commercial decisions'.[12] This also represents the origin of what has been the focus of the

---

[6] Louise Amoore, *The Politics of Possibility: Risk and Security Beyond Probability* (Duke University Press, 2013) 36.
[7] Ibid 39.
[8] Paul Edwards, *The Closed World: Computers and the Politics of Discourse in Cold War America* (MIT Press, 1996). The installation of a US business school Dean as a military commander to enact that approach is demonstrative of the belief that lack of domain knowledge can be overcome with sufficient data and tools for calculation.
[9] Amoore, above n 6, 39.
[10] Ibid 40.
[11] Ibid.
[12] Louise Amoore, 'Algorithmic War' (2009) 41(1) *Antipode* 49, 55.

technological discipline of data science for the last several decades: the statistical interrogation of massive datasets.

In February 2002, advocates for this type of large-scale pattern recognition suggested in a US House Sub-Committee hearing that, had algorithmic search facilities been available to security forces, the September 11 attacks may have been averted. Lobbyists (including IBM and Accenture, among others) argued that 'our enemies are hiding in open and available information',[13] suggesting their own computational pattern matching technologies were now integral to the war on terror.[14] The acceptance of data mining technologies and practices in the security and law enforcement expansion that followed ushered in a new relationship between citizens and states, and new modalities of governance. Techniques first used to merchandise milk had now substantially altered the way governments would monitor and assess individuals.

LOW-LEVEL AUTOMATION

There are many different ways that profiling analytics occur, but they often follow a similar logic. Large datasets are parsed through models which break down and recombine information to 'determine and discover patterns and relations with some other element gathered from other subjects and events'.[15] These statistical patterns and connections can then be used to assess and make decisions about a person. Different applications use different datasets and different levels of complexity. In 'lower-level' systems, these models operate on the basis of statistical extrapolations from targeted questioning. A profile is based on a limited and human-engineered dataset, with measures taken to validate or invalidate 'already proposed correlations believed to be relevant and pertinent' by answering preceding questions.[16] For example, Bernard Harcourt outlines the questions used in parole prediction under categories like: criminal history, education and employment, financial position, family and marital status, accommodation, leisure and recreational interests, companions, alcohol and drug status, emotional and personal characteristics, and attitude and orientation.[17] Using a scoring system based on responses to those questions, it was believed statistical likelihood of re-offending could be calculated, and parole decisions improved accordingly.

Many automated systems replicate and moderately extend these actuarial approaches for the sake of bail, sentencing, and parole, using more complex statistical methods to identify correlations within what are still relatively constrained

[13] J Kestelyn, 'For Want of a Nail' (2002) 5(7) *Intelligence Enterprise* 8, 8.
[14] Amoore, above n 6, 41.
[15] Ibid 51.
[16] Serge Gutwirth and Mireille Hildebrandt, 'Some Caveats on Profiling' in Serge Gutwirth et al (eds) *Data Protection in a Profiled World* (Springer 2010) 31, 32–33.
[17] Bernard Harcourt, *Against Prediction: Profiling, Policing, and Punishing in an Actuarial Age* (University of Chicago Press, 2006), 80.

datasets. These systems analyse information available to law enforcement, such as incident, health, prison administration, and intelligence files, as well as data from existing clinical instruments used by corrections agencies in order to classify individuals according to risk.[18] Models are created from sets of relationships within the data, which are then 'employed to automate the process of classifying entities or activities of interest, estimating the value of unobserved variables, or predicting future outcomes'.[19] Although it is difficult to know what specific 'features' in this data (data points that are used as measurements of the phenomena that a machine learning system is analysing) are relevant for various risk assessment tools, as these are typically trade secrets which courts seem happy to protect (something discussed in more detail later in the chapter),[20] these profiling systems are not necessarily very complex or sophisticated. They do not focus as much on detecting patterns hidden in the data, as they do on encoding some particular existing calculation of relevance.[21] Nonetheless, automating this type of profiling in criminal justice applications, particularly risk assessments for bail, parole, and sentencing decisions, has become a pivotal social justice issue, and an exemplar of the risks of inherent biases in the data informing these systems and the calculations they perform.

To that end, many of the automated systems at work today are very similar to the actuarial prediction mechanisms that have been around for some time. Law enforcement and criminal justice used data-oriented prediction mechanisms throughout the twentieth century. Much like judicial photography, actuarial prediction emerged in systems of prison administration,[22] and was an outgrowth 'of a turn to individualisation in law at the dawn of the twentieth century'.[23] In his book *Against Prediction*, Harcourt describes the evolution of 'penalogical modernism' that emerged around the end of the nineteenth century as a historical break from the Victorian system. Harcourt claims, on the basis of developments in statistics and data collection, the prison as a sanctioning mechanism became increasingly tailored to each individual convict. The turn to probabilistic reasoning was intended to increase control over the individual by disciplining uncertainty. Decisions about what to do in the present were thus increasingly based on a quantifiable probability of the occurrence of a future event. Based on 'the laws of chance', this predictive knowledge supposedly allowed for 'more control over individual behaviour'.[24] By the middle of the twentieth century, actuarial approaches had been deployed in

---

[18] Walter Perry et al, 'Predictive Policing: The Role of Crime Forecasting in Law Enforcement Operations' *Rand Corporation* (2013) at xvi.
[19] Solon Barocas and Andrew Selbst, 'Big Data's Disparate Impact' 104(3) *California Law Review* (2016) 7.
[20] *State v. Loomis*, 2015AP157-CR (WI, 2016).
[21] Some applications that include machine learning do parse that data for new statistical relationships.
[22] Harcourt, above n 17, 39.
[23] Ibid 41.
[24] Ibid 44.

sentencing, parole prediction and even active policing. They eventually became common practice in criminal profiling, using correlations between specific group-based traits and group-based offending rates to help 'law enforcement officers identify potential suspects for investigation'.[25]

Alongside 'penological modernism' and its turn to individual treatment, there was (and continues to be) a great deal of research that deployed statistical and actuarial thinking towards the role of incarceration as a method of general crime prevention and control.[26] This was not so much an interrogation of the utility of preventative detention, but rather the measurement of whether a social benefit is achieved through focusing penological and policing resources on particular offenders who supposedly commit the majority of crime. Indeed, 'statistical sentencing' is based on an ideological premise of the ability to predict dangerousness and introduce selective incapacitation as social welfare mechanisms. The risks attendant on those practices are typically dismissed as the cost of an otherwise more socially optimal distribution of resources. However, instead of being a simple objective approach, these techniques represents a penological and criminological argument as to the relationship between sentencing and crime-reduction that clearly echoes and evolved out of the ideologies of preventative detention discussed by statisticians and criminologists in the 19th century like Galton and Lombroso.

It is this line of thinking that has informed the continuing basic research behind automated bail, parole, and sentencing recommendation and prediction systems. The RAND Corporation pioneered this early research on risk assessment tools, 'including the INSLAW instrument (developed for U.S. federal prosecutors to carry out risk assessment of offenders), the Salient Factor Score (developed as a risk assessment scale for U.S. Parole Commission), and the Canadian Dangerous Behaviour Rating Scale for Metropolitan Toronto Forensic Service'.[27] Statistical risk assessment based on predicting dangerousness is now typically called 'evidence-based practices'.

'Predictive policing' represents another application of that actuarial logic. To date, predictive policing has been more 'successful' with techniques focusing on geographical and temporal crime prediction – that is, the *when* and *where* of crime, although techniques predicting the *who* of criminal behaviour, while less mature, do exist, and are developing.[28] In predictive policing, the question of *who* is not merely

---

[25] Ibid 103.
[26] See, e.g., Jacqueline Cohen, 'Incapacitation as a Strategy for Crime Control: Possibilities and Pitfalls' (1983) 5 *Crime and Justice* 1.
[27] Danielle Kehl et al 'Algorithms in the Criminal Justice System: Assessing the Use of Risk Assessments in Sentencing' (2017) Responsive Communities Initiative, Berkman Klein Center for Internet and Society.
[28] See Perry, above n 18, 81. There are several more examples in the literature. See, e.g., Craig Uchida, 'Predictive Policing' in Gerben Bruinsma and David Weisburd (eds) *Encyclopedia of Criminology and Criminal Justice* (Springer 2013) 3871; Journalists have also discussed the issue in Matt Stroud, 'The Minority Report: Chicago's New Police Computer Predicts Crimes, but Is It Racist?' (19 February 2014) *The Verge* www.theverge.com/2014/2/19/5419854/the-minority-report-this-computer-predicts-crime-but-is-it-racist; and Joe Nicholson, 'Detroit Law Enforcement's Secret

an assessment that a person sharing particular characteristics is likely to commit a crime (i.e. general profile),[29] but relies on analytics of behavioural information to produce risk assessments for specific individuals.[30] Systems produced for those purposes by vendors like Palantir, a company launched shortly after the September 11 attacks, have been trialled in cities like New Orleans, Los Angeles, and Chicago, and even Sydney, Australia with limited government oversight.[31] The New Orleans system primarily operationalised criminal databases looking at ballistics, gang, probation and parole data, jail telephone records, as well as central case management histories, and a repository of 'field interview cards'. Field interview cards are a mechanism for collecting structured data from suspect and non-suspect persons expressly for the purpose of intelligence gathering. They greatly expanded the scope of the input data for Palantir's systems, and have since been used in other predictive policing exercises such as Chronic Offender Bulletins listing 'probable' and 'potential' repeat offenders.[32] The primary profiling mechanisms in New Orleans, however, appears to have been social network analysis of shooting victims to generate a 'heat list' of 3,900 people at the highest risk of involvement in gun violence due to their connections to shooters or victims.

The Verge reported that in 2016 the Danish national police and intelligence services also signed an 84-month contract with Palantir for a similar predictive technology package to identify potential terrorists.[33] They report that this system also uses law enforcement data taken from automated number plate readers and CCTV video to make predictions about individuals.[34]

Weapon: Big Data Analytics' (16 May 2014) *Venture Beat* http://venturebeat.com/2014/05/16/detroit-law-enforcements-secret-weapon-big-data-analytics.

[29] See, e.g., Andrew Ferguson, 'Predictive Policing and Reasonable Suspicion' (2012) 62 *Emory Law Journal* 259, 293.

[30] Perry, above n 18, 90.

[31] In Australia, the NSW Police have been using an algorithmic risk assessment and predictive policing system called the 'Suspect Target Management Plan' (STMP), that generates lists of suspects for police targeting. Investigation into the system identified that 44 per cent of individuals targeted were indigenous (although being only 3.3. per cent of the Australian population). When questioned by the legislative assembly, the NSW police (or rather the Minister for Police) refused to release any details on the procurement process or system itself. See Vicki Sentas and Camilla Pandolfini, 'Policing Young People in NSW: A Study of the Suspect Targeting Management Plan' (2017) *A Report of the Youth Justice Coalition NSW*.

[32] Mark Harris, 'How Peter Thiel's Secretive Data Company Pushed into Policing' *Wired* (9 August 2017). www.wired.com/story/how-peter-thiels-secretive-data-company-pushed-into-policing/.

[33] Ali Winston, 'Palantir Has Secretly Been Using New Orleans to Test Its Predictive Policing Technology' (27 February 2018) *The Verge* www.theverge.com/2018/2/27/17054740/palantir-predictive-policing-tool-new-orleans-nopd.

[34] Palantir's systems also offer police departments, in the United States at least, access to massive databases of crime data, including telecommunications data, automated number plate reader data, FBI terrorism reports, and local traffic citations. They also offered the ability to search the system by name, vehicle, keyword, location or even tattoo (a continuation of the nineteenth-century Distinctive Marks Register). These systems also produce automated intelligence updates for policing personnel by geography.

Although lab-based tests of these techniques often show good results (i.e. higher accuracy than predictions through clinical – or human expert – methods),[35] sober assessments of predictive policing in practice typically identify no benefit in terms of reduction in crime rate or violence. For instance, Jessica Saunders and others from RAND evaluated Chicago's person-based (rather than location-based) Strategic Subjects List programme. Like the New Orleans programme, this was a relatively simple, actuarial model, rather than a highly complex machine learning model using vast datasets. It effectively deployed a form of social network analysis using co-arrestees and linked associates of homicide victims to predict the likelihood of someone becoming a victim themselves. The evaluation looked at homicide trends, and found the programme had no effect on homicide rates but did drastically increase arrest rates. In other words, the predictive policing mechanism became an investigatory tool rather than a mechanism for improving community outcomes. However, it also contributed directly to greater policing of specific populations by increasing the number of arrests, which is often used problematically as a proxy for criminality in other predictive policing and risk assessment systems.[36]

Based on those lab studies showing higher accuracy than clinical models, some insist that these techniques represent a necessary step in contemporary policing because they are (or could be) more accurate than biased officers.[37] Proponents also characterise PredPol, Strategic Subjects List, and others as 'first stage' crime prediction algorithms because, while they guide the deployment of resources, they are not yet used to make specific legal determinations.[38] In other words, those commentators see the end-point of this trajectory as 'police officers and judges ... mak[ing] their decisions based solely on the outputs of the algorithms without exercising any of their own independent judgments'.[39] This type of formalisation raises an entirely different spectrum of issues – for instance, whether perfect prevention of crime is a desirable social goal,[40] or whether 'inefficiency' needs to be preserved in criminal justice processes, let alone whether it might be technically possible.[41] However, prior to those more abstract concerns, there remain a litany of issues associated with the technical and ideological dimensions of these systems, as well as the political economy of their development and deployment.

---

[35] Jessica Saunders, Priscilla Hunt and John S Hollywood, 'Predictions Put into Practice: A Quasi-Experimental Evaluation of Chicago's Predictive Policing Pilot' (2016) 12(3) *Journal of Experimental Criminology* 347.

[36] Kristian Lum and William Isaac, 'To Predict and Serve?' (2016) 13 *Significance* 14; David G. Robinson, 'The Challenges of Prediction: Lessons from Criminal Justice' (2018) 14(2) *I/S: A Journal of Law and Policy for the Information Society* 151.

[37] Ric Simmons, 'Quantifying Criminal Procedure: How to Unlock the Potential of Big Data in Our Criminal Justice System' (2016) *Michigan State Law Review* 947.

[38] Ibid 996.

[39] Ibid 965.

[40] Michael Rich, 'Limits on the Perfect Preventive State' (2013) 46 *Connecticut Law Review* 883.

[41] Woodrow Hartzog et al, 'Inefficiently Automated Law Enforcement' (2015) *Michigan State Law Review* 1763.

Critiques of risks assessments are broad, and can be generally divided into a few meaningful themes. On one hand, there are a range of issues associated with the procurement of these systems from private industry, as well as the lack of transparency associated with algorithms protected by trade secrets.[42] In the high profile *Loomis* case, for instance, the court refused to provide access to the vendor's 'trade secrets' for the sake of fairness auditing, with the court acknowledging and accepting that it could not evaluate how features such as gender were used in the assessment. Scholars have also criticised the influence of tech vendors in this domain, arguing that their dominance constitutes a form of undue influence – especially as customers (often cities) primarily obtain the results of analyses as part of a contract but do not obtain access to the proprietary algorithms that perform them, or the data collected during their operation.[43] That also means that governments may have limited input into the design, parameterisation, and specification of these products, including what datasets are appropriate or not appropriate to include. That one-sidedness generates due process risks associated with ensuring equality under the law, as what variables are taken into consideration remain unknown.

Another focus is the problematic selection of data that informs these systems – for instance, the use of arrest data as a proxy for criminal activity while ignoring the vast disparity in arrest rates across population segments when compared to conviction rates. Others discuss how these instruments over-criminalise particular populations. Some have also argued that tools like COMPAS, the recidivism prediction system created by Northpointe Inc. and implicated in the *Loomis* case, are no more accurate or fair than predictions made by individuals, even those with no criminal justice experience. To that end, authors have performed experiments suggesting a person with no experience would make the same decision as the algorithm, and they extrapolate that finding to argue that an experienced person should therefore make a *better* decision.[44] Those authors also argue that while the COMPAS system uses 137 features to make a prediction, the same predictive accuracy can be achieved with only two features, thus challenging the value of automated statistical approaches altogether, or at least suggesting that traditional actuarial methods are just as good as these automated 'unstructured' methods.

These are all critically important questions concerning the use of technologies representing actuarial and probabilistic logics for assessing, understanding, and identifying individuals, refracted through a similar criminological rationality to that encountered in Chapter 2. The use of computational logic, technical opacity, and political cooperation make interrogating this growing

---

[42] Teresa Scassa, 'Law Enforcement in the Age of Big Data and Surveillance Intermediaries: Transparency Challenges' (2017) 14 SCRIPTed 239.
[43] Elizabeth Joh, 'The Undue Influence of Surveillance Technology Companies on Policing' (2017) 92 NYU Law Review 101.
[44] Julia Dressel and Hany Farid, 'The Accuracy, Fairness, and Limits of Predicting Recidivism' (2017) 4 Science Advances.

practice absolutely critical. However, these techniques can be explored further, in particular, by looking at more complex systems parsing behavioural data on a larger scale.

HIGH-LEVEL PROFILING

Not all of these profiling products and processes use structured information, like police reports, as their input data. As Bryce Goodman describes, 'Traditional analyses (i.e. actuarial predictions) typically employ a small number of theoretically important variables with known distributions. By contrast, machine learning techniques are agnostic to the theoretical importance of variables, making them suitable for very large, high-dimensional datasets'.[45] Those techniques mean statistical assessments of criminal propensity might be meaningfully extracted from any correlatable biometric or behavioural data. The proxy for behavioural data in this context is effectively 'transactions' within informational environments. Some of these profiling systems thus use very expansive datasets that include data on individuals who have not had any contact with the criminal justice system. For instance, Elizabeth Joh discusses Intrudo's 'Beware' software, which ostensibly analyses billions of data points 'including property records, commercial databases, recent purchases, and social media posts, to assign threat scores for people'.[46] To that end, Twitter and Facebook APIs have become powerful policing tools, aided by private companies offering analytics of social media, geographic, financial, demographic, and consumer data.

The proliferation of these techniques through national security apparatuses was made clear when Edward Snowden disclosed the existence of international intelligence programs such as XkeyScore, UpStream, PRISM, and TEMPORA, among others. Data collected by those programs 'not only include emails, chats, and web-browsing traffic, but also pictures, documents, voice calls, webcam photos, web searches, advertising analytics traffic, social media traffic, botnet traffic, logged keystrokes, computer network exploitation targeting, intercepted username and password pairs, file uploads to online services, Skype sessions, and more'.[47] Data was gathered from telecommunication companies, large technology companies, as well as splicing and mirroring of underwater fibre-optic cables. These programs not only demonstrate the sheer scale of data collection, but also the co-option and

---

[45] Bryce Goodman, 'A Step Towards Accountable Algorithms? Algorithmic Discrimination and the European Union General Data Protection' (Paper presented at the 29th Conference on Neural Information Processing Systems, Barcelona, 2016).
[46] Joh, above n 43, 119.
[47] The security surveillance programs exposed by Snowden, such as PRISM, UPSTREAM, XkeyScore and Tempora are well described, for example, by John Lanchester in 'The Snowden Files: Why the British Public Should Be Worried About GCHQ' in the *Guardian* (4 October 2013) www.theguardian.com/world/2013/oct/03/edward-snowden-files-john-lanchester; see, e.g., Glen Greenwald, *No Place to Hide: Edward Snowden, the NSA, and the US Surveillance State* (Picador, 2015).

cooperation of the private sector. Palantir, for instance, not only supplies predictive policing products to cities, it also provides intelligence agencies throughout the Five Eyes communities with analytics software through which data is aggregated and inferences generated.[48] To that end, Palantir has become infrastructural in government intelligence and data analytics, with states becoming 'users' of technology platforms that provide governance 'services' across the entire data ecosystem.

In their deployment for decision-making systems around the state's distributive and criminal justice functions, the legal problems associated with these systems are often conceptualised in terms of prejudice, bias, and discrimination. Related critiques highlight the problematic belief that the numbers 'speak for themselves',[49] as well as inaccuracy, de-individualisation, and information asymmetry.[50] These problems are compounded through what Rouvroy argues is the inability 'to contest or resist the autonomic assignation of profiles and the practical consequences ensuing in terms of access to places, opportunities, and benefits'.[51] However, the use of pattern matching across large data sets within the more complex profiling mechanisms also highlights the knowledge logic of the exercise. As compared to the speculative profiling of early intelligence surveillance, or even the automation of actuarial decisions, data analytics on diverse datasets means moving from interrogating individuals through specific questions, to privileging statistical correlation.[52] The epistemological move is made clear by Serge Gutwirth and Paul de Hert:

---

[48] Sam Biddle, 'How Peter Thiel's Palantir Helped the NSA Spy on the Whole World' (22 February 2017) *The Intercept* https://theintercept.com/2017/02/22/how-peter-thiels-palantir-helped-the-nsa-spy-on-the-whole-world/.

[49] Lyria Bennett Moses and Janet Chan, 'Using Big Data for Legal and Law Enforcement Decisions: Testing the New Tools' (2014) 37 *UNSW Law Journal* 643, 666.

[50] See, e.g., Alessandro Mantelero, 'Social Control, Transparency and Participation in the Big Data World' (2014) *Journal of Internet Law*, 23; Schermer, above n 5, 46–47; Hildebrandt and Koops similarly classify this in terms of 'incorrect categorization, privacy and autonomy, discrimination and stigmatization, and the lack of due process' in Mireille Hildebrandt and Bert-Jaap Koops, 'The Challenges of Ambient Law and Legal Protection in the Profiling Era' (2010) 73(3) *The Modern Law Review* 428, 433. For instance, in their article 'Big Data's Disparate Impact', Solon Barocas and Andrew Selbst give examples of how an algorithm used to mine data might produce unfair results. Of note in their analysis is how the specification of 'target variables', the attributes of data that serve as proxies for the outcomes or qualities of interest, can be troubling. Barocas and Selbst describe how the data mining programmer's task of defining a target variable requires translation of 'some amorphous problem into a question that can be expressed in more formal terms that computers can parse'. This is an inherently subjective and open exercise through which the target variables can be expressed in ways that affect some people (individuals and groups) less favourably than others. (Barocas and Selbst above n 19.)

[51] Antoinette Rouvroy, 'Technology, Virtuality and Utopia: Governmentality in an Age of Autonomic Computing' in Mireille Hildebrandt and Antoinette Rouvroy (eds) *Law, Human Agency and Autonomic Computing: The Philosophy of Law meets the Philosophy of Technology* (Routledge, 2011) 7.

[52] Ibid 33.

[T]he correlations established by 19th century scientists were the result of oriented questioning: the chosen parameters or variables were presupposed to explain the problem at hand. Today, however, such preceding questions (and the structuration/ stratification of parameters they imply) are no longer needed to organise the search for correlations. On the contrary, the emergence in itself of a correlation has become the pertinent or interesting information or knowledge, which in its turn will launch questions, suppositions and hypotheses. Things are going the other way around now: the upsurge of a correlation *is* the information.[53]

Analytics using unconstrained data sources thus generate a complex relation between accuracy, knowledge, and identity. As Bigo and Bauman argue, stigmatisation through 'guilt by association' is clearly one risk of the state coming to know individuals through this type of surveillance, but it also reflects a new reality by which 'any communicating being, any user of late modern communication technologies, is rendered a suspect'.[54] For Bigo and Bauman, this is because a 'suspect' is no longer limited to a security, criminal, or juridical context, but rather takes shape through being the location or node of 'potential informational value or utility'.[55] This shifts the nature of the profile to something that incorporates not only statistical probability, but also 'possibility'. For Amoore, data mining is intended to facilitate a 'system that could identify the incipient, the potential, the merely possible'.[56] The change in knowledge process to forward-looking pre-emption on the basis of correlation and association thus generates a new type of representational logic.

Some authors argue that the representations produced by data mining and algorithmic profiling have a more attenuated relation to 'the real' than surveillance images produced by other techniques. While there is, of course, no 'uncoded reality' or truly 'natural' representation of the physical world, there is still a qualitative difference between a profile produced by an investigator on the basis of hypothesis and narrative, using information drawn from sources like observation, recordings (of sound and image), or informants, compared to the purely arithmetic construction of meaning, drawn from data found in discrete and disaggregated databases, on the basis of mathematical convention or protocols. Rouvroy similarly comments on how these 'new information infrastructures "translate" or "transcript" the physical space and its inhabitants (that's us) into constantly evolving sets of data points'.[57] In other words, the meaningful difference between the profiling exercises described here and those described in previous chapters is located in the mechanism by which 'the real world' or 'the truth' presents itself into the world of the sensible. In this case, not by

---

[53] Serge Gutwirth and Paul De Hert, 'Regulating Profiling in a Democratic Constitutional State' in Mireille Hildebrandt and Serge Gurtwirth (eds) *Profiling the European Citizen: Cross-Disciplinary Perspectives* (Springer 2008) 287.
[54] Zygmunt Bauman, Didier Bigo et al, 'After Snowden: Rethinking the Impact of Surveillance' (2014) 8(2) *International Political Sociology* 121, 131.
[55] Ibid 138.
[56] Amoore, above n 6, 43.
[57] Rouvroy, above n 51, 7.

slavish mechanical representation, nor through narrativisation, but through a quantifiable language of logic.[58]

Describing this as an ontological feature of digital media, Justin Clemens and Adam Nash, for instance, explain how information 'must first be digitised to data, then modulated between storage and display in an endless protocol-based negotiation that both severs any link to the data's semantic source and creates an ever-growing excess of data weirdly related to, but ontologically distinct from, its originating data source'.[59] They argue that the mathematical codes and conventions used to analyse and parse already hyper-mediated digital information seem to omit any 'natural' starting point from which a subjective assessment or reading is drawn. Instead, formless but machine-readable data is decontextualised and recontextualised according to protocols, ready for subsequent manipulations by software. Identity and subjectivity in this context are no longer constituted through images or linguistic discourses, but through a series of positive (+) and negative (−) inscriptions and the polarity of neodymium magnets. In fact, this is why Clemens and Nash claim that with digital convergence, there are no more media, only one single medium.[60] Only through modulation into a display register does digital information obtain meaning, thus speaking more to the process of modulation than to what the data supposedly represents. For Clemens and Nash logic (and its protocols) become the medium of being.[61]

On one hand, when data becomes decontextualised, when it is no longer interpreted according to the purpose for which it was generated, it becomes amendable to operations on the register of mere possibilities. In other words, there are fewer limitations on how that data can be translated into meaningful information. This 'virtual' register is not about actuarial assessments of probability, it is not about statistical likelihood, but rather the repeated posing of the question of how reality can expand itself.[62] 'It is a (potentially infinite) bundle of possibilities, living an existence which is *parallel* to the actual world of things and matters.'[63] And while some scholars believe '[t]he virtual reality of computer space is fundamentally no different from the virtual reality of writing, reading, drawing, or even thinking',[64] it is *practically* profoundly different because this 'supplementary', 'unrealised' digital world is liable to recording, registration, and manipulation at a very fine-grained level of detail. Unlike analogue recording media such as writing, data mining

[58] An example of the use of logic in the description of reality can be found in George Spencer-Brown, *Laws of Form* (Allen & Unwin, 1969).
[59] Justin Clemens and Adam Nash, 'Being and Media: Digital Ontology After the Event of the End of Media' (2015) 24 *The Fibreculture Journal* 6, 9.
[60] Ibid, 10.
[61] Ibid 24.
[62] Elizabeth Grosz, 'Cyberspace, Virtuality and the Real: Some Architectural Reflections' in Elizabeth Grosz and Peter Eisenman (eds) *Architecture from the Outside: Essays on Virtual and Real Space* (MIT, 2001).
[63] Rouvroy, above n 51, 23.
[64] Grosz, above n 62, 77.

technologies 'process real time as a temporal event',[65] and include detail that would otherwise evade ordinary human perception. Operating on the virtual plane means embracing representations of individuals on the basis of an 'indeterminate, unspecifiable future', and affording 'pre-eminence of futurity over the present and past'.[66]

When logic is the medium of being, and representation includes the register of possibility, Rouvroy goes further and asks the critical political question:

> [W]hat are the specificities of the new modes of intelligibility of the 'real', or of the new rationality that such technologies inaugurate? What 'axial principles' does autonomic computing serve? The politically relevant question is thus: what is the kind of power that the new regimes of (in)visibility and intelligibility accompanying the deployment of such technologies are aimed at and/or are capable of bringing forward? To what type of governmental rationality are these regimes instrumental?[67]

For Rouvroy, it is a world 'liberated from contingency and unpredictability', but at the cost of 'the potential, the inactual'.[68] Removing chance, as contemporary surveillance shows, requires knowing (or making) the meaning of every piece of information in its relation to all other pieces of information. Rouvroy sees that elimination of unpredictability or spontaneity as de-humanizing.[69] In an analysis of Bentham's panopticon prison, far removed from Foucault's *disciplinary* perspective and discourse on visibility, Jacques-Alain Miller wrote of the political reality behind Bentham's surveillance device, associating it with 'logic' (i.e. the proto-computational knowledge system) becoming the primary framing for understanding the world.[70] Miller describes how, because 'all chance must be controlled, banished', the panopticon 'is to be an area of totalitarian control'.[71] For Miller, spaces devoid of the unpredictable, the unknown, are intrinsically totalitarian spaces because if 'nothing is without effect, everything can be calculated', making logic 'the sole imperative in the panoptic universe'.[72] As Miller notes:

> [T]otalitarian mastery of the environment excludes anything irrational. Henceforth, logic can be brought to bear upon everything ... It's a kind of madness, of course –

---

[65] Vagias Karavas, 'The Force of Code: Laws Transformation Under Technological Conditions' (2009) 10 *German Law Journal* 463, 469. Karavas offers a good example: 'If one tries to store with the help of written media the temporal event of a chain of speech, one can principally only write down what has been said. In the era of technological media, though, one can also store singular and contingent events, such as the vocal tone of the speaking person by transforming it for example in the case of the computer, into a series of 0s and 1s.'

[66] Antoinette Rouvroy, 'Technology, Virtuality and Utopia: Governmentality in an age of Autonomic Computing' in Mireille Hildebrandt and Antoinette Rouvroy (eds) *Law, Human Agency and Autonomic Computing: The Philosophy of Law meets the Philosophy of Technology*, 88.

[67] Rouvroy, above n 51, 5.

[68] Ibid 21.

[69] Ibid 25.

[70] Jacques-Alain Miller, 'Jeremy Bentham's Panoptic Device' (1987) 41 *October* 3, 4.

[71] Ibid 5.

[72] Ibid 6.

analytical insanity ... it is the insanity proper to logic, which, conceiving a world in which all things are relative, makes itself absolute and denying the whole of nature, establishes its own artifices.[73]

Logic is also the sole imperative of the algorithmic universe. Indeed, the 'logical universe' can be read as pre-cursor to increasingly computational physical environments, which place their own demands on identities – by reconfiguring them into 'users'. Miller similarly argues '[g]eneral transparency, general classification, general utilisation – these values demand that absolutely no uncertainty shall exist with regard to identities'.[74] The rationale being, 'once life is totally reflected in the mirror of its exhaustive inscription, the government will be in a better position to take informed and scientific decisions'.[75]

In Chapter 8, we encounter biometric data science applications that take the logic of logic even further. These technological approaches further contest the legitimacy of narrative identity as the privileged site of subjectivity on the basis that the technology has greater access to the self than a self-reflexive human mind. Accordingly, the conflict between the profiler's and the profiled's understandings of identity takes on new complexity. Beyond the simple notion of internal and external, beyond the division between 'substance' vs 'form', the dichotomy increasingly becomes one of 'materiality' vs 'information' and 'narrative' vs 'logic'. That is to say, what distinguishes the profiled subject in their own mind and in the profilers' mind is a radical schism in world view between narrative, embodiment, and materiality on one hand, and logic, information, and quantifiability on the other.

CONCLUSION

This chapter has outlined certain features of automated profiling and the growing scale of the contemporary archive, along with some of its social, political, and technical dimensions. When 'transactional' information, drawn from sources completely unrelated to traditional law enforcement categories, is used to assess individuals, with consequences for status and rights, information law becomes a material concern, and the law, as we will see, has responded. Newer ideas of 'algorithmic accountability' have emerged that shift the information law narrative again from transparency of how individuals are profiled, to requirements that such profiling occurs according to a mathematical understanding of satisfactory measurement, computation, and classification of persons. What we also see in the evolution of these doctrines is another shift in the technologies of legal enforcement, into the computational architectures themselves.

[73] Ibid 7.
[74] Ibid 17.
[75] Ibid 19.

7

Algorithmic Accountability and the Statistical Legal Subject

When addressing profiling by states, privacy law's legal subject is the nineteenth-century liberal 'citizen', objecting to the consequences of being identified by the state in improper ways. Data protection's legal subject, on the other hand, is the twentieth-century data subject who contests how their data representation in centralised repositories creates information asymmetry, and how it facilitates being understood and known by impenetrable analysis and evaluation. Data protection thus created a rights-bearing entity whose representation in those repositories should not usurp the self-image of the physical person. For both these legal persons, the broad rationale behind legal intervention is protection from institutional misinterpretation, miscategorisation, or 'poor' profiling decisions. Poor because the information on which a profiling decision is based unfairly produces an interpretation about criminal propensity, poor because the data on which a profiling decision is based is itself inaccurate or irrelevant, or poor, in the case of automated systems, on the basis that the quality and opacity of the decision-making process itself (i.e. the algorithmic analysis, and the manner in which it decontextualises and manipulates data points) generates classifications and predictions too divorced from their semantic referents. But where and what is the twenty-first-century legal person? The implications for identity associated with the ways contemporary data science and machine learning produce the subjects of their analysis are markedly different from older profiling technologies, systems, and practices. As Seda Gürses and her co-authors remind us:

> In the 90s, software engineering shifted from packaged software and PCs to services and clouds, enabling distributed architectures that incorporate real-time feedback from users. In the process, digital systems became layers of technologies metricized under the authority of optimization functions. These functions drive the selection of software features, service integration, cloud usage, user interaction and growth, customer service, and environmental capture, among others. Whereas information systems focused on storage, processing and transport of information, and organizing knowledge – with associated risks of surveillance – contemporary systems leverage the knowledge they gather to not only understand the world, but also optimize it, seeking maximum

extraction of economic value through capture and manipulation of people's activities and environments.[1]

Optimisation through data science is a virtualised form of cybernetic control. The 'teleology' or purpose of a cybernetic system, in which pressure or force is exerted to shift the system's behaviour towards a goal, is replicated in the statistical methods of data science. And while Gürses identifies the risks these technologies pose in terms of 'social sorting, mass manipulation, asymmetrical concentration of resources, majority dominance and minority erasure', the previous chapters have demonstrated (and the following chapters expands further) the ways they also significantly shift ideas of identity and selfhood. This reality prompts the question of whether insisting on the distinction between the physical and informational person that emerged in the legal architectures addressing earlier file keeping and information processing systems is still appropriate. The strengthening of data protection and its consent regimes may prove effective against online behavioural advertising, and it may (hopefully) extinguish the parasitic data-brokering business, but whether it affects profiling, or automated decision-making operating on the register of governance, especially in the more complex information processing regimes of the 'world state', remains questionable.

Other legal ideas, however, have begun to emerge over the past decade that influence and limit profiling practices in other ways. These are grouped here under the heading of 'algorithmic accountability'. There are many examples, however this chapter focuses on only a small selection that are especially relevant to profiling. First are some efforts at institutional transparency, that push for oversight, auditing, and making automated decision-making processes more understandable. Second is the regulation of automated decision-making (and profiling) in the GDPR which extends data subject rights further. Third, also related to the GDPR but likely to become a general accountability norm, is a right to explanation of automated decisions. Fourth is the emerging technical discipline of 'fairness' in machine learning. Some of these mechanisms also deploy new *technologies* of legal enforcement. Alongside the individual rights to judicial remedy and the bureaucratic infrastructure of monitoring and compliance in privacy and data protection, these legal ideas are increasingly incorporated into the profiling technologies themselves, thus sometimes falling under the rubric of 'legal protection by design'.

These legal tools offer another shift in the philosophy behind regulating profiling. Whereas privacy is about preventing individuals from being seen in a certain way, and data subject rights are about giving individuals the capacity to participate in how they are seen, algorithmic accountability mechanisms seem to express a position of: whatever decision you are making about me, please judge me fairly or appropriately

---

[1] Seda Gürses, Rebekah Overdorf, and Ero Balsa, 'Stirring the POTS: Protective Optimization Technologies' in Emre Bayamlıoğlu et al (eds) *Being Profiled: Cogitas Ergo Sum (10 Years of 'Profiling the European Citizen')* (Amsterdam University Press, 2018) 24, 24.

compared to everyone else. As such, the legal subject generated by these mechanisms is generally capable of enforcing their will only against a statistical notion of appropriateness, rather than a narrative self-account. In enforcing a more ethical or fairer translation of self into the computational register, the legal person becomes a filter rather than a mask. It becomes a mechanism for ensuring a decision made about a person abides by a set of normative commitments expressed statistically, rather than privileging the subjective truth of an individual capable of actioning those rights.

INSTITUTIONAL TRANSPARENCY

In certain formulations, algorithmic accountability is premised on transparency. In many ways the push for transparency stems from the various types of opacity that inhere in automated decision-making systems. Jenna Burrell traces, for instance, three forms of opacity: corporate concealment or trade secrets that may ultimately constitute some type of knowing deception; the reality that few people are sufficiently literate with relevant programming languages and coding; and most significantly, that 'mathematical optimisation in high-dimensionality characteristic of machine learning' is inconsistent with the demands of human-scale reasoning and styles of semantic interpretation.[2] Transparency in algorithmic accountability thus goes beyond data subject rights' focus on access to data pertaining to data subjects, and instead directs the need for transparency at the actual practices and tools of profilers. Optimally, it requires clarity in the procurement, implementation, and technical mechanisms associated with automated decision-making systems, sometimes for the sake of compliance with certification, auditing, or due process requirements. This type of transparency is useful for keeping track of the impacts of decision systems over time, and achieving some public disclosure on their purpose, reach, policies, and technologies. How to actively achieve this type of transparency in a meaningful way requires understanding what needs to be exposed, to who, and when.[3] Some have accordingly proposed a 'how', 'what', 'why' model for thinking about the different types of understanding necessary for regulating automated decision-making systems.[4] The 'what' question asks for the reasons behind a specific outcome – i.e. for a given input, what led to the output? The 'how' question is the set of rules that govern the decision process and may involve exposure of its logic, including particular algorithms and approaches.

---

[2] Jenna Burrell, 'How the Machine Thinks: Understanding Opacity in Machine Learning Algorithms' (2016) 3(1) *Big Data & Society* 1, 2.

[3] See, e.g., Bruno Lepri et al, 'Fair, Transparent, and Accountable Algorithmic Decision-making Processes: The Premise, the Proposed Solutions, and the Open Challenges' (2018) 31(4) *Philosophy & Technology* 611; Michael Veale, Max Van Kleek, and Reuben Binns, 'Fairness and Accountability Design Needs for Algorithmic Support in High Stakes Public Sector Decision Making' (Paper presented at the ACM Conference of Human Factors in Computing Systems, Montreal, 21–26 April 2018).

[4] Andrew D Selbst and Solon Barocas, 'The Intuitive Appeal of Explainable Machines' (2018) 87 *Fordham Law Review* 1085.

The 'why' question looks to the ultimate goals of the system, the assumptions made in its implementation, data selection, and compliance with legal standards. Researchers working in this area have, however, demonstrated that both governments and corporate actors are extremely reluctant to expose this information.[5] Indeed, trade secrets remain a critical obstacle when governments use systems created by private software providers. And the law does not always help. For instance, the preamble to the GDPR acknowledges that transparency and access rights must be balanced against the rights of those who generated the profiles, including copyright or trade secrets in the intellectual property of the profiling code.[6]

Addressing this opacity would go a long way to improving the structural conditions that affect profiled individuals. There have been some successes in the courts with freedom of information actions.[7] Some have also attempted to develop ideas of algorithmic accountability and compliance without requiring transparency; for instance, what Joshua Kroll and his collaborators call 'procedural regularity'. These systems would enable individuals to know that the procedure applied to them was the same procedure as applied to everyone else (perhaps a variant of 'natural justice'), that the same policy is used for each decision, that those decisions are reproducible, and that the decision policy was specified before the particular subjects of the decision were known. Proponents of that approach cite the whole toolbox of computer science tools used for testing and verification of software, and mechanisms like zero-knowledge proofs, that can prove the existence of some feature of the data without revealing the whole system's operation. That approach, however, is primarily targeted at clearly egregious or abusive uses of those technologies, not necessarily for ensuring accountability in routine ordinary operation.

Other accountability approaches take the form of bureaucratic and structural compliance mechanisms, such as algorithmic auditing, certification, and impact assessments. To that end, the GDPR, for instance, includes requirements for data protection impact assessments (Article 24), codes of conduct (Article 40), and certification (Article 42) in certain situations. In the United States, a proposed *Algorithmic Accountability Act* would require automated decision and data protection impact assessments for private companies using learning systems. Those compliance obligations would apply to any system affecting consumers' legal rights, any system involving large amounts of sensitive data, or involving systematic monitoring of a publicly accessible physical space. With respect to the public sector, others have argued for 'public agency accountability' that involves self-assessments with respect

---

[5] See, e.g., Robert Brauneis and Ellen P Goodman, 'Algorithmic Transparency for the Smart City' (2018) 20 *Yale Journal of Law and Technology* 103.

[6] *Regulation (EU) 2016/679 of the European Parliament and of the Council of 27 April 2016 on the Protection of Natural Persons with Regard to the Processing of Personal Data and on the Free Movement of Such Data, and Repealing Directive 95/46/EC (General Data Protection Regulation)* [2016] OJ L 119/1, Recital 63.

[7] See, e.g., *Millions March NYC v. New York City Police Department* (NY Sup Ct, 100690/2017, 23 May 2017).

to fairness, justice, and bias.[8] Some have framed these bureaucratic requirements as an 'FDA for algorithms',[9] intended to bring public administrative and public law types of accountability to automated decision-making systems.[10] This has been put into practice, for example, with the creation of the New York City taskforce on algorithmic accountability, introduced by legislation,[11] that coordinated a fact-finding group of researchers to evaluate the city's use of automated decision-making systems, without necessarily exposing their technical details to the public, and without interfering with the trade secrets of the companies that build those technologies.[12] The taskforce's purview is systems used by the city for automated decision-making including policing and criminal justice, welfare entitlements, public housing, and education. It is unclear, however, whether disclosure to this taskforce has yet had any meaningful regulatory impact, or in fact whether the taskforce has even received any meaningful disclosures, suggesting it may ultimately be a cynical political exercise.

Similar ideas have also been proposed by researchers in the form of 'technological due process'. The idea involves extending the administrative law requirements to automated decision-making systems. Danielle Keats Citron advocated for these mechanisms as early as 2008, noting then that automated computer systems were becoming *primary* decision-makers in administrative decisions.[13] She sees a system of technological due process as necessary to bolster the procedural safeguards being undermined by automation, and considers the 'due process' clauses of the US Constitution (and other US federal and state laws) an appropriate way to do so. This position was then expanded by Citron with Frank Pasquale in the case of scoring algorithms, typically operationalised by private entities, the archetype of which is the US credit score.[14] They argue that 'technological due process' – 'procedures ensuring that predictive algorithms live up to some standard of review and revision to ensure their fairness and accuracy' – is the proper path to accountability.

---

[8] Dillon Reisman et al, *Algorithmic Impact Assessments: A Practical Framework for Public Agency Accountability* (April 2018) AI Now Institute https://ainowinstitute.org/aiareport2018.pdf.
[9] Andrew Tutt, 'An FDA for Algorithms' (2017) 69 *Administrative Law Review* 83.
[10] See Danielle Keats Citron, 'Technological Due Process' (2008) 85 *Washington University Law Review* 1249.
[11] *A Local Law in Relation to Automated Decision Systems Used by Agencies*, Pub L No 2018/049, NY City Council (2018).
[12] See, e.g., Julia Powles, 'New York City's Bold, Flawed Attempt to Make Algorithms Accountable', *New Yorker* (online), 20 December 2017 www.newyorker.com/tech/annals-of-technology/new-york-citys-bold-flawed-attempt-to-make-algorithms-accountable.
[13] Citron, above n 10.
[14] Danielle Keats Citron and Frank Pasquale, 'The Scored Society: Due Process for Automated Predictions' (2014) 89 *Washington Law Review* 1; See also Kate Crawford and Jason Schultz, 'Big Data and Due Process: Toward a Framework to Redress Predictive Privacy Harms' (2014) 55 *Boston College Law Review* 93.

AUTOMATED DECISION-MAKING AND PROFILING IN THE GDPR AND LED

Margot Kominski correctly describes the GDPR as a regime of algorithmic accountability.[15] Data sanitisation, anonymity, restrictions around using protected categories of data, and principles of legality, fairness, and minimisation, when applied to automated decision-making, fall clearly into that category. There are, however, even more explicit accountability mechanisms for profiling, such as Article 22 of the GDPR, which gives data subjects the right to *not* be subject to automated profiling decisions based *solely* on automated processing where those decisions produce legal or similar effects. The Article 29 Working Party's Automated Decision Making Guidelines are helpful for understanding those terms.[16] For the sake of GDPR and LED, the Working Party specifies that profiling must be automated, and carried out on personal data with the objective of evaluating a personal trait of a natural person. Automated Decision Making, in their definition, has a slightly different, though overlapping scope, and can be based on data provided by an individual, data observed or collected about them, or data derived or inferred such as a profile that has already been created (like a credit score) but does not necessarily require personal evaluation. That means automated decision-making can occur with or without profiling, but could become profiling if used to evaluate a personal trait.

European data protection law has, since at least 1995, included limitations on automated decision-making and profiling,[17] recognising such decision-making as a threat to informational privacy.[18] There are similar provisions in the LED that *enable* automated processing and profiling, but only when authorised by law that provides appropriate safeguards to the data subject, including, at least, the right to obtain human intervention on the part of the controller.[19] These rights have been interpreted as meaning that there must be a 'human-in-the-loop' when automated profiling occurs, and indeed Article 22(3) of the GDPR specifies that data controllers should afford data subjects a right to obtain human intervention, express their view,

---

[15] Margot Kaminski, 'The Right to Explanation, Explained' (2019) 34(1) *Berkeley Technology Law Journal*.

[16] Article 29 Data Protection Working Party, 'Guidelines on Automated Individual Decision-Making and Profiling for the Purposes of Regulation 2016/679' (Working Paper No WP251) European Commission, 3 October 2017.

[17] Council Directive 95/13/EC of 23 November 1993 *on the protection of individuals with regard to the processing of personal data and on the free movement of such data (Data Protection Directive)* [1995] OJ L281/31, art 15; *General Data Protection Regulation* [2016] OJ L 119/1, art 22.

[18] See, e.g., Bart Schermer, 'The Limits of Privacy in Automated Profiling and Data Mining' (2011) 27(1) *Computer Law & Security Review*, 45.

[19] Directive (EU) 2016/680 of the European Parliament and of the Council of 27 April 2016 *on the protection of natural persons with regard to the processing of personal data by competent authorities for the purposes of the prevention, investigation, detection or prosecution of criminal offences or the execution of criminal penalties, and on the free movement of such data, and repealing Council Framework Decision 2008/977/JHA* (Law Enforcement Directive) [2016] OJ L 119/89, art 11(1).

and *contest* a decision when profiling is permitted by consent of the data subject, or in performance of a contract between the controller and data subject. But even though such provisions have been law (in Europe at least) since 1995, they remain very vague and entirely underused.

Lee Bygrave offers some sensible insight into the scope of both the older and newer provisions, highlighting how many of the questions plaguing the older law continue unanswered. For instance, does a human decision-maker *anywhere* in the relevant information processing chain avoid the law's effect?[20] That a human decision-maker anywhere in the process might remove an automated system from the reach of the law seems a problematic limitation, especially considering the growing evidence of human decision-makers deference to the outcomes of automated 'decision support systems'. Some have argued that 'decision based solely on automated processing' should not be interpreted as a loophole (as the German Federal Court of Justice seemed to suggest in a decision on credit scores),[21] and instead be understood as allowing a certain degree of human action without removing a decision from the scope of the provision.[22] What degrees of human intervention might be permissible is, however, also unclear.

The same lack of clarity shrouds what constitutes 'legal or similar effects'. Further, what do the terms 'significantly', 'solely', and 'certain personal aspects' mean in the context of defining what type of decisions are covered? Again, some have argued for broad understandings of 'legal or similarly significant effects' that *could* even include types of behavioural manipulation through information filtering.[23] However, that likely includes a very substantial amount of online activity, including search. Guidance by the Court of Justice of the European Union will be essential to a more complete understanding of those provisions, and how the competing tensions will be resolved.

These provisions also do not prohibit automated decisions, instead offering data subjects a right to object, which itself may be of limited value if the automated decisions are authorised by law (which is likely the case for government deployment of any automated decision-making system). Even that right to object disappears if the profiling occurs according to explicit consent, enabling legislation, or satisfaction of

---

[20] Isak Mendoza and Lee A Bygrave, 'The Right Not to Be Subject to Automated Decisions Based on Profiling' in Tatiana-Eleni Synodinou et al (eds) *EU Internet Law: Regulation and Enforcement* (Springer, 2017) 77.

[21] *Bundesgerichtshof* [German Federal Court of Justice], VI ZR 156/13, 28 January 2014 reported in (2014 BGHZ) in the so-called SCHUFA case concerning the use of automated credit-scoring systems, concerning DPD Article 15.

[22] See, e.g., Emre Bayamlıoğlu, 'Transparency of Automated Decisions in the GDPR: An Attempt for Systemisation' (Working Paper, 16 January 2018); see, e.g., UK Information Commissioner's Office, *Guide to the General Data Protection Regulation/Automated Decision-Making and Profiling* https://ico .org.uk/for-organisations/guide-to-data-protection/guide-to-the-general-data-protection-regulation-gdpr /automated-decision-making-and-profiling/what-else-do-we-need-to-consider-if-article-22-applies.

[23] Bayamlıoğlu, above n 22.

a contract.[24] That said, Article 22(4) does prohibit automated processing based on special categories of data that reveal: race or ethnic origin, political opinions, religion or beliefs, trade union membership, genetic or biometric data for the purpose of identifying a natural person, or data concerning health or sex life without appropriate safeguards.[25] But this restriction is constrained by Article 9(2), where processing is for 'reasons of substantial public interest', which likely include prevention or investigation of crime as well as matters of national security.[26] The limitations based on special categories of data are also problematic for failing to forbid the combination or aggregation of other non-protected data to produce inferences that can stand in for processing of restricted data. For instance, a prohibition on including religious information in profiling inputs is likely ineffective when profiles can include geolocation data that regularly locates a subject at, for instance, a mosque.[27]

Rules governing automated profiling in the LED are also equivocal.[28] Limitations in the Directive on 'automated processing of personal data intended to evaluate certain personal aspects relating to the data subject' exclude what Paul de Hert and Vagelis Papakonstantinou call 'incidental profiling' – that is, 'applying "profiling type" search criteria within the search results of already executed, normal, processing'[29] – and 'non-evaluatory profiling' – that is, 'not evaluating, but merely identifying data'.[30] Further, the restrictions in Article 9(2) that automated processing not be based *solely* on data revealing race, ethnic origin, political opinion, religion or belief, trade union membership, genetic data or data concerning health or sex life, do not apply when authorised by a law providing adequate safeguards,[31] or when the processing is necessary to protect the vital interests of the data subject or another person,[32] a claim that could easily be made through narratives of public safety. The ways in which the LED will apply to target-based predictive policing and risk assessments thus remains unclear. To what degree could it limit the assignment of risk-scores or render them transparent? To what degree might it constrain the categories of data information in those systems? How do these automatically generated and recursive profiles and assessments fit into data subject rights' relationship to identity? Indeed, in the context of data protection rationales concerning the reconciliation of documentary reality with personal experience, such limitations are to be expected. Put another way, the right to challenge an assessment or decision on its

---

[24] GDPR Article 22(2)(a), (b), (c).
[25] Ibid Article 22(4) referring to Article 9(1).
[26] Ibid Article 9(2).
[27] Schermer, above n 18, 49.
[28] *Law Enforcement Directive* [2016] OJ L 119/89.
[29] Paul De Hert and Vagelis Papakonstantinou, 'The Police and Criminal Justice Data Protection Directive: Comment and Analysis' (2012) 22(6) *Computers and Law Magazine of SCL* 1, 3.
[30] Ibid 4.
[31] *Law Enforcement Directive* [2016] OJ L 119/89.
[32] Ibid Article 8(2)(b).

quality cannot really be read out of 'data sovereignty', 'informational self-determination' or the language of data protection generally.

That data protection does not address assessments, inferences or profiles adequately is part of a broader critique that data protection may not be geared to deal with issues around the production and management of *knowledge*.[33] This was Hildebrandt's insightful criticism from 2008, which Sandra Wachter and Brett Mittelstadt have reiterated and updated in their work arguing for a right to 'reasonable inferences'.[34] Those authors use CJEU caselaw to illustrate what they see as the inability of data protection law to adequately protect inferences drawn from data. These cases present the relatively non-controversial boundaries to the scope of access, in particular that access rights do not penetrate into documents representing decision-making processes. This is made clear, for instance, in the *YS v. Minister Voor Immigratie* case, where the advocate general opined, and the court decided, that *minutes* in a case file, including primary legal analysis used in an internal decision-making process for residence applications in the Netherlands, were not personal data for the sake of claims for access. Indeed, the advocate general argued that 'only information relating to facts about an individual can be personal data', whether they were expressed objectively or subjectively (while also recognising the blurry distinction between facts and opinions relevant to such an assessment).[35] The court decision thus noted that 'extending the right of access of the application for a residence permit to that legal analysis would not in fact serve the directive's purpose of guaranteeing the protection of the applicant's right to privacy with regard to the processing of data relating to him, but would serve the purpose of guaranteeing him a right of access to administrative documents, which is not however covered by [data protection law]'.[36] Ultimately, these cases demonstrate that informational self-determination will not transcend relatively established principles in administrative law with respect to exposing decision-making processes and the subjective nature of assessment, especially in immigration decisions, or any other exercise that involves intelligence or security materials and sources. To that end, introducing a right that exposed decision-making processes would be very radical.

As with data subject rights, authors have noted how these limitations on profiling, particularly requiring a 'human-in-the-loop', and the right to object

---

[33] See, e.g., Mireille Hildebrandt, 'Defining Profiling: A New Type of Knowledge?' in Mireille Hildebrandt and Serge Gutwirth (eds) *Profiling the European Citizen: Cross-Disciplinary Perspectives* (Springer 2008) 17; Mireille Hildebrandt and Bert-Jaap Koops, 'The Challenges of Ambient Law and Legal Protection in the Profiling Era' (2011) 73(3) *The Modern Law Review* 428; and Ronald Leenes, 'Mind My Step?' in Mireille Hildebrandt and Serge Gutwirth (eds) *Profiling the European Citizen: Cross-Disciplinary Perspectives* (Springer, 2008) 197.

[34] Sandra Wachter and Brent Mittelstadt, 'A Right to Reasonable Inferences: Re-Thinking Data Protection Law in the Age of Big Data and AI' (2019) *Columbia Business Law Review*.

[35] Opinion Advocate General, *YS v. Minister Voor Immigratie and Minister Voor Immigratie v. M and S*, 12 December 2013, Joined Cases C-141/12 and C-372/12.

[36] Judgment of the Court, *YS v. Minister Voor Immigratie and Minister Voor Immigratie v. M and S*, 17 July 2014, Joined Cases C-141/12 and C-372/12 [46].

or contest, demonstrate 'a concern to uphold human dignity by ensuring that humans (and not their "data shadows") maintain the primary role in "constituting" themselves'.[37] Such authors see these limitations on profiling as an extension of the principles behind data subject rights, indicating that this type of control extends not simply over data, but over identity, and that risks to identity are what constitute the harm of automated profiling.[38] However, the requirement of a human-in-the-loop also exposes a problematic tension behind these provisions and their protection of identity. Amongst the growing number of automated decisions that define contemporary life, it becomes necessary to ask in what contexts will such rights to contest and object be sufficient to reinstate meaningful control in a physical person? Put another way, how many automated decisions do we encounter or experience daily that satisfy the criteria to make contestation available, and how difficult is it for an individual to engage those rights? It is also unclear what such that contestation might look like?[39] What different information could a person present to a decision-maker other than correcting the data on which the decision was made? Could an individual present alternative computations and assessments using different measurements and analytics? The human-in-the-loop paradigm may make sense in certain very high-level applications, but it is hardly the structural panacea of algorithmic accountability some might wish it to be. The provisions still operate on very static notions of data and processing, while still placing a great deal of weight on individuals to look after their own interests. That is why other provisions in the GDPR, operating with fewer limitations than Article 22, like the specific access rights dealing with the logic of decision-making systems (what is sometimes called a right to explanation), may be more meaningful within the algorithmic accountability paradigm.

A RIGHT TO EXPLANATION?

A right to explanation, another dimension to the regulation of automated systems, has also been read out of Article 15(1)(h) of the GDPR. There is, however, rigorous debate over what that provision truly affords data subjects, and how useful it may be. The Article provides that in the case of automated decision-making and profiling, data subjects should have access to 'meaningful information about the logic involved, as well as the significance and the envisaged consequences of such

---

[37] Mendoza and Bygrave, above n 20.
[38] See, e.g., Frederike Kaltheuner and Elettra Bietti, 'Data Is Power: Towards Additional Guidance on Profiling and Automated Decision-Making in the GDPR' (2018) 2(2) *Journal of Information Rights, Policy and Practice*.
[39] See, e.g., Dimitra Kamarinou, Christopher Millard, and Jatinder Singh, 'Machine Learning with Personal Data' (Working Paper, No 247/2016, Queen Mary School of Law, November 2016) where the authors argue it should involve the right to appeal to a machine rather than a human.

processing for the data subject'. Like the limitation on automated decision-making and profiling discussed above, this provision also had a precursor in the 1995 Data Protection Directive.[40] Unfortunately, the history of that provision offers no clarity as to how it should be interpreted, and it has never received judicial edification. What constitutes logic here is thus disputed.[41] What the GDPR amendment requires to make a disclosure about that logic *meaningful* also baffles. The current debate focuses on whether the provision requires explanation of system functionality ('the logic, significance, envisaged consequences and general functionality of an automated decision-making system, e.g. the system's requirements specification, decision trees, pre-defined models, criteria, and classification structure') or explanation of specific decisions ('the rationale, reasons, and individual circumstances of a specific automated decision, e.g. the weightings of features, machine-defined case-specific decision rules, information about reference or profile groups').[42] Authors arguing for the former interpretation note that the term 'explanation' is not actually present in Article 15, only in Recital 71, which cannot establish a legally binding right. Wachter, Mittelstadt, and Floridi argue that even reading Articles 13, 14, and 15 together does not indicate an *ex post* right to explanation of the logic, significance, and consequences of a decision. They claim the access provision only requires an *ex ante* explanation of system functionality rather than account of why any particular decision was made. This argument situates explanation as another transparency right concerning the functioning of automated systems rather than a new requirement for explainable decision outputs.

On the other hand, authors like Andrew Selbst and Julia Powles suggest that read together, these articles do constitute something better described as a right to explanation, because the requirement of meaningfulness within the right to be informed should be tied to the right to contest a decision in Article 22(3). This approach frames the right in terms of a necessary procedural requirement for contesting a decision *after* such a decision has been made. Those authors' more flexible reading suggests meaningfulness should be interpreted as what is required to facilitate the data subject's exercise of other rights guaranteed by the GDPR such as the right to object in Article 22. This interpretation would greatly enhance the utility of the law.[43]

[40] *Data Protection Directive* [1995] OJ L281/31, art 12.
[41] Clive Norris and Xavier L'Hoiry, 'What Do They Know? Exercising Subject Access Rights in Democratic Societies' (Paper presented at the 6th Biannual Surveillance and Society Conference, 24–26 April 2014); See also Mireille Hildebrandt, 'Legal Protection by Design: Objections and Refutations' (2011) 5(2) *Legisprudence* 223, 236, where she says in respect of Article 12: 'Since it is technically impossible to provide such access in a way that is comprehensible for ordinary citizens, the normativity that is inherent in the computational infrastructure overrules the normativity of the written law.'
[42] Sandra Wachter, Brent Mittelstadt, and Luciano Floridi, 'Why a Right to Explanation of Automated Decision-Making Does Not Exist in the General Data Protection Regulation' (2017) 7(2) *International Data Privacy Law* 76.
[43] Others have argued that a right to explainability might be better understood as a right to 'legibility', contextualising it as another form of access right, though one geared towards understanding systems rather than access to data. But the difference between a right to the logic of a decision, a right to be

Without further clarification, this all hinges on speculation as to the meaning of 'meaningful', which may have been somewhat haphazardly included in the provision because of the ongoing uncertainty around the unclear definition of 'logic'. If a right to explanation does exist, there are still questions as to what that explanation should communicate. Must it involve disclosures about the creation and design of an algorithm? How the machine learning models were built? How feedback is incorporated? Details on an algorithm's function? What its weightings and features are? What kind of outputs it generates? The specifications and parameters of the procurement request? Whether it was certified or audited? It is also unclear to what degree any of these are meaningful questions for data subjects.[44]

Others have downplayed the utility of a right to explanation at all. Lilian Edwards and Michael Veale, for instance, argue that explanation is unlikely to present a complete remedy because it is only triggered in limited circumstances, and the legal conception of explanation may not be what technical systems, such as explanatory artificial intelligence (XAI) systems (discussed below), can foreseeably provide.[45] They also recognise that focusing on transparency might be a misdirection. For those authors looking at the history of transparency approaches, 'subject-centric explanations' may be very difficult to provide in the face of machine learning dimensionality and opacity, and thus may not be feasible, nor truly match user needs. Edwards and Veale warn that 'we are in danger of creating a "meaningless transparency" paradigm to match the already well known "meaningless consent" trope'.[46] Ultimately, it is unclear whether this right would enable any or all of: exposing the normative basis of the system, procedural regularity, exposing the causality behind decisions, depicting an understanding of the impact of the decision, or making actors accountable for their thinking. Despite the ambiguity however, the computer science community is taking on board the possibility that machine learning-based profiling may need to be explainable to be legally acceptable, which has caused a renewed explosion of interest in XAI, an increasingly prominent sub-field of computer science.[47]

XAI re-entered the mainstream agenda after DARPA's 2016 grant solicitation funded multiple research laboratories to address the problem that the development

    informed, a right to explainability, or a right to legibility is not necessarily helpful (Gianclaudio Malgieri and Giovanni Comandé, 'Why a Right to Legibility of Automated Decision-Making Exists in the General Data Protection Regulation' [2017] 7[4] *International Data Privacy Law* 243).
[44] See, e.g., ibid.
[45] Lilian Edwards and Michael Veale, 'Slave to the Algorithm? Why a "Right to Explanation" is Probably Not the Remedy You Are Looking For' (2017) 16 *Duke Law & Technology Review* 18.
[46] Ibid 23.
[47] See, e.g., Ashraf Abdul et al, 'Trends and Trajectories for Explainable, Accountable, and Intelligible Systems: An HCI Research Agenda' (Paper presented at the ACM Conference of Human Factors in Computing Systems, Montreal, 21–26 April 2018), who offer a survey of the greater trends in the field.

and effectiveness of machine learning technologies are limited by their opacity.[48] XAI is seen as useful for system verification and improvement, enabling human learning from how machine learning systems perform tasks, and for legal compliance.[49] Different explanatory approaches have produced a rough hierarchy of unintelligible 'opaque systems', 'interpretable systems' that facilitate mathematical analysis of algorithmic mechanisms, and 'comprehensible systems' that produce symbolic outputs for users about what the system is doing.[50] There are, as a result, a growing number of XAI models and a great deal of competing theorisations of the value, function, and proper expression of computational explanation. But what constitutes explanation amongst the computer science community, let alone the broader scholarly community that has long considered that question, or the communities that would procure XAI systems, is itself drearily confused.

Some projects describe explanation as 'presenting textual or visual artefacts that provide qualitative understanding of the relationship between the instance's components (e.g. words in text, patches in an image) and the model's prediction'.[51] A prominent example is the Local Interpretable Model-agnostic Explanations (LIME) system, capable of describing what elements of an image pushed the classifier to make a particular prediction, by identifying local elements of the image connected with those predictions.[52] Some XAI systems attempt to derive more comprehensible, intelligible, or simplified descriptions of a model which can then be communicated to users. Some argue that beyond simplified approximations of how a system works, explaining the line of reasoning a system engages is also necessary.[53] Others have proposed 'what', 'why', and 'how' models (again), noting that 'reasons' are not necessarily 'explanations' unless they give insight into the mechanisms at play in any particular decision.[54] Some approaches look for relationships between participant, task, and effect, and others focus on 'counter-factual' approaches that account for how a model has behaved in a particular context or application rather than how it functions.

---

[48] David Gunning, *Explainable Artificial Intelligence (XAI)* (November 2017) DARPA/I2o www.darpa.mil/attachments/XAIProgramUpdate.pdf.
[49] Wojciech Samek, Thomas Wiegand, and Klaus-Robert Müller, 'Explainable Artificial Intelligence: Understanding, Visualizing, and Interpreting Deep Learning Models' (2017) *ITU Journal: ICT Discoveries, Special Issue No 1*, 11.
[50] Derek Doran, Sarah Schulz, and Tarek R Besold, 'What Does Explainable AI Really Mean? A New Conceptualization of Perspectives' (Paper presented at the International Workshop on Comprehensibility and Explainability in Artificial Intelligence and Machine Learning, Bari, Italy, November 2017).
[51] Marco Tulio Ribeiro, Sameer Singh, and Carlos Guestrin, '"Why Should I Trust You?" Explaining the Predictions of Any Classifier' (Paper presented at the 22nd ACM SIGKDD International Conference on Knowledge Discovery and Data Mining, San Francisco, CA, August 2016), 1135.
[52] Ibid.
[53] Doran, above n 50.
[54] Tarek R Besold and Sara L Uckelman, 'The What, the Why, and the How of Artificial Explanations in Automated Decision-Making' (Working Paper, arXiv:1808.07074, 21 August 2018).

In 'Accountability of AI under the Law', Finale Doshi-Velez and her co-authors describe what they understand as the three core elements of explanation in the counter-factual approach: What were the main factors in a decision? Would changing a certain factor have changed the decision? And why did two similar-looking cases get different decisions, or vice versa?[55] For them, the goal of explanation is to produce post-hoc analysis of decision output rather than necessarily exposing how a model works.[56] Interest in counter-factual approaches follows a contemporary fascination in cognitive science and statistical causality with the significance of counter-factual reasoning.[57] These approaches seem to embrace the idea that counter-factual and causal statistical methods better simulate human explanatory processes. However, counter-factual methods are primarily 'justification' rather than 'introspection' methods. Their utility thus hinges on who is the recipient of the explanation. This might be very useful in the medical or military context (where justifying an output to a supervisor or senior is the primary task), but less so when it comes to profiling, law enforcement, or administrative decision-making – i.e. where the explanation ought serve as the basis to contest a decision by the subject of the decision. Indeed, counter-factual approaches are not the best for demonstrating how a particular decision-maker has interpreted and dealt with a particular rule – i.e. the rule a contesting party might argue the decision-maker has failed to abide by, or has improperly interpreted. If the goal of explanation is to give ammunition for an appeal, a piece of software explaining how the system would have computed other input data may not be enough to build an argument that the decision was made incorrectly or illegally.

Also important for our purposes here, counter-factual approaches do not easily accommodate the automated analysis of sound or images (i.e. computer vision or audition for entity analysis, behavioural analysis, emotion evaluation, or personality computation described further in Chapter 8). It is difficult to alter the data of an image to embody a 'what if' counter-factual question. That is why image analysis is explored by systems more akin to 'point and justify' models,[58] working out the meaning of intermediate representations, or automated captioning.[59] To that end, other ideas like 'disentangled representations'[60] that attempt to elucidate what

[55] Finale Doshi-Velez et al, 'Accountability of AI Under the Law: The Role of Explanation' (Working Paper, arXiv:1711.01134v2, 21 November 2017).

[56] See, e.g., Sandra Wachter, Brent Mittelstadt, and Chris Russell, 'Counterfactual Explanations Without Opening the Black Box: Automated Decisions and the GDPR' (2018) 31 *Harvard Journal of Law & Technology* 841.

[57] Yuval N Harari, *Sapiens: A Brief History of Humankind* (Random House, 2014); Judea Pearl and Dana Mackenzie, *The Book of Why: The New Science of Cause and Effect* (Basic Books, 2018).

[58] See, e.g., Dong Huk Park et al, 'Attentive Explanations: Justifying Decisions and Pointing to the Evidence' (Working Paper, arXiv:1612.04757, 14 December 2016); Ribeiro et al, above n 51.

[59] See, e.g., Lisa Anne Hendricks et al, 'Generating Visual Explanations' (2016) 9908 *Lecture Notes in Computer Science: ECCV 2016* 3.

[60] Irina Higgins et al, 'Towards a Definition of Disentangled Representations' (Working Paper, arXiv:1812.02230, 5 December 2018); William Whitney, 'Disentangled Representations in Neural Models' (Working Paper, arXiv:1602.02383, 7 February 2016).

elements of a representation, or how different representations generated throughout a computational process, are connected to decision outputs, may be more useful for contesting decisions that are relevant to behaviour, personality, or emotion evaluation through computer vision, audition, or other sensing.

Ultimately each of these systems include inherent trade-offs, perform better or worse in certain situations, provide one type of information at the expense of another, and end up being arbitrary when pushed too far.[61] Without arguing for what might be the most appropriate XAI approach, offering another unified theory of explanation, suggesting a theory of what notions of explanation in the philosophical literature are best amenable to machine learning, or even arguing as to what might constitute adequate explanation in machine learning for the sake of legal compliance, it is noted here that explainability actually risks becoming a harmful mechanism if limited to the counter-factual format, and in fact antithetical to the regulatory trajectory of the GDPR. XAI has the potential to entrench problematic automated decision-making by narrowing the types of reasons that are given for decisions, thus narrowing the grounds for legitimate contestation. XAI also generates a risk of ceding to data scientists the epistemological terrain of what constitutes explanatory information.[62] Being subjected to automated decisions without understanding how or why that decision was made may be problematic, but receiving automated explanations that, while designed to increase your trust and acceptance of a decision, do not provide a premise on which to base an appeal or contest, might be worse. In such a case what explanation means for law, a long-discussed subject in legal theory, may be ultimately reduced to what a computational system is capable of explaining about itself, or what the entities that build and commercialise machine learning systems would prefer to constitute an explanation. To that end, the dual motivations behind XAI of legal compliance on one hand, and enhancing trust in a system on the other, might be contradictory, depending on how that notion of legal compliance is configured.

In legal thinking, the connection between an explanation and the utility of that explanation for contesting a decision is where focus should be directed. When computer scientists generate 'interpretable models', it is important to recognise that 'interpretable' in that sense is a purely mathematical and quantified concept.[63] As Mittelstadt and co-authors rightly note, XAI is more akin to scientific modelling than explanation-giving.[64] If the function of explanation is similar to the

---

[61] See Brett Mittelstadt, Chris Russell, and Sandra Wachter, 'Explaining Explanations in AI' (Paper presented at FAT* 2019, Atlanta, GA, January 2019), for examples of the various limitations associated with linear models.

[62] See, e.g., Tim Miller, Piers Howe, and Liz Sonenberg, 'Explainable AI: Beware of Inmates Running the Asylum or: How I learnt to Stop Worrying and Love the Social and Behavioural Sciences' (Working Paper, arXiv:1712.00547, 5 December 2017); Tim Miller 'Explanation in Artificial Intelligence: Insights from the Social Sciences' (Working Paper, arXiv:1706.07269, 22 June 2017).

[63] See, e.g., Zachary C Lipton, 'The Mythos of Model Interpretability' (Paper presented at the 2016 Workshop on Human Interpretability in Machine Learning, New York, NY, 23 June 2016).

[64] Mittelstadt, above n 61.

provision of legal reasons, then this is a very precarious trajectory.[65] Of course, not all explanatory systems are geared for that goal – but those built to satisfy Article 15 of the GDPR should be. Explanations that are intended only to build trust in automated decision-making systems are inevitably part of the agenda behind the proliferation of automated decision-making systems, but not necessarily developing the capacity to contest them.

This critique of explainability follows similar commentary as to the limitations of transparency generally. For instance, Gloria González Fuster has argued:

> In European data protection law ... transparency is fundamentally not about a vague, utopic state of objective clarity, but about something else. It is not about letting data subjects sneak into the real life of their data and into the algorithms that move them, but about providing individuals with a certain narrative about all this processing; a narrative de facto constructed for data subjects on the basis of the interests of the data controllers, and adapted to fit a certain idea of the data subject's presumed needs and ability to discern.[66]

Fuster thus describes how transparency is about translation, in the sense of delivering to data subjects an account of what is being done to their personal data, tailored to a certain idea of what individuals might want to hear, and what they can perceive. That 'the information provided by controllers to data subjects reflects the controller's perception of the individuals whose data they are about to process' goes a long way to describing the limitations of transparency to any meaningful exercise of control.[67] Fuster's point here is that transparency can become an instrument that distracts us or even actively undermines the capacity to challenge or bring oversight to these decision-making processes.

FAIRNESS

For these reasons transparency, in any form, including XAI only takes us so far. An alternative register of legal intervention is thus emerging, focused on ensuring that automated profiling occurs according to statistically acceptable parameters of human calculation. The goal of this approach is to achieve a 'fairer' computational translation and assessment of the world, and the people in it, by exposing and limiting bias and prejudice in the data sets used in machine learning or produced by the working of machine learning models. The fairness in machine learning paradigm grew predominantly out of the US legal environment's prohibitions on

---

[65] See, e.g., Karen Yeung and Adrian Weller, 'How Is "Transparency" Understood by Legal Scholars and the Machine Learning Community?' in Emre Bayamlıoğlu et al (eds) *Being Profiled: Cogitas Ergo Sum* (10 Years of 'Profiling the European Citizen') (Amsterdam University Press, 2018) 36.
[66] Gloria González Fuster, 'Transparency as Translation in Data Protection' in Emre Bayamlıoğlu et al (eds) *Being Profiled: Cogitas Ergo Sum* (10 Years of 'Profiling the European Citizen') (Amsterdam University Press, 2018) 52, 52.
[67] Ibid 53.

discrimination, although proscriptions on the use of sensitive data types in automated profiling in the GDPR and LED and other anti-discrimination laws suggest fairness is a global concern.[68]

Unfair discrimination finds its way into automated systems in multiple ways,[69] and improving the outcomes of automated decision systems by removing the impact or influence of sensitive data types on automated decision-making is a critically important exercise. We are inundated with scandal after scandal about discriminatory systems that embody problematic bias, knowingly or unknowingly. Prominent examples include Amazon's experimental automated human resources system that appeared to marginalise applications from women. There, the training data demonstrated a preference for male candidates, reflecting the organisation's historic employment culture and practices. When assessing new applications, the system accordingly penalised the word 'women's' or other indications the applicant was female, such as attendance at a women's college or university. Another canonical example is the racial bias associated with the COMPAS risk analysis tool described in Chapter 6. That tool, its use, and the opacity of its operation are all highly problematic. But the discussion amongst researchers that followed the case and the subsequent analysis in *Pro Publica* was interesting for how it highlighted the multiple possible interpretations of fairness in statistical applications, the impossibility of embedding multiple ideas of fairness concurrently, and that a system's optimisation will inevitably reflect a political agenda. In other words, fairness has to be optimised towards one outcome or another. This might be, for instance, 'predictive parity' (ratio of true positives to those labelled high-risk generally), which would be preferred by risk assessment system designers, or 'error rate balance' (the distribution of false positives and negatives for specific groups), which better reflects a social justice paradigm of substantive equality in outcomes.[70] These goals likely cannot be implemented simultaneously.

Investigations of fairness have dramatically improved insight into the ways in which automated systems generate unwanted outcomes, and have produced an entire catalogue of techniques for identifying 'unfairness' and correcting it within mathematical models. But this technical approach to fairness also has very real limits. As luminaries in the field like John Kleinberg and Arvind Narayanan have demonstrated, there are now somewhere between 15 and 25 plausible definitions of 'fairness' that are being used in the literature, each optimising for different things.

---

[68] Bryce W Goodman, 'A Step Towards Accountable Algorithms? Algorithmic Discrimination and the European Union General Data Protection' (Paper presented at the 29th Conference on Neural Information Processing Systems, Barcelona, Spain, December 2016).
[69] Solon Borocas and Andrew Selbst, 'Big Data's Disparate Impact' (2016) *California Law Review* 104.
[70] See Arvind Narayanan, 'Translation Tutorial: 21 Fairness Definitions and Their Politics' (Tutorial delivered at FAT* 2018, New York, NY, 23 February 2018, citing Alexandra Chouldechova, 'Fair Prediction with Disparate Impact: A Study of Bias in Recidivism Prediction Instruments' [2017] 5[2] *Big Data* 153).

Further, the selection of more than two optimisation goals may be impossible.[71] Inevitably, there is a limit on how fair any system can be, and political choices must be made about what the goal of fairness optimisation is, and what stakeholders it will benefit. Further, the elimination of specific proxies (like sensitive or protected data) from a data set may be a fraught and counter-productive exercise, as the structural inequality associated with those features lingers on in other non-protected data categories. Eventually, tracking the effect of protected features through an entire dataset becomes an intractable mathematical problem.[72] To that end, it needs to be understood that there is a limit to the ways in which the subtle political questions behind fairness can be conceptualised as mathematical optimisation problems.

To offer a little more insight, fairness definitions typically fall into three categories: 'statistical', 'similarity', and 'causal' based reasoning methods.[73] Statistical measures describe fairness metrics that can be calculated from observational data, such as how a range of features is distributed across a population. Statistical fairness measures attempt to equalise a certain property across the population, however they often mask unfairness towards smaller minority or sub-groups within the population that are not identified by the attribute being equalised for. These measures are therefore only fair for an average member of a protected group. 'Similarity'-based approaches look at 'individual' fairness by analysing the similarity of treatment between two individuals. Similarity is measured by a 'distance metric' or 'statistical distance' between the distribution of outcomes for those two individuals. But this is difficult to translate into a meaningful notion of fairness because the relationship between that 'distance' and some tangible fairness criterion is highly abstracted. Finally, 'causal reasoning' fairness systems take unobservable variables into account in order to understand the influence of different attributes on each other. The most common example is 'counter-factual fairness', which involves changing the value of any one protected attribute while keeping non-causally dependent attributes constant to examine any influence on the outcome. A system will be counter-factually fair if it generates the same outcome in both the 'real world' and a 'counter-factual world' where the individual belonged to a different demographic group.[74] But as noted, this does not address how protected features typically represent structural inequalities that will be expressed through the entirety of an individual's representation in a dataset.

Another important limitation to the fairness paradigm is its co-opting by industrial interests. These fairness metrics, and the particular politics they embody, are now

---

[71] Jon Kleinberg, Sendhil Mullainathan, and Manish Raghavan, 'Inherent Trade-Offs in the Fair Determination of Risk Scores' (Paper presented at the 8th Innovations in Theoretical Computer Science Conference, San Diego, CA, 10–12 January 2019).
[72] See Goodman, above n 68, citing Y Dodge, 'Interaction effect' *Oxford Dictionary of Statistical Terms* (Oxford, 2003).
[73] Sahil Verma and Julia Rubin, 'Fairness Definitions Explained' (2018) *ACM/IEEE International Workshop on Software Fairness* 1.
[74] Matt J Kusner et al, 'Counterfactual Fairness' (Working Paper, arXiv:1703.06856, 20 March 2017).

being created and marketed by large tech firms like Google and IBM as 'fairness solutions'. Those companies are producing an ecosystem of fairness auditing tools, and claim to have 'solved' the fairness problem. Such companies clearly have an interest in removing discrimination from their products, as fairer machine learning is more legitimate machine learning, which of course, also legitimises the epistemological claim to the quality of knowledge generated by the systems they sell. But there is a risk that the valuable work of this academic community is being used to justify the proliferation of these systems and their social acceptance. Sebastian Benthall has described this cooperation of the academic community working on fairness in machine learning, and corporate interests, as an example of Nancy Fraser's idea of 'progressive neoliberalism' – the alliance of neoliberalism with progressive political movements.[75]

To that end, scholars like Frank Pasquale have begun to ask whether this form of accountability adequately considers the question of 'accountability to whom'.[76] Indeed, without proper attention to that question, this form of accountability risks becoming part of the feedback mechanism that continually improves and thus proliferates automated decision-making. We therefore have to ask to whom this gives political and decision-making power. Yarden Katz has suggested that 'If AI runs society, then grievances with society's institutions can get reframed as questions of "algorithmic accountability." This move paves the way for AI experts and entrepreneurs to present themselves as the architects of society'.[77] The risk associated with computational notions of explainability is thus replicated here – there is an epistemological territory that needs defending from purely statistical frameworks, such that the power to govern is not limited to a particular group building and implementing statistical tools.[78]

THE TECHNOLOGIES OF ALGORITHMIC ACCOUNTABILITY

Ironically, the degree to which these legal compliance mechanisms have become highly technical is simultaneously their most challenging and most interesting development. That there are large computer science and data science communities working in these areas demonstrates how the technologies of legal compliance are again changing – from judicial supervision of states in privacy, to distributed

---

[75] Sebastian Benthall, 'Critical Reflections on FAT* 2018: A Historical Idealist Perspective', *Datactive* (11 April 2018) https://data-activism.net/2018/04/critical-reflections-on-fat-2018-a-historical-idealist-perspective/.
[76] Frank Pasquale, 'Odd Numbers', *Real Life Magazine* (online), (20 August 2018) http://reallifemag.com/odd-numbers/.
[77] Yarden Katz, 'Manufacturing an Artificial Intelligence Revolution' available https://papers.ssrn.com/sol3/papers.cfm?abstract_id=3078224, 2.
[78] See, e.g., Julia Powles and Helen Nissenbaum, 'The Seductive Diversion of "Solving" Bias in Artificial Intelligence' (7 December 2018) https://medium.com/s/story/the-seductive-diversion-of-solving-bias-in-artificial-intelligence-890df5e5ef53.

bureaucratic compliance and enforcement mechanisms in data protection, to (in this case) computationally embedded and executed compliance. Those computational accountability mechanisms concerning fairness, explainability, and transparency are thus connected to ideas about privacy and data protection by design, as well the more holistic question of the possibility of 'computational law'. While some authors have argued that these types of computational implementations should never be thought of as anything other than compliance 'by design', the problem of 'by design' is that its indeterminacy leaves room for industry actors to use political and market power to shape norms according to their own interests.

As Laurence Diver and Burkhard Schafer suggest:

> Bearing in mind the conflicts inherent in a market where the data controllers creating the systems that PbD is intended to regulate are often the same controllers who stand to gain from gathering personal data, there is a potentially concomitant effect arising from a centralisation of PbD innovation in those same companies. In the absence of true competition between PbD approaches there is perhaps an incentive for powerful entrenched market players to form cartels, agreeing amongst themselves on commercially favourable PbD standards which minimise regulatory limitations on data processing as far as possible within the elastic limits of a mercurial legal norm.[79]

To that end, it has been suggested that the extreme indeterminacy of the 'by design' requirements in, for instance, the GDPR, is the product of industry lobbying designed to soften applicable standards.

Where the discussion about 'by design' becomes more interesting, for our purposes at least, is when they perform what Ira Rubinstein has described as a 'complimentary' function – the *implementation* of statutory principles or other legal requirements.[80] These approaches take us closer to the idea that such tools might be defined as 'legal' technologies in and of themselves, rather than simply tools of compliance. Indeed, this moves us from a discussion of how law addresses automation to a discussion of the automation of law – the distillation of legal specification into computational representation for the sake of automated enforcement. This is taken up further in Chapter 9 and Chapter 10.

While privacy law offers opacity and the idea of not being seen in a certain way, and data subject rights offer transparency in the sense of knowing how one is being seen and the chance to participate in the construction of one's own identity, algorithmic accountability offers something else. For instance, the legal subject of fair machine learning is less a unique private person and more a statistical node whose 'distance metric' from other statistical nodes is deemed appropriate. Legal

---

[79] Laurence Diver and Burkhard Schafer, 'Opening the Black Box: Petri Nets and Privacy by Design' (2017) 31 *International Review of Law, Computers & Technology* 68, at 72, quoting Sarah Spiekermann and Lorrie Faith Cranor, 'Engineering Privacy' (2009) 35 *IEEE Transactions on Software Engineering* 67, 72.

[80] Ira S Rubinstein, 'Regulating Privacy by Design' (2011) 26 *Berkeley Technology Law Journal* 1409.

subjectivity, and what it means to bear rights when profiled in this way, may merely be an assurance of an appropriate channelling through these statistical filters, or the reception of automatically generated explanations of a particular profiling decision. If that is the case, the philosophy animating algorithmic accountability appears to be something along the lines of 'whatever you are doing to me, do it gently'. That may also describe the limit of the political potential of this legal subject and these legal tools. This is a legal subject that has exchanged the capacity to affirm its own discursive account of identity over that of a profile, for a type of computational guarantee that the identity generated, in all its intricacies, will not leave them worse-off than others because of the influence of certain types or categories of data like race, sexuality, or gender. But despite the ineptitude of that particular legal guarantee, this type of legal subjectivity, as is discussed in the following chapters perhaps takes us closer to a meaningful response to the problem of profiling, especially in the context of cyber-physical systems of the 'world state'.

CONCLUSION

All of the mechanisms described under the heading of algorithmic accountability, just like privacy and data protection, are limited in very significant ways. But importantly, some of these approaches, through their embedding in the data scientific operation of profiling, address what is the emerging critical issue of optimisation. That is, they interrupt how machine learning optimisation occurs or what can be optimised for. Increasing control over optimisation, as we'll see in the next chapters, is central to producing an effective legal paradigm in this area. The other lingering feature of these algorithmic accountability mechanisms is their structural susceptibility to industrial or corporate cooption. As law and computer science interface more profoundly and productively, the communities that decide on what constitutes appropriate ways for computer science to satisfy or enact legal obligations has a difficult and highly political task. In is unsurprising then that corporate interests fund a great deal of both the computer science and legal research in this area, as they have a great deal at stake when it comes to determining what constitutes a fair encoding of the world, or what constitutes explanatory information. As the world moves towards further quantification and computation, it is critical to remember that although legal ideas may be implementable in computational mechanisms, those computational mechanisms do not exhaust the totality of that legal idea. In other words, law is always more than its expression be it in software or spoken language. Law remains a series of practices that stand outside of computation, even as computational mechanisms adopt increasingly computational characteristics.

8

From Photographic Image to Computer Vision

Neural Networks and Identity in the World State

In 2012, Alex Krizhevsky, then a PhD student at the University of Toronto under Geoffrey Hinton, won the annual 'ImageNet' automated image labelling competition by an impressive 10.8 per cent margin.[1] This use of a neural network-based object classification algorithm also triggered a major shift the way computers relate to images and the physical world more generally. ImageNet is an image database, labelled primarily by Amazon Mechanical Turk workers, first published by computer scientist Fei-Fei Li in 2009. Her intention was to 'map out the entire world of objects'[2] for the sake of training machine learning systems. The first winner of the ImageNet competition in 2010 achieved a labelling accuracy of 71.8 per cent. By 2017, the majority of teams had surpassed 95 per cent, with many today considering ImageNet 'solved'. That leap in accuracy from adoption and subsequent improvement of Krizhevsky's deep convolutional neural network architecture for image classification. These techniques, discussed in more detail later in the chapter, are a subset of machine learning algorithms that are highly effective for pattern recognition in vision tasks.

Now, image classification competitions focus more on labelling 3D data (a task highly relevant to technologies like augmented reality) or videos of humans performing various actions.[3] But the deep neural network architectures that stunned the world in the 2012 ImageNet competition have become the bread and butter of image interpretation and classification. Although neural networks are used in all types of automated profiling, 'computer vision' applications are the focus in this chapter, as they connect these profiling practices to a history of visual technologies, and situate

---

[1] See Alex Krizhevsky, Ilya Sutskever, and Geoffrey E. Hinton, 'ImageNet Classification with Deep Convolutional Neural Networks' (2012) *Advances in Neural Information Processing Systems* 1097; Timothy B Lee, 'How Computers Got Shockingly Good at Recognizing Images', *Ars Technica* (online), 18 December 2018 https://arstechnica.com/science/2018/12/how-computers-got-shockingly-good-at-recognizing-images/.

[2] Dave Gershgorn, 'The Data that Transformed AI Research – And Possibly the World', *Quartz* (online), 26 July 2017 https://qz.com/1034972/the-data-that-changed-the-direction-of-ai-research-and-possibly-the-world/.

[3] Will Kay et al, 'The Kinetics Human Action Video Dataset', *ArXiv* https://arxiv.org/abs/1705.06950.

the analysis within Western thought's continuing reflections on 'the connection between actuality and photo'.[4] Computer vision and neural networks have also generated new systems of measurement and classification for persons echoing earlier practices of police photography and automated profiling, bringing together biological and behavioural analysis, with new consequences for its subjects.

Judicial photography and its related practices measured and archived the body, generating novel institutional identities that Agamben described as reducing humans to 'naked life'. When refracted through computation, massive data collection and analysis, and the unique character of neural networks, computer vision similarly produces new mechanisms for identity formation that amplify that effect. They extend the notion of logic as the medium of being, and seek to further transcend the separation between image and referent discussed in the previous chapters. Whereas photography became the standard-bearer of 'mechanical objectivity', slavishly reproducing nature, certain computer vision practitioners have started to suggest the technology not only 'understands' the content of images, but actually reveals the truth of their content. Rather than approximation and speculation by profiling with 'transaction-generated information' created from interactions with informational environments,[5] some researchers have begun to argue that *only through computation* are we able to access all the information available in human faces, bodies, and behaviours. In other words, only through computation can the excesses of the physical world and the people within it be perceived, processed, and known.

The capacity for new visual technologies to access truth is a familiar trope in the history of media technologies. However, in the context of computer vision, some new distinctive features complement those historical continuities. Although there are multiple plausible epistemic bases for decision-making with neural networks and computer vision, the knowledge-logic depicted in this chapter is described as a form of 'computational empiricism' that draws on a confluence of automating the production of representations, the opacity of neural networks, the influence of the corporate data science infrastructure, and the dramatic capacities of these technologies. This chapter tracks those logics in computer vision and biometrics applications, with a particular focus on what is called 'personality computation'.[6] It also traces these ideas back to the intellectual tradition of cybernetics that emerged in the middle of the twentieth century, and has continued to influence how individuals are conceptualised and known in informational environments. In particular, the

---

[4] Walter Benjamin, 'A Short History of Photography (1934)' in Alan Trachtenberg (ed) *Classic Essays on Photography* (Leete Island Books, 1980).

[5] Oscar H Gandy Jr, 'Statistical Surveillance: Remote Sensing in the Digital Age' in Kristie Ball, Kevin D Haggerty, and David Lyon (eds) *Routledge Handbook of Surveillance Studies* (Routledge 2012).

[6] See, e.g., Julio CS Jacques Junior et al, 'First Impressions: A Survey on Computer Vision-Based Apparent Personality Trait Analysis', arXiv:1804.08046v1 [cs.CV] (21 April 2018).

chapter describes the theoretical lens of cybernetics that interprets the world as information, and the people within it as information processing nodes, whose true selves are expressed as patterns of behaviour. Profiling with computer vision, by translating the 'real world' into numbers for sensing, classification, and decision-making, participates in this tradition at the critical interface between the physical and informational worlds, and introduces new mechanisms for understanding people, with new consequences for legal thinking.

PERSONALITY COMPUTATION

Computer vision is a family of technologies and practices by which computational systems understand and make decisions about the physical world and the people within it. Computer vision can produce classifications and knowledge about scenes, objects, events, and people, or anything else that can be sensed with a camera. A great number of applications are already operating, for instance: autonomous vehicle control; optical character recognition; augmented reality; automated target recognition in military and industrial situations; contextual image classification; medical imaging and diagnostics; and traffic rule enforcement, amongst many others. When 'looking at people', however, there are many more. Facial recognition, for instance, currently the most notorious application of computer vision to people, links a person's image to some form of institutional identity such as a driver's licence, passport, or police portrait.[7] By connecting an individual to their behaviour in physical space,[8] facial recognition couples identity across physical and computational registers, enabling automated decisions about identity to be expressed into physical environments, for instance to authorise access, flag suspicion, or grant privileges.

There is already much more that computer vision can do when 'looking at people', however.[9] Alongside 'identification', computer vision can also 'classify'.[10] That is, as well as linking image and spatial location to an institutional identity, computer vision can generate classifications about *non-visual* human attributes such

---

[7] See, e.g., Jordan G Teicher, 'What Do Facial Recognition Technologies Mean for Our Privacy?' *New York Times* (18 July 2018) www.nytimes.com/2018/07/18/lens/what-do-facial-recognition-technologies-mean-for-our-privacy.html; Clare Garvie, Alvaro Bedoya, and Jonathan Frankle, 'The Perpetual Lineup: Unregulated Police Face Recognition in America' (18 October 2018) www.perpetuallineup.org; Monique Mann and Marcus Smith, 'Automated Facial Recognition Technology: Recent Developments and Approaches to Oversight' (2017) 40(1) *University of New South Wales Law Journal* 121.

[8] A similar process happens with vehicle registration and automated number plate recognition. See, e.g., James Bridle, 'How Britain Exported Next-Generation Surveillance' (18 December 2013) https://medium.com/matter/how-britain-exported-next-generation-surveillance-d15b5801b79e.

[9] See, e.g., Sergio Escalera et al, 'ChaLearn Looking at People: A Review of Events and Resources' *Proceedings of the 2017 International Joint Conference on Neural Networks* (IJCNN 2017), IEEE, 2017.

[10] Gandy, above n 5.

as personality, emotion, and (future) behaviour. More controversial classifiers have also addressed questions of sexuality, criminal propensity, political position, IQ, and paedophilic tendencies. Many of these fall under the heading of 'personality computation', and are researched in the computer science subfields of Automated Personality Analysis (APA) and Automated Personality Recognition (APR). Whereas APA avoids interrogating the accuracy of its claims, instead focusing on personality traits attributed by others (often Amazon Turk workers), APR seeks to identify the true character of the individual by locating stable statistical relationships between visual stimuli and personality.

Computational personality analysis tracks faces, postures, movements, actions, gestures, voices, interactions, and emotions (as well as whether those emotions and expressions are real or fake) to infer personality traits.[11] Different analytic techniques operate on different data inputs. Some use dynamic information such as what a person *does*, or the way a physical morphology changes. Some use static information such as how a person *looks*. Some use multiple modalities – like combinations of visual and audio data in different configurations. Indeed, the biometric modality of computer audition demonstrates many of the characteristics discussed in this chapter.[12] With the growing success of neural networks for image classification, explorations of facial morphology through statistical methods appear to be gaining disciplinary legitimacy, with APA and APR becoming the fodder of entire fields and competitions, sponsored by industry actors like Microsoft, Facebook, Amazon, and even Disney.[13]

Although these disciplines explore multiple stimuli including dynamic facial information, handwriting, and speech, they also include what could be called 'computational physiognomy'. Despite Galton's failure in the nineteenth century, and the ongoing stigma associated with eugenics and 'Social Darwinism', physiognomic experiments have, since that time, been continually rehearsed with new photographic techniques, statistical methodologies, and biological theories. In parallel with ongoing physiognomic experimentation, there has been a growing psychological literature exploring how 'first impressions' are generated from looking at faces (including impressions of criminality).[14] That material explores how faces

---

[11] Jacques Junior et al, above n 6.
[12] See, e.g., Emily Apter, 'Shibboleth: Policing by Ear and Forensic Listening in Projects by Lawrence Abu Hamdan' (2016) 156 *October* 100.
[13] The 2018 International Conference on Pattern Recognition ran a competition on computer vision for recognition of complex personality characteristics.
[14] See, e.g., Janine Willis and Alexander Todorov, 'First Impressions: Making Up Your Mind After a 100ms Exposure to a Face' (2006) 17(7) *Psychological Science* 592; Nalini Ambady and John Skowronski (eds) *First Impressions* (The Guilford Press, 2008); Christopher Y Olivola and Alexander Todorov, 'Fooled by First Impressions? Re-Examining the Diagnostic Value of Appearance-Based Inference' (2010) 46(2) *Journal of Experimental Social Psychology* 315; Thomas Alley, 'Physiognomy and Social Perception' in Thomas Alley (ed) *Social and Applied Aspects of Perceiving Faces* (Laurence Erlbaum Publishers, 1988).

are a form of non-verbal communication, and part of the intrinsic heuristics we use to navigate daily social interactions. The experimental success of that research, however, has also facilitated the claim that 'research on appearance-based accuracy might seem more credible if society were "not so enamoured of the idea that because a person's appearance *ought* not to make a difference, it *does* not," blaming the dearth of this research on the "naturalistic fallacy" (that is, confusing how things *are* with how they *ought* to be)'.[15]

Early work in computational physiognomy was based on very simplistic models using Euclidean distances (the straight-line measurement between two points in a geometric plane) and geometric angles to classify facial features, corresponding with the pioneering physiognomer Lavator's division of the face into 32 classes.[16] Initially, these experiments were framed in terms of investigating whether computers could replicate the trait evaluation performed by humans (i.e. first impressions analysis). There were no complex machine learning methods, or assessments of accuracy. It was simply a translation of the task of physiognomic measurement into a computer vision system. Beginning in 2012, however, this type of personality computation became far more sophisticated, and it was not long until convolutional neural networks were predicting intelligence and other personality characteristics based on portraits.[17] Competitions for computational personality analysis (both

---

[15] Jeffrey M Valla, Stephen J Ceci, Wendy M Williams, 'The Accuracy of Inferences about Criminality Based on Facial Appearance' (2011) 5(2) *Journal of Social, Evolutionary, and Cultural Psychology* 66, 68 (quoting E. Berschied, 'An Overview of the Psychological Effects of Physical Attractiveness' in G. Lucker et al [eds] *Psychological Aspects of Facial Form* [University of Michigan Press, 1981]). The theoretical justifications for this work have moved away from the biological or genetic determinisms of Social Darwinism, however (see, e.g., Alexander Todorov, *Face Value* [Princeton University Press 2017]). In their study of the accuracy of physiognomic interpretation, they cite multiple studies showing that accurate physiognomic judgements can be made by humans. One example is a 1962 study on inferences of criminality that claimed success in replicating Galton's process. Kozeny's 'Experimental Investigation of Physiognomy Utilizing a Photographic-Statistical Method' used 730 criminal portraits to create composites for 16 crime categories, which were then physiognomically classified (from the visual information) (E Kozeny 'Experimentelle Untersuchungen zur Ausdruckskunde mittel photographisch-statisticher Methode' [1962] 114 *Archive für die Gesamte Psychologie* 55). And Valla, Ceci, and Williams also claim success in measuring inferences of criminality from cropped facial images. But significantly, those authors argue that movement to the ecological perspective (environmental adaptation studies) as a justification means the question of criminal identification remains an open one, and further, that there should not be any political impediment to investigating the accuracy of inferences.

[16] Hee-Deok Yang and Seong-Wang Lee, 'Automatic Physiognomic Analysis by Classifying Facial Component Feature' (2006) *IEEE The 18th International Conference on Pattern Recognition (ICPR'06)* – although they reference statistical work from 1997 in V Dominique et al, 'What Represents a Face? A Computational Approach for the Integration of Physiological and Psychological Data' (1997) 26 *Perception* 1271. And material on computer vision for expression analysis has also been continuing since the 1990s; See, e.g., John Graham, 'Lavater's "Physiognomy": A Checklist' (1961) 55(4) *The Papers of the Bibliographical Society of America* 297. This pioneering work was initially published in 1806.

[17] See, e.g., Ting Zhang et al, 'Physiognomy: Personality Traits Prediction by Learning' (2017) 14(4) *International Journal of Automation and Computing* 386. Work of this type often uses the OCEAN model for personality description.

apparent and true) began in 2012, with the use of neural networks and deep learning dramatically improving on the early unimpressive results in classifier accuracy.[18] As is described below, deep learning and neural networks enable measurement at a radically different scale than earlier classifiers that use human engineered low-level image 'features' (like facial landmarks) or intermediate level 'attributes' (like nose, glasses, moustache, hair, and forehead height).

The significance of these technical advances for personality computation, and the epistemological platform of some practicioners is demonstrated clearly in Wu and Zhang's 2016 paper 'Automated Inference on Criminality Using Face Images'.[19] That research used 1856 government ID images, about half of which included individuals with a criminal conviction, as a dataset for a criminal-propensity classifier, built with a convolutional neural network. The authors argue it identifies criminal persons with 89.51 per cent accuracy. The theoretical grounding of this research is similar to other APR exercises. The authors claimed to be testing the social inference hypothesis, noting, 'As modern machine learning algorithms can match and exceed human performance in face recognition, it seems irresistible to pursue automated inference on criminality.' Both the ideological and methodological problems with this research are easy to identify.[20] Nevertheless, the research is revealing in terms of how certain practitioners understand the relationship between computer vision and human characteristics as chaneled through these statistical methods. Most telling is the authors' acknowledgment that the variance between criminal and non-criminal populations was not evident from visual assessments or simple Euclidean measurements. The paper noted that, 'quite surprisingly, the average faces of the two populations ... appear hardly distinguishable'. Visual information, in the sense of information that is visually perceivable and interpretable, what Galton had unsuccessfully relied on to identify the criminal 'mean', was and remains insufficient for physiognomic purposes. Only through the high-dimensional computational analysis of granular measurements was this statistical separation

---

[18] Jacques Junior et al, above n 7, discussing the Interspeech, MAPTRAITS, WCPR, and ChaLearn competitions.
[19] Xiaolin Wu and Xi Zhang, 'Automated Inference on Criminality using Face Images' (13 November 2016) https://arxiv.org/abs/1611.04135.
[20] This is coupled with an intrinsic criminological approach to understanding criminality on the basis of 'abnormality' (note this leads to the inverse conclusion that there is a law of normality of faces for non-criminals; i.e. a return to ideas of criminal biopathology), rather than structural causes. In a response to criticisms of this work, the authors acknowledged that they could not control for socioeconomic status of image subjects (as given away in the example datasets by white collars) as well as the problematic belief that 'Unlike a human examiner/judge, a computer vision algorithm or classifier has absolutely no subjective baggages [sic], having no emotions, no biases whatsoever due to past experience, race, religion, political doctrine, gender, age, etc., no mental fatigue, no preconditioning of a bad sleep or meal. The automated inference on criminality eliminates the variable of meta-accuracy (the competence of the human judge/examiner) altogether.'

discernible. The finding represents the premise and utility of neural networks for this application,[21] and is highly illustrative of the shift from qualitative visual understanding to quantitative statistical ways of knowing.

The claim was made even more explicitly in Wang and Kosinski's controversial paper 'Deep Neural Networks are More Accurate than Humans at Detecting Sexual Orientation From Facial Images'.[22] That project used 14,438 facial images extracted from an existing database, of which 6,076 were identifiably gay according to correlation with a Facebook Audience Insights platform, and self-declared sexual interest on Facebook. A deep neural network called VGG-Face (originally deployed for facial recognition), which transforms facial images into 4,096 particular scores, was used for pattern analysis and classification. While the authors begin from the proposition that 'DNNs are increasingly outperforming humans in visual tasks such as image classification, facial recognition, or diagnosing skin cancer', they ultimately conclude that 'our faces contain more information about sexual orientation than can be perceived or interpreted by the human brain'.

Although these are highly ideological, politically and theoretically naïve, and otherwise problematic applications of computer vision profiling, it is less the particular application that is of interest here, and more the epistemological platform being invoked. Indeed, the family of profiling practices described above also includes much less sensitive or controversial applications, many of which are already in broad use. And while some of those particular applications have been challenged as scientifically flawed, there remains a growing demand for new computational biometrics. Now, both behavioural and biological data, including 'soft' biometrics such as 'ambiguous or not concretely measurable traits' like gait, voice or nonconscious body movement are used to determine all sorts of characteristics.[23] In human resources, for instance, automated analysis of video resumes and interviews are used for employment decisions.[24] Similarly, the health insurance industry is increasingly interested in new forms of data collection and analysis to further individualise its risk calculations, including piggybacking on the diagnostic potential of computer vision in healthcare applications to individualise policies and police compliance with medical directions.[25]

---

[21] Yann LeCun, 'Deep Learning' (2015) 521 *Nature* 436.
[22] Yilun Wang and Michal Kosinski, 'Deep Neural Networks Are More Accurate than Humans at Detecting Sexual Orientation from Facial Images' (2018) 114(2) Journal of Personality and Social Psychology 246.
[23] R Joshua Scannell, 'Controlled Measures' *Real Life* (17 September 2018) https://reallifemag.com/controlled-measures/.
[24] Escalera, above n 9.
[25] David Schatsky, Plamen Petrov, and Rajeev Ronanki, 'Cognitive Technologies for Health Plans' (Report, Deloitte LLP, 2015) www2.deloitte.com/content/dam/insights/us/articles/artificial-intelligence-health-plans/DUP_1087-Cognitive-Technologies_Health-Plans_MASTER.pdf; Junfeng Gao et al, 'Computer Vision in Healthcare Applications' (2018) *Journal of Healthcare Engineering* (online), available www.ncbi.nlm.nih.gov/pmc/articles/PMC5857319/pdf/JHE2018-5157020.pdf.

Law enforcement is, of course, another large consumer of computer vision. Companies like NEC, IDEMIA, Amazon, and Microsoft are producing computer vision products for a large variety of applications including policing and security. Echoing the nineteenth-century problem of not being able to locate individuals within the growing registers of police portraits, many of these computer vision applications developed out of the reality that humans could not monitor the increasing amounts of footage produced by CCTV cameras. To that end, beyond facial recognition and automated number plate recognition, computer vision has been put to work in object tracking, as well as naming and annotating human actions, both in real-time video analysis and post-hoc image searches.[26] The explosion of body-worn cameras in policing also raises the possibility that facial morphology, posture, pose, and movement analysis might inform real-time decisions about pre-violent or pre-flight behaviours using behavioural and biological inputs derived from image analysis.[27] Indeed, body-worn camera analytics is becoming big business for companies like TASER (who have rebranded as a body-worn camera and analytics company called AXON), NTechLab, and IBM,[28] with ongoing work into the analysis of suspicious behaviour from that footage.

It can be argued that one should not deduce a general epistemological platform from those applications in computational physiognomy or personality computation. While that is a fair interjection, there are two responses to this claim. First, the political ideas animating physiognomy and phrenology have never gone away. Instead, they have been modernised and dissimulated into actuarial systems and statistical methodologies that increasingly inform automated decision-making systems.[29] The point being that computer vision systems, by virtue of their classification function in commerce and governance, are always ideological. Second, physiognomy's role as a mechanism for understanding humans is, and continues to be, historically relevant. Physiognomy was an early interface for the application of methods from the physical sciences to the social sciences, including the analysis of human behaviour. To that end, criminologist Nicole Rafter has brilliantly argued, with respect to the earlier practices of physiognomy and phrenology, that their scientific invalidity was somewhat insignificant when compared to the epistemological and methodological paradigms that they ushered in.[30] Those pseudo-sciences shifted how we understand

---

[26] Haroon Idres and Mubarak Shah, 'Enhancing Camera Surveillance Using Computer Vision: A Research Note' (2017) 41(2) *Policing: An International Journal of Police Strategies & Management* 292.

[27] See, e.g., Alex Pasternack, 'Police Body Cameras Will Do More than Just Record You' *Fast Company* (3 March 2017) www.fastcompany.com/3061935/police-body-cameras-livestreaming-face-recognition-and-ai; Jason Corso et al, 'Video Analysis for Body-Worn Cameras in Law Enforcement' (2016) *CoRR* abs/1604.03130 discussing 'early warning systems'.

[28] Ava Kofman, 'Taser Will Use Police Body Camera Videos "To Anticipate Criminal Activity"' *The Intercept* (30 April 2017) https://theintercept.com/2017/04/30/taser-will-use-police-body-camera-videos-to-anticipate-criminal-activity/.

[29] Joi Ito, 'Supposedly "Fair" Algorithms Can Perpetuate Discrimination' *Wired* (5 February 2019) www.wired.com/story/ideas-joi-ito-insurance-algorithms/.

[30] Nicole Rafter, 'The Murderous Dutch Fiddler: Criminology, History and the Problem of Phrenology' (2005) 9(1) *Theoretical Criminology* 65.

people and their behaviour away from metaphysics and theology, and towards 'analytical empiricism'. Rafter shows how phrenology, the discredited science of 'the correspondences between the external and internal man, the visible superficies and the invisible contents'[31] based on reading character traits from skull morphology, 'produced one of the most radical reorientations in ideas about crime and punishment ever proposed in the Western world'. It was radical for its providing a *measurable* explanation of criminal behaviour and other social phenomena on the basis of positivist reasoning with empirical methods, and it transformed criminology, penology, and jurisprudence because it changed how we produce knowledge about people.

It is argued that the profiling exercises described above should be thought of as data points in the movement towards *computational empiricism* as a dominant knowledge system. Computational physiognomy, whether or not it is accurate is a harbinger of computational and data scientific methods applied to the analysis of human behaviour that can be measured through sensing the physical world. Beyond 'laundering' various ideological, even eugenicist, politics through technological neutrality,[32] the claim here is that the foundational knowledge claims of these technical systems exhibit their own political and philosophical positions. Following that line of reasoning, this form of biometric empiricism takes its legitimacy, not from its accuracy, but from its deployment to determine political, juridical, civic, and commercial subjectivities in the manner deemed desirable by the entities that build, sell, and use those systems.

COMPUTATIONAL EMPIRICISM

The claim that nature can only be accessed through computation is an attempt to divine a 'statistical law' premised on the reduction of the real into numbers – an attempt to access the hidden mathematical sub-structures of reality. In many respects, this claim is neither unique nor controversial, but it remains significant in the context of a technological capacity that is proliferating so rapidly and widely.[33] It is also far from universally accepted. Some computer scientists sensibly argue that 'deep learning can't extract information that isn't there, and we should be suspicious of claims that it can reliably extract hidden meaning from images that eludes human judges'.[34] But such admissions seem peculiar when, really, deriving meaning from measurements too granular for non-computational analysis is the very premise of machine learning, and unquestionably, computer vision *can* expose what would evade ordinary visual analysis.

---

[31] Ibid 71 quoting John Caspar Lavater, *Essays on Physiognomy* (Thomas Holcroft trans, William Tegg & Co, 1810).

[32] Blaise Agüera y Arcas, Margaret Mitchell, and Alexander Todorov, 'Physiognomy's New Clothes' (7 May 2017) https://medium.com/@blaisea/physiognomys-new-clothes-f2d4b59fdd6a.

[33] See, e.g., Pedro Domingos, *The Master Algorithm* (Basic Books, 2015).

[34] Agüera y Arcas et al, above n 33, although those authors there propose the contradictory argument that 'On a scientific level, machine learning can give us an unprecedented window into nature and human behaviour, allowing us to introspect and systematically analyze patterns that used to be in the domain of intuition or folk wisdom.'

To that end, some have begun to argue that access to the hidden structures of reality has now become the organising principle of data science.[35]

Many representational technologies are premised on revealing previously inaccessible information. Photography, for instance, was understood as a way to 'see into nature's cabinet'.[36] It challenged the 'optical unconscious'.[37] Walter Benjamin describes this access to nature as opening up 'in this material the physiognomic aspects of the world of images, which reside in the smallest details, clear and yet hidden enough to have found shelter in daydreams'.[38] Other optical technologies project similar narratives. The telescope gave access to celestial knowledge, the microscope to cellular knowledge. X-ray imaging and radiographic measurements of material density afforded a 'New Sight'[39] that could reveal 'hidden existence'.[40] For some commentators, the X-ray was the beginning of a form of a-visuality, in which sensing technologies 'transgress the physical thresholds of an optically available world'.[41] Roberta McGrath has described public attitudes around X-rays, noting 'The body itself is thus perceived as literally ghostlike, immaterial, only flesh, as being merely a thin veneer, literally a skin, covering a hidden, deeper reality which will, like truth, be uncovered, revealed.'[42] Artists and intellectuals similarly responded, 'Who can still believe in the opacity of bodies, since our sharpened and multiplied sensibilities have already penetrated the obscure manifestation of mediums?'[43] The idea of the body as readable medium, and the transgression of the optically available world, are highlighted again in Mark Andrejevic's analysis of 'neuromarketing', where he notes:

> The notion that bodies are, for marketing purposes, more truthful than the words they utter is emerging as a recurring theme in the promotion of neuromarketing, which promises to render obsolete the allegedly quaint and outdated techniques of surveys and focus groups … They can, thanks to new technologies, cut through directly to the underlying truths revealed by the brain.[44]

Andrejevic places this claim within 'The appeal of techniques for bypassing discursive forms of representation (by cutting "straight to the brain")' against 'the popularised and

---

[35] Dan McQuillan, 'Data Science as Machinic Neoplatonism' (2018) 31 *Philosophy of Technology* 253.
[36] Roberta McGrath, *Seeing Her Sex: Medical Archives and the Female Body* (Manchester University Press, 2002) 114.
[37] Benjamin, above n 4.
[38] Ibid.
[39] 'The New Sight and the New Photography', *The Photogram* (1898).
[40] Mary Warner Marien, *Photography: A Cultural History* (Laurence King Publishing, 2nd ed, 2006) 216.
[41] Susan Schuppli, 'Atmospheric Correction' in Daniel Rubinstein et al (eds) *On the Verge of Photography: Imaging Beyond Representation* (ARTicle Press, 2013) 23, quoting Akira Mizuta Lippit, *Atomic Light: Shadow Optics* (University of Minnesota Press, 2005) 44.
[42] McGrath, above n 37, 115.
[43] Umberto Boccioni, quoted in Didier Ottinger (ed) *Futurism* (Centre Pompidou/5 Continent Editions, 2008) 154.
[44] Mark Andrejevic, 'Brain Whisperers: Cutting Through the Clutter with Neuromarketing' (2012) 2(2) *Somatechnics* 198, 199.

reflexive mediated critiques of discursive forms of representation for their potentially deceptive, indeterminate, and constructed character'. These approaches are also echoed in the behavioural sciences, wherein the premise of stable relationship between stimuli and character afforded mechanisms for personality and behaviour calculation like 'digital phenotyping'.[45] Those techniques for transcending the body, like neuroimaging, often use statistical systems as the basis of their knowledge claims rather than images alone. To that end, even neurological images are visualizations of statistical probabilities rather than direct images of the biological system studied. Peter Galison's distinction of the 'image' and 'logic' traditions in the context of physical sciences also helps clarify the epistemological significance of computer vision. He discusses the 'image tradition', wherein 'the fundamental authority of the individual event stood, sometimes explicitly, sometimes implicitly, as the epistemic foundation of the edifice of argument'. This is counter-posed to the increasingly statistical modes of sensing, detecting, and measuring the world he describes as the hes 'logic tradition'.[46] The data input for logic tradition processes is typically 'counting' performed by electronic detectors trained to capture and measure particular phenomena. Importantly, the quantitative epistemological paradigm often dismisses the visual paradigm because of the polysemic nature of images and the proliferation of visual meaning.[47]

Computer vision, in its unique mediation of the physical and information worlds, and when refracted through a particular politics, takes these narratives further. Computer vision seems to fulfil conditions described as early as 1990 by media theorist Vilèm Flusser when warning of a world coded by automation and 'technical images'. For Flusser, the programme of technical images involves surfaces being abstracted out of the four dimensions of space and time and then re-projected, still encoded, onto the world 'out there'. The result being that the world 'itself becomes like an image – a context of scenes, of states of things.'[48] The use of images to write the world rather than interpret it thus becomes a form of 'idolatry', wherein humans forget they created images in order to orientate themselves in the world, and 'their lives become a function of their own images . . . '. In other words, computer vision offers the potential to not only understand the world, but through its growing use in creating our cyber-physical environments, to also redraw the world autonomously. Within this imagined world, all knowledge becomes a probabilistic infill, and all relations between image and referent become stochastic.

An element of this discontinuity with previous visual technologies is that within computer vision systems, especially those animated by neural networks, the

[45] See, e.g., Luke Stark, 'Algorithmic Psychometrics and the Scalable Subject' (2018) 42(2) *Social Studies of Science* 204.
[46] Peter Galison, *Image and Logic: A Material Culture of Microphysics* (University of Chicago Press, 1997) 436, 453.
[47] Anne Beaulieu, 'Images Are Not the (Only) Truth: Brain Mapping, Visual Knowledge and Iconoclasm' (2002) 27(1) *Science, Technology, and Human Values* 53.
[48] Vilém Flusser, *Towards a Philosophy of Photography* (Anthony Mathews trans in Reaktion Books, 2000) originally published as *Für Eine Philosophie der Fotographie* (European Photography, 1983).

measurement, encoding and decoding, and knowledge discovery are increasingly automated. The selection of representations – that is, the mechanisms by which the world is presented for analysis – is also increasingly performed by the technical system itself. The elements of images from which meaning is derived in machine learning, the relevant features, are selected through automated learning processes, rather than through the laborious manual process of 'feature engineering'. This is sometimes called 'automated machine learning' or 'end-to-end machine learning'. Through these processes, the clinical is replaced with the empirical, image comprehension is replaced by image computation, observation with measurement, with the truth – the deeper hidden reality – becoming only available in the high-dimensionality that neural networks can access and process.[49]

MEASUREMENT AND REPRESENTATION

Accessing the mathematical substructures of reality requires measurement. Accordingly, computer vision systems do not see – they measure. They measure visual data (x) in order to determine a 'world state' (w).[50] As Sheila Jasanoff notes, 'Any form of data collection involves, to begin with, an act of seeing and recording something that was previously hidden and possibly nameless.'[51] In the same way that photography bypassed the optical unconscious, computer vision profiling is about noticing, measuring, and analysing that which was previously not available to human perception and cognition.[52] The process is complex, however, because the relationship between x and w is not one-to-one. Photographic images are reductions of the three- (or four-)dimensional world into two-dimensions. There are therefore multiple configurations of the three-dimensional world that might result in any particular two-dimensional output. In other words, 'there may be many real-world configurations that are compatible with the same measurements'.[53] Thus the chance that any possible world state is present or true is describable only through probability. Similarly, to recover what is lost in the

[49] Rob Kitchen, 'Big Data, New Epistemologies and Paradigm Shifts' (2014) *Big Data and Society* 1, at 2, where he says, 'Big Data analytics enables an entirely new epistemological approach for making sense of the world; rather than testing a theory by analysing relevant data, new data analytics seeks to gain insights "born from the data".'
[50] Simon J D Prince, *Computer Vision: Models, Learning and Inference* (Cambridge University Press, 2012); Note Rob Kitchen, 'Big Data, New Epistemologies and Paradigm Shifts' (2014) *Big Data and Society* 1, where he quotes Sinan Aral, who states, 'Revolutions in science have often been preceded by revolutions in measurement.'
[51] Sheila Jasanoff, 'Virtual, Visible, and Actionable: Data Assemblages and the Sightlines of Justice' (2017) 4(2) *Big Data and Society* (online), http://journals.sagepub.com/doi/full/10.1177/2053951717724477.
[52] A good example is Professor William T Freeman's work at MIT and Google, where his teams have turned computer vision systems into visual and auditory movement microscopes, highlighting previously undetectable motion in video.
[53] Prince, above n 50. Further, measurements are noisy. And there needs to be a way to separate relevant information for the sake of knowledge production from the recorded image. Probability is also useful for describing noise in recorded data.

dimensional reduction of image-making, computer vision uses very high dimensional systems of measurement, and the statistical relations by which meaning is attributed only become discernible at that high dimensionality.[54]

'Dimensions' are the number of data points in a sample, and can be thought of in the same way that we might think of a person as multi-dimensional, that is, having many different attributes. Image dimensions are typically the Red-Green-Blue (RGB) values for each pixel in an image, inscribed by the translation (or transduction) of light energy to voltage in a sensor, provided as a numerical measurement. These do not have any intrinsic semantic content or meaning. Machine learning systems are, however, able to attribute meaning to those measurements by clustering those high dimensional data points across samples (i.e. images). Different machine learning techniques are simply different ways of clustering these data points. The data that produces classifications (like criminal or non-criminal) are therefore not measurements of facial features within two- or three-dimensional space. Rather, the statistical correlations that give this data meaning exist at higher dimensionality – in statistical environments beyond the visual (three-dimensional) field. It is a hyper-dimensional space based on probabilistic statistical maps that humans cannot navigate without computational systems. In fact, it has been said that if we could see in higher dimensions we wouldn't need machine learning![55] This is how the world becomes 'world state' (w).

Machine learning is computationally demanding, however, and it cannot operate on absolutely all the data that could be derived from an image. Instead, it is necessary to marshal selections of data into 'representations'. When computer vision emerged as a discipline in the 1960s, it became apparent that those technical systems could not respond to the totality of recorded signal (an image). The computational resources required to perform statistical analysis on that amount of data are too immense. Therefore, instead of 'image level computation', computational economy required transformations into symbolic representations.[56]

The inability of computer vision systems to respond directly to the totality of a registered signal has been acknowledged by some as a failure,[57] and others as a fundamental limitation.[58] Nevertheless, it remains the primary mechanism by which computer vision translates measurements of the world into the computational register. As Yoshua Bengio and his co-authors note,

---

[54] This has also been discussed as one of the reasons for machine learning's opacity by Jenna Burrell, 'How the Machine "Thinks": Understanding Opacity in Machine Learning Algorithms' (2016) 3(1) *Big Data and Society* 1.
[55] Pedro Domingos, 'A Few Useful Things to Know about Machine Learning' (2012) 55(10) *Communications of the ACM*.
[56] CM Brown, 'Computer Vision and Natural Constraints' (1984) 224 *Science* 1299.
[57] Prince, above n 50.
[58] Herbert Dreyfus, 'Why Heideggerian AI Failed and How Fixing It Would Require Making It More Heideggerian' (2007) 171(18) *Artificial Intelligence* 1137, where he argues that the use of representations rather than direct sensory input is a limiting factor for artificial intelligence.

much of the actual effort in deploying machine learning algorithms goes into the design of preprocessing pipelines and data transformations that result in a representation of the data that can support effective machine learning. Such feature engineering is important but labour-intensive, and highlights the weakness of current learning algorithms: their inability to extract and organize the discriminative information from the data.[59]

Neural network architectures, however, deploy a different register of representation than the symbolic AI of the 1960s and 1970s as well as earlier machine learning systems. In the last few years, significant research has gone into ways to avoid manual assessments of images to identify what might be relevant for building classifiers (i.e. feature engineering) in favour of a statistical pattern recognition that can identify a relevant feature on the basis of its probabilistic relationship to other features in the environment.[60] This is sometimes called 'representation learning', where a system is fed with raw data 'to automatically discover the representations needed for detection or classification'.[61] This technique reached new heights with deep learning and the convolutional neural networks described above. Deep learning means multiple layers of representation, automatically generated, where each level of representation is more complex and abstract than the previous one. As Yan LeCun explains:

> An image, for example, comes in the form of an array of pixel values, and the learned features in the first layer of representation typically represent the presence or absence of edges at particular orientations and locations in the image. The second layer typically detects motifs by spotting particular arrangements of edges, regardless of small variations in the edge positions. The third layer may assemble motifs into larger combinations that correspond to parts of familiar objects, and subsequent layers would detect objects as combinations of these parts. The key aspect of deep learning is that these layers of features are not designed by human engineers: they are learned from data using a general-purpose learning procedure.[62]

The final layers of representation in neural networks typically represent concepts and classifications. Within these systems, the creation of the representation is performed by the opaque computational processes of the convolutional neural network itself. Put another way, the representation can only really be described as the neural network. Accordingly, the inherent paradox of the technology is the use of correlation to create invisible or inaccessible automated representations in order to surpass the use of manual representation. Neural networks thus overcome the limits of representation with more representations – what Andrejevic has described as

---

[59] Yoshua Bengio, Aaron Courville, and Pascal Vincent, 'Representation Learning: A Review and New Perspectives' (2014) arXiv:1206.5538v3 [cs.LG] 23 April 2014.
[60] See, e.g., Hairong Qi and Wesley E Snyder, *Machine Vision* (Cambridge University Press, 2004).
[61] LeCun, above n 21.
[62] Ibid.

a logic of 'framelessness'.[63] Just like photography, it is a mechanical process of abstraction, though one that operates beyond human comprehension and cognition. As a consequence, some have argued that the deference in data science to probabilistic assessments of what elements of an image are meaningful is part of an insistence that these statistical processes are accessing '[a] hidden layer of reality which is ontologically superior, expressed mathematically and apprehended by going against direct experience'.[64] That position is a radical extrapolation of the enlightenment idea that the better the system of measurement, the more insight it affords,[65] and the better its claim to 'metaphysical objectivity' – i.e. the relationship between representation and truth.[66]

COMPUTATIONAL EMPIRICISM AS A DOMINANT EPISTEMOLOGY

From the above, we can begin to outline various elements of computational empiricism, as a method from the physical sciences applied to people.[67] First, it operates on the basis that external measurement is a more reliable pathway to knowledge than the discursive output of a subject or any expression of self-image. This is, of course, not unique to these practices or technologies, it is simply one element of the empirical schema presented here. It is also not a uniquely visual phenomenon. In addition to the techniques described above, the technology of the stethoscope, for instance, and the practice of 'auscultation' – listening to the body at a physical distance – offers another useful example of technological mediation making the body an object of knowledge. Histories of diagnostic practices with stethoscopes have been invoked to demonstrate the movement from theoretical to perceptual ways of knowing the body, achieved through the combination of rationality and empiricism.[68] This line of thinking describes the ascendance of empiricism in this (medical) context as entwined with

---

[63] Mark Andrejevic, '"Framelessness," or the Cultural Logic of Big Data' in Michael Daubs and Vincent Manzarolle (eds) *Mobile or Ubiquitous Media* (Peter Lang, 2018).
[64] McQuillan, above n 35, 261.
[65] See, e.g., James Bridle, *New Dark Age: Technology and the End of the Future* (Verso, 2018).
[66] Lorraine Daston and Peter Galison, 'The Image of Objectivity' (1992) 40 *Representations* 81.
[67] Note the term 'computational empiricism' was used by Paul Humphries in 'Computational Empiricism' in Bas C van Fraasen (ed) *Topics in the Foundation of Statistics* (1997, Springer) at 119, where he discussed the idea in the context of changing scientific methods associated with the adoption of powerful instrumentation and powerful computational devices. His point is to suggest notions of 'logical empiricism' require updating by computationally oriented methods. The term 'computational positivism' is best described in Roddam Narasimha, 'Axiomatism and Computational Positivism: Two Mathematical Cultures in Pursuit of Exact Sciences' (2003) 38(35) *Economic and Political Weekly* 3650, where he uses the term to describe methodologies in exact sciences and mathematics that focus on matching algorithms to observations rather than drawing conclusions from axioms and models.
[68] See Jonathan Sterne, 'Mediate Auscultation, the Stethoscope, and the "Autopsy of the Living": Medicine's Acoustic Culture' (2001) 22(2) *Journal of Medical Humanities* 115, where he locates this in the work of Michel Foucault's *The Birth of the Clinic* (Pantheon Books, 1973), and S J Reiser's *Medicine and the Reign of Technology* (Cambridge University Press, 1978).

the construction of a new object, and productive of a new medical epistemology of pathological anatomy.[69] The updating of remote sensing in medical applications with new sensors and data science is oriented towards constructing similar epistemologies of pathological behaviours.[70] These forms of empiricism thus go beyond merely extending our perceptual abilities through computational instruments,[71] but also include marginalising the subject's accounting for its own experience.

A second element to the schema is a specific type of computational intervention in the relationship between measurement and classification. On one hand, computational systems differ from other representational technologies because of their capacity to both measure and process quantities of data that are too large for human tabulation, too discrete for human perception, and too complex for human cognitive analysis. This is also not unique in computer vision or data science. Where these techniques differ, however, is the degree of automation in the selection of elements (or features, or dimensions) of a measurement deemed to be meaningful. While the camera is a much older form of 'black box', in computer vision, decisions about what elements of a measurement inform each layer of representation are increasingly displaced into automated learning systems. Those highly political decisions of how the real world is translated into the symbolic register of computation are thus automated according to impenetrable logics. Of course, humans participate in selecting input data (i.e. what the sensor captures) and defining the accuracy of outputs, which each participate in tuning the selection of representations and their parameters, and there is a growing discipline focused on probing how those decisions are made, but the process of producing representations is increasingly dissimulated into the architecture of the system.

A third element of the schema is the implicit claim evident in some work that this process is working towards exposing the fundamental substructures of reality. While there are many other plausible epistemic foundations to data analytics, including the notion that models are always wrong, but sometimes useful,[72] that they are a form of C.S. Peirce's 'abductive reasoning' (i.e. they infer plausible hypotheses rather than verifiable conclusions), or that they enact a form of logic that satisfies the Kantian transcendental ideal,[73] the profound capacities of these systems seem to create, within some communities at least, a reorientation of organising principle towards the belief that increasingly granular measurement and high dimensionality analysis

---

[69] Sterne, above n 68, 117.
[70] See, e.g., Saeed Abdullah and Tanzeem Choudhury, 'Sensing Technologies for Monitoring Serious Mental Illnesses' (2018) 25(1) *IEEE MultiMedia* 61; Rui Wang et al, 'Predicting Symptom Trajectories of Schizophrenia Using Mobile Sensing' (2017) 1(3) *Proceedings of the ACM on Interactive, Mobile, Wearable and Ubiquitous Technologies* 110.
[71] Humphries, above n 68.
[72] George E P Box and Norman R Draper, *Empirical Model Building and Response Surfaces* (Wiley, 1987).
[73] Sebastian Benthall, 'Philosophy of Computational Social Science' (2016) 12(2) *Cosmos and History: The Journal of Natural and Social Philosophy* 13.

has the capacity to reveal hidden truths. This computational variant of realism has been described by Dan McQuillan as 'machinic neoplatonism'.[74] That is, a metaphysical commitment to a world of truth, form, and idea existing behind, and only imperfectly imprinting on, the world of the humanly sensible, accessible only through mathematics. Rather than being a particular method, for McQuillan, it represents an automated applied philosophy.

A fourth element is the growing connection between states and the private and corporate entities that create, disseminate, promote, and sell data science products and services. Beyond whatever contestable epistemological framework a data scientist invokes, the political power to implement it as a knowledge-logic stems from these relations. When photography rose to prominence, the companies selling film and cameras were not the largest corporations in the world. Today, the company with the highest commercial evaluation in the United States is Amazon – a company that not only sells data science and computer vision products and services (including to police forces), but also controls the infrastructure that carries the majority of data storage and computation in North America.[75] Indeed, Amazon is attempting to establish itself as part of the broader state governance apparatus, and may potentially control the US Department of Defence data cloud if it wins the $10 billion JEDI bid. While Amazon and Microsoft have become major purveyors of data analytics, other technology companies like Facebook and Google control massive data collection infrastructures, and together, these companies control the majority of the technological systems that structure the very means of information dissemination and interpersonal exchange. Some have described these conditions in terms of 'data power',[76] but this could also be extended to 'computational power' (in its political as well as technical meaning), 'analytics power', and even 'epistemological power' – the capacity to validate a knowledge claim or system. Indeed, if the phenomenal advances in artificial intelligence in recent times are the product of massive amounts of data collection and computational power, then these private entities control the tools for the production of knowledge, and have an agenda of securing its legitimacy.

The epistemological character of these practices, then, cannot be attributed to the technological systems alone, but rather to a mix of the inherent 'program' of the technical 'apparatus',[77] and political context. Sabina Leonelli, for instance, has argued that the interest in big data in the sciences is not just a matter of its novel

[74] McQuillan, above n 35.
[75] See, e.g., Lina M Khan 'Amazon's Antitrust Paradox' (2016) 126 *Yale Law Journal* 710.
[76] Orla Lynskey, 'Grappling with "Data Power": Normative Nudges from Data Protection and Privacy' (2019) 20(1) *Theoretical Inquiries in Law* 189.
[77] These terms are intended to follow the definitions provided by Vilém Flusser, the book includes a Glossary. At (83) '*Apparatus* (pl. *-es*): a plaything or game that simulates thought [*trans.* An overarching term for a non-human agency, e.g. the camera, the computer and the "apparatus" of the State or of the market]; organization or system that enables something to function.' At (84) '*Program: a* combination game with clear and distinct elements [*trans.* A term whose associations include computer programs, hence the US spelling].'

technological characteristics, but its status in the scientific community, which is epistemologically generative. Indeed, the same could be said for how these commercial entities have influenced the reception of data science in service of governance and law enforcement, which thus produce their own epistemic communities around the production of knowledge about people through machine learning and computer vision profiling. Indeed, university professors and researchers are increasingly funded by these companies, with key figures establishing data science schools and institutes (as well as social science, law, and humanities groups that propose ethical and regulatory limitations to their application). To that end, these companies have an interest (and indeed pursue an agenda) in the quality and legitimacy of knowledge claims produced through machine learning technologies.

In democratic society we outsource so much decision-making to regulatory bodies that not only do we not know how they come to their conclusions about what technologies are safe and fair, but we also do not know how to evaluate those questions. But this computational empiricist agenda is not necessarily being driven by states and regulatory agencies.[78] It is being driven by a new weird composite of states and the private sector. This amalgam becomes determinative of what it means to know, who is entitled to know, and with what tools. In this context, the science of government is cybernetics, which has its own understanding of the human, identity, and the self. As summarised neatly by 'The Invisible Committee':

> Officially, we continue to be governed by the old dualistic Western paradigm where there is the subject and the world, the individual and society, men and machines, the mind and the body, the living and the nonliving. These are distinctions that are still generally taken to be valid. In reality, cybernetized capitalism does practice an ontology, and hence an anthropology, whose key elements are reserved for its initiates. The rational Western subject, aspiring to master the world and governable thereby, gives way to the cybernetic conception of a being without an interiority, of a selfless self, an emergent, climatic being, constituted by its exteriority, by its relations.[79]

The application of those logics is now approaching a new crescendo with the understanding of personal data, and its relationship to identity, not merely as a representation, but as a pattern as to behaviour, emotion, and desire, computed recursively in real-time, and optimised towards particular goals.

SUBJECTIVITY AND CYBERNETICS

In the introduction to this book, narrative identity was discussed as a privileged notion of self. There are multiple ideas as to what constitutes narrative identity, but

---

[78] Sheila Jasanoff, 'The Practices of Objectivity in Regulatory Science' in Charles Camic, Neil Gross, and Michèle Lamont (eds) *Social Knowledge in the Making* (University of Chicago Press, 2011) 307.
[79] The Invisible Committee, 'Fuck Off, Google' (2014) www.anonymous-france.eu/IMG/pdf/the-invisible-committee-fuck-off-google.pdf.

they seem to share a general foundation that humans are fundamentally self-interpreting beings. 'Self' in these ideas is based on the notion that 'there is a form of explanation necessary to describing human lives that does not reduce to physical or biological explanation and gives events and actions significance'.[80] But as argued above, identity and self should not be conceptualised in the abstract. Identity is a product of practices, forms of governance, and scientific discourse.[81] The internal and external, or narrative and categorical, ideas of identity that have been operationalised in the law are also products of particular social and technological environments. Specifically, these definitions of identity are deeply connected to the idea of the image and the persona, the role of writing, certain scientific, philosophical accounts of mind, and of specific citizen–state configurations. In other words, the narrative notion of self is intuitive primarily in the context of static documentary systems of representation. The techno-political shifts that have emerged over the past century, however, mean that we now inhabit a very different technological, social, scientific, and political environment, with new consequences for the structuring of identity.

A recent example may help clarify how computational systems address persons in emerging technological environments. While this example describes speculative rather than mainstream data science applications, it also exposes the horizon of inside thinking about the nature of humans under contemporary conditions. In May 2018, *The Verge* and *Fortune* published a leaked internal video produced in 2016 by designers at 'X' – one of Google's (or rather Alphabet's) experimental research labs – called 'The Selfish Ledger'.[82] Subsequently dismissed by Google as 'speculative design', the video expressed the idea that user data might be best understood as analogous to a Lamarckian epigenome. This theorisation posits user data as a 'ledger', analogous to a genetic code, that evolves and adapts through interaction with the environment. Genetic adaptation through environmental interaction (rather than natural selection) was the basis of Lamarck's evolutionary theory.[83] Lamarck wrote of evolution in 1809, before Darwin, and neo-Lamarckism emerged in the middle of the nineteenth century to attack Darwin's theory of natural selection. Lamarckian evolutionary ideas interpreted genetic adaptations as *ecological* rather than innate or endogenous (as is the case with natural selection). Lamarck's model looked at the interplay of habitats (the conditions under which an organism lives, which provide environmental pressures) and habits (the process for adapting the organism to new needs). Modification through habits then proliferate through reproduction. The essence of Lamarckism, then, is 'that the controlling factor or

---

[80] Sydney Shoemaker 'On What We Are' and Marya Schechtman, 'The Narrative Self' in Shaun Gallagher (ed) *The Oxford Handbook of the Self* (Oxford University Press, 2011).
[81] Nikolas Rose, *Inventing the Self: Psychology, Power, and Personhood* (Cambridge University Press, 1998).
[82] Vlad Savov 'Google's Selfish Ledger Is an Unsettling Vision of Silicon Valley Social Engineering' *The Verge* (17 May 2018) www.theverge.com/2018/5/17/17344250/google-x-selfish-ledger-video-data-privacy.
[83] Edward J Pfeifer, 'The Genesis of American Neo-Lamarckism' (1965) 56(2) *Isis* 156, 157.

process in evolution is functional, and that acquired characters are readily transmissible'.[84]

The Selfish Ledger video combines the Lamarckian idea of data as 'genetic' with ideas from the life sciences made famous by Richard Dawkins in The Selfish Gene that interpret animal behaviours as determined by benefit to genes rather than individuals. In that model, the human is reconceptualised as a vehicle for genetic content.[85] The Selfish Ledger thus interrogates the possibility of a 'data ledger' as the critical content of self that is adapted through environmental interaction, made possible by the human 'custodian'. Critically, the ledger is no longer a historical register of behaviour or transactions, but a volitional or teleological artefact. The data ledger becomes less an 'index' and more an agent capable of participating in goal satisfaction. This figures the individual as amenable for behavioural optimisation, wherein human behaviours are engineered to satisfy the ledger, or at least shift behaviour closer to the ledger's target. The ledger eventually becomes a site of agency within the person, generating its own suggestions as to appropriate goals, even directing behaviours towards producing more data to assist with further behavioural optimisation. The ledger, when informed by multiple generations of users, is pitched at affording a richer understanding of 'who we are as people', with the idea that we can sequence human behaviour in much the same way as we were able to sequence the human genome – and edit that sequence in a similar way for desirable consequences. This example is not to raise the trite observation that we are being 'conditioned to obey.' The purpose is to highlight how, from the perspective of the profilers (and to a certain undeniable extent, to ourselves), the boundaries of human identity and experience are expanding in a systemic and informational way. In the view of the profilers, data is not simply an index or static representation. In fact, it highlights the need for a new language to describe the relationship between informaiton and embodied self.

The video also connects to twentieth-century cybernetics ideas that have greatly influenced the development of computing and governance, and arguably continue to influence the epistemological commitments of data science. These ideas structure the self as an information processing node that receives inputs and produces outputs. This is the legacy of an intellectual movement focused on understanding humans as defined by behavioural patterns. Norbert Weiner speaks to this conception of humanity, for instance, in his famous quote:

> Our tissues change as we live: the food we eat and the air we breathe become flesh of our flesh and bone of our bone, and the momentary elements of our flesh and bone pass out of our body every day with our excreta. We are but whirlpools in a river of ever-flowing water. We are not stuff that abides but patterns that endure.[86]

---

[84] See, e.g., L H Bailey 'Neo-Lamarckism and Neo-Darwinism' (1894) 28(332) The American Naturalist 661, 662.
[85] Richard Dawkins, The Selfish Gene (Oxford University Press, 1976).
[86] Norbert Weiner, The Human Use of Human Beings: Cybernetics and Society (Doubleday, 1950).

The origins of this thinking are laid out in the essay Weiner wrote, along with Arturo Rosenblueth and Julian Bigelow, entitled 'Behavior, Purpose and Teleology'.[87] By acknowledging the concept of 'purpose', the authors were introducing ideas of voluntary activity into machinic understandings, or rather extending machinic process to include notions of purpose, voluntariness, and in a sense, agency. In other words, they bring the metaphors of servomechanisms, negative feedback (i.e. teleological feedback), and self-guiding torpedoes to bear on human behaviour as a way of understanding the relationship between input and output.

This approach was intended to reveal 'that a uniform behavioristic analysis is applicable to both machines and living organisms, regardless of the complexity of the behavior',[88] for which the essay then becomes a treatise. This early work, for which Wiener was the primary protagonist, investigated human–machine integration, often conceptualising humans as the 'machine in the middle' that could offer corrective feedback to the machinic elements. 'Effective human-machine integration required that people and machines be comprehended in similar terms, so that human-machine systems could be engineered to maximise the performance of both kinds of components.'[89] These ideas then led to the question, posed by neuropsychiatrist Warren McCulloch at the 1948 Hixon Symposium on Cerebral Mechanisms in Behaviour at California Institute of Technology, 'Why is the mind in the head?'[90]

Associated understandings of self, mind, and identity along these lines became more concrete cognitivist philosophies and psychologies in the 1950s and 1960s. These disciplines recast cognition as fundamentally symbolic information processing or computation of physically represented symbols. Information theory gave new terminologies and systems of quantification to facilitate human integration into control systems by reconfiguring human action as a combination of sensory devices, computational processes, amplifications, and mechanical linkages into other systems. McCulloch, along with his colleague Walter Pitts, developed mathematical formulations for artificial neurons and neuronal networks as heuristics for understanding human cognitive function, operating through firing or inhibition as a product of stimulation from surrounding neurons' activity.[91] Social scientists like Gregory Bateson began arguing that mental processes such as 'ideas, communication, differentiation, pattern, and so on, are matters of form rather than substance'.[92]

[87] Arturo Rosenblueth, Norbert Wiener, and Julian Bigelow, 'Behavior, Purpose and Teleology' (1943) 10(1) *Philosophy of Science* 18.
[88] Ibid 22.
[89] Paul Edwards, *The Closed World: Computers and the Politics of Discourse in Cold War America* (MIT Press, 1996) 148.
[90] Warren S McCulloch, 'Why Is the Mind in the Head?' in L A Jeffress (ed) *The Hixon Symposium* (John Wiley, 1951).
[91] Warren McCulloch and Walter Pitts, 'A Logical Calculus of the Ideas Immanent in Nervous Activity' (1943) 5 *Bulletin of Mathematical Biophysics* 115.
[92] Gregory Bateson, *Steps to an Ecology of Mind* (University of Chicago Press, 2000) xxiii.

In doing so, he challenged the idea of self as a transcendent entity, instead insisting that 'the total self-corrective unit which processes information, or, as I say, "thinks" and "acts" and "decides", is a *system* whose boundaries do not at all coincide with the boundaries either of the body or of what is popularly called the "self" or "consciousness"'.[93] Donna Haraway has discussed these changes in terms of biology being reconfigured from a 'science of sexual organisms to one of reproducing genetic assemblages' with 'engineering [becoming] the guiding logic of life science in the 20th century.'[94]

In a world understood, narrativised, and operationalised this way, the nature of identity dramatically changes.[95] In an information processing environment, identities become composites of inter-related parts, with the specific patterns of inter-relation constituting the structures that sustain identity, rather than identity being some 'supernatural entity that exists irrespective of what happens between its components'.[96] Theorists like Paul Stokes, for instance, thus challenge the ideas of internal/external, *ipse/idem*, and narrative/categorical identity, with more ecological, multi-layered understandings. Stokes's account of identity, for instance, begins with an enactive level of operational units that produce the system in question, including the behavioural elements that represent us contextually from situation to situation. This proceeds to the pattern level of related enactive layer elements, which produces a meta-identity or personality. A coherence and integration level follows, a homeostatic idea concerned with systemic cohesion and internal regulation, which engages in the real-time control of actual events and achieves the real-time cohesion of the composite elements. Next is an anticipatory level, which anticipates patterns by projecting forward into the future. Last, self-reference levels generate self-image and sense of self, attribute behaviour as metaphor to the identity in question, and generate the ongoing 'truth' (i.e. fiction) of self by managing interactions between the coherence and anticipatory levels. These ideas are not entirely inconsistent with certain notions of narrative self and identity, especially if it is understood that 'human brains are narrative generating machines and selves are the protagonists of the narratives they generate'.[97] But in this view, neither the brain nor the biological human organism are essential to self.

This thinking is thus better understood as inverting narrative identity, positing self-referential accounts as a fiction, used to maintain a psychologically integrated perception of self as an individual by dismissing the true self's deeply composite nature. The argument made here is that by continuing to enact and enforce laws on

---

[93] Gregory Bateson, 'The Cybernetics of "Self": A Theory of Alcoholics Anonymous' in Gregory Bateson (ed) *Steps to an Ecology of Mind* (University of Chicago Press, 2000) 309.
[94] Donna Haraway, 'The Biological Enterprise: Sex, Mind, and Profit from Human Engineering to Sociobiology' (1979) 20 *Radical History Review* 206.
[95] See, e.g., Gerald Adams, 'Identity: A Brief Critique of a Cybernetic Model' (1997) 12(3) *Journal of Adolescent Research* 358.
[96] Paul Stokes, 'Identity: Articulating Cybernetics and Sociology' (2006) 35 *Kybernetes* 124.
[97] Ibid.

the basis of ideas of identity produced in dynamic relations with older 'representational' technologies, we may be distracting ourselves from the political reality of what identity and self mean (or how they are constructed and operationalised) in the contemporary milieu of real-time computation, data science, and optimisation. For the sake of clarification, this is not to argue that human identity or the notion of self necessarily reflect these ideas, but rather that these are part of the ways humans are constructed and construct themselves through contemporary knowledge-generating practices. These are the 'truth games',[98] the pragmatic operations and rhetorics of identity that the law must contend with in the contemporary context. Thinking about the proper register of legal intervention means facing the question, what are humans now from the (data) scientific standpoint? What is the meaning of identity usurpation when identity is understood as a pattern of behaviour? Does this offend fundamental notions or values in similar ways? Does this problematise legal notions centred on 'taking back control' as fantastical?

CONCLUSION

This chapter has attempted to outline some emerging challenges produced by a profound new technical capacity. Lawmakers now have to contend with new iterations of a philosophy insisting that measuring everything and drawing knowledge from those measurements is the path to truth. Addressing this reality means clarifying how computer vision systems and data science applications are merely apparatuses, combining and computing symbols that encode the world a particular way, according to particular programs. Without intervention at that level, digital systems risk simultaneously constituting both the world and the dominant understanding of it.[99] Constraining data science through law therefore means exposing the difference between world and 'world state', and challenging the idea that such systems access a 'hidden reality' instead of producing and operationalising a *para*-reality built from *para*-visual representations. But it also means understanding what the subject actively situated within complex webs of technical and computational (and potentially legal) relations might want from the law, and what existing legal regimes might not be tooled to provide.

---

[98] Luther H Martin, Huck Gutman, and Patrick H Hutton (eds) *Technologies of the Self: A Seminar with Michel Foucault* (University of Massachusetts Press, 1988).

[99] See, e.g., Leif Weatherby, 'Digital Metaphysics: The Cybernetic Idealism of Warren McCulloch' (2018) 20(1) *The Hedgehog Review* (online), https://iasc-culture.org/THR/THR_article_2018_Spring_Weatherby.php.

9

Person, Place, and Contest in the World State

How should law address the conversion of the body into information? How should law address the computational empiricist position in which the quantitative is the path to knowledge, and the world of infinite possibility exists in the data rather than the human spirit? How should law address the move from a logic of 'approximation' to a logic of 'revelation' in data science practices? How should it deal with profiles built not from disaggregated datasets but the application of machine learning models to data collected from the 'real world'? In other words, how should law address the 'world state'? The following chapter first outlines some of the new legal ideas gaining prominence in this context, and then presents a series of further strategies, including introducing new mechanisms into information environments to build boundaries and increase friction with respect to the processing of data. Introducing more structure into information environments is intended to contest or limit the ability to build meaning and knowledge through systems that treat data as ontologically flat and indiscriminate, whereby knowledge becomes a product exclusively of statistical operations on data rather than any connection to a semantic referent. A second strategy is extending the mechanisms of algorithmic accountability, such as fairness and explainability, into mechanisms for contestation, giving individuals greater participation in how statistical systems measure and analyse them. A final strategy for addressing emerging types of profiling involves extending the ways we have typically thought about protecting identity in, and exploring different ways of thinking through, the connection between an embodied person and their data. This is not an investigation of 'virtual personhood', but rather the possibility of 'composite identities' premised on linkages between the physical and virtual, that might be useful for law. In particular, the discussion imagines a new 'legal person', capable of addressing profiling in cyber-physical systems, not defined by the capacity to impose an internal narrative self-truth over an external representation, but rather by defining identity as an *interface* to the world. While these are by no means trivial engineering tasks, and their precise formulations would require considerable further research, these strategies are hopefully useful for guiding further thinking about the building of accountable systems.

NEW NORMS IN THE WORLD STATE

There have been multiple attempts to rethink what law could do in the contemporary technological environment. Below is an outline of some of the more compelling ideas for defining meaningful restrictions of profiling in this context.

A Right to Reasonable Inferences

One register of legal thinking tells us to dig-in harder – to keep arguing for the primacy of the autonomous liberal subject capable of exercising control over their external sites of identity. This first approach discussed briefly in Chapter 7, extends data subject rights from the capacity to shape the data on which decisions are made, into the capacity to contest the quality of a profile directly. Building on Hildebrandt's critique of data protection's application to data rather than 'knowledge' from 2008,[1] Wachter and her collaborators suggest a 'right to reasonable inferences' that would constrain the type of inferences or profiles may be produced about a person.[2] Those authors see the introduction of a reasonableness standard as a complement to the right to contest profiling and automated decision-making in Article 22 of the GDPR. They suggest that presently, the capacity to challenge automated decisions will only be successful if the input data is incorrect or incomplete in some way, or if the processing violates some external principle like anti-discrimination law. However, a right to reasonable inferences would allow making the argument to the human-in-the-loop provided by Article 22 that a conclusion, inference, or profile is not reasonable based on the 'reasoning' or 'parameters' of the decision itself.

This seems a sensible, non-controversial, and in many ways intuitive approach. If an entity produces profiles of people, those profiles or inferences *should* be 'reasonable'. However, this proposal also highlights the tension between data protection's logic of privileging the discursive subject, and the profiling logic of looking beyond the discursive subject to find the truth about them. For instance, the authors see this right as 'derived from the right to privacy when viewed as a mechanism intended to protect identity, reputation, and capacities for self-presentation'.[3] Reasonableness would thus be measured through a comparison of the data subject's self-image and how the profiler interprets them, with the goal of constraining the boundaries of that interpretation according to what the data subject might see in themselves. However, actuarial and statistical thinking now dominate profiling decisions across domains like policing, criminal justice, finance, insurance, or any other field that involves measuring a person in terms of comparative risk. The entire premise of those systems

---

[1] Mireille Hildebrandt, 'Defining Profiling: A New Type of Knowledge?' in Mireille Hildebrandt and Serge Gutwirth (eds) *Profiling the European Citizen* (Springer, 2008) 17.
[2] Sandra Wachter and Brett Mittelstadt, 'A Right to Reasonable Inferences: Re-Thinking Data Protection law in the Age of Big Data and AI' (2019) 2 *Columbia Business Law Review* 494.
[3] Ibid 580.

is rejecting an individual's account of self in favour of a socialised statistical account. Statistical society insists that we *are* representable and interpretable beyond our understandings of self, and that those representations *ought* to be put to work establishing our rights and obligations. A right to reasonable inferences thus faces the challenge of finding a way to impose a discursive logic in that statistical terrain.

Human Non-computability

Beyond the imposition of an internal narrative self over the images and representations produced by others, some have suggested ways to protect what is uncountable, incalculable or *incomputable* about individual persons.[4] These are typically framed as ways of insisting that there is no 'true' or correct account of an individual, and therefore that the patterns or representations constituting how we are known must not be overly rigid or determinative. At a basic level, this idea is visible in discussions of 'obfuscation' and 'inaccuracy' as privacy protecting.[5] There is a privacy value in undermining the capacity to precisely target individuals. Similar ideas animate techniques like 'adversarial machine learning' that introduce noise into machine learning classification systems. Those approaches can successfully confuse computer vision classifiers, for instance, by perturbing digital images in ways that are undetectable to humans. Hildebrandt takes these ideas further however, and directs them precisely at data science's program of quantification – what she describes as the 'overcomplete datafication of anything and everything based on the idea that the mathematics that grounds all these machines reveals the ultimate layer of a hidden reality'.[6] She thus suggests a right to human non-computability built on the philosophical principle of indeterminate identity. This is not necessarily a return to older opacity paradigms of privacy – a relocation of the black box to the level of the individual – but rather a mechanism for limiting certain classes of knowledge claims, and thus challenging the epistemological primacy of data science. In one compelling expression, it is achieved through 'agonistic machine learning' systems, as a way of 'demanding that companies or governments that base decisions on machine learning must explore and enable alternative ways of datafying and modelling the same event, person or action'.[7] Agonistic systems would demonstrate how each act of computation relies on a particular system of measurements, representations, and analytics. Rather than challenging human computability wholesale, the project highlights how humans can be computed in multiple ways, in order to 'ward off monopolistic claims about the "true" or the "real" representation of human

[4] Mireille Hildebrandt, 'Privacy as Protection of the Incomputable Self: From Agnostic to Agonistic Machine Learning' (2019) 20 *Theoretical Inquiries in Law* 83.
[5] Gloria Gomez Fuster, 'Inaccuracy as a Privacy Enhancing Tool' (2010) 12 *Ethics of Information Technology* 87; see also Finn Brunton and Helen Nissenbaum, *Obfuscation: A User's Guide for Privacy and Protest* (MIT Press, 2015).
[6] Hildebrandt, above n 4, 95–96.
[7] Ibid 106.

beings'.[8] This is arguably also a form of 'explanation', but importantly one targeted at the decision-making process itself rather than how different inputs might produce different outputs. In other words, it is an explanation mechanism informing how to transcend the solution space of any particular decision. Such an approach facilitates 'a say in the conditions of our own legibility',[9] and a 'right to co-determine how we are read',[10] highlighting the role individuals could play in protecting themselves. How such an approach might become the basis for computational mechanisms of contestation is discussed later in the chapter. However, before outlining that strategy, it is important to point out some other emerging themes in the legal thinking.

Manipulation

The nature of profiling, the measurement and analysis of behavioural, emotional, and psychological information, the use of 'dark patterns' in interface design, and the growing disciplines of 'behavioural informatics' and 'mechanism design', are about more than simply creating representations – they are about actively shaping behaviour. Dark patterns involve the design of user interfaces to engineer certain interactions that are not necessarily in the user's best interest.[11] Examples include frustrating or channelling user choice through the presentation of an interface, by making desirable options difficult to find, guilting users into compliance with emotive language, or outright trickery. Similarly, mechanism design, while not necessarily nefarious or negative, also includes the computational governance of behaviour. This discipline considers the design of mediating structures between interacting agents, such that the equilibrium behaviour of the agents is optimised towards some objective. The typical example is online auctions. However, in light of these techniques, it becomes clear that behaviour in informational environments is no longer only controlled through mechanisms of access and denial or automated rule enforcement. Instead, 'code' means designing mathematically mediated, game-theoretically informed environments, platforms, and infrastructures that engineer *rational* behaviour of the interacting agents towards certain purposes. Beyond e-commerce, these techniques are being explored in public health, the design of public spaces, energy regulation,[12] criminal justice systems,[13] among others. It is not

[8] Ibid 106.
[9] Julie E Cohen, 'Turning Privacy Inside Out' (2019) 20 *Theoretical Inquiries in Law* 1, 12.
[10] Mireille Hildebrandt, 'Law as an Affordance: The Devil Is in the Vanishing Point' (2017) 4(1) *Critical Analysis of Law* 116, 124.
[11] Colin M Gray et al, 'The Dark (Patterns) Side of UX Design' (Paper presented at the 2018 CHI Conference on Human Factors in Computing Systems, Montreal QC, Canada, 21–26 April, 2018).
[12] See, e.g., Phillip Cash, Charlotte Gram Hartley, and Christine Boysen Durazo, 'Behavioural Design: A Process for Integrating Behavior Change and Design' (2017) 48 *Design Studies* 96.
[13] See, e.g., Werner Güth, 'Mechanism Design and the Law' in Francesco Parisi (ed) *The Oxford Handbook of Law and Economics: Volume 1: Methodology and Concepts* (Oxford University Press, 2017) 483; Ron Siegel and Bruno Strulovici 'Judicial Mechanism Design' (Working Paper, August 2018).

impossible to imagine them extended into mechanisms for guiding decisions on healthcare, education, policing, civic participation, navigating borders, sanctioning conduct, and general administrative governance.

Another relevant example gaining attention is 'personalised law'. This branch of law and economics thinking involves data collection and profiling to personalise the communication or execution of legal obligations.[14] The idea is that legal norms can be made more granular than in their present 'impersonal' form, with normative obligations crafted to the profile of the legal 'user' in order to best achieve compliance. In many ways, this makes a great deal of sense. Why do we distinguish, for instance, legal obligations as dependent on whether an individual is older or younger than 18 rather than by their actual age? Beyond age however, Ariel Porat and Lior Strahilevitz have argued that legal duties and rules could be based on different psychological personality types. The majority of research in this area has considered applications such as mandatory disclosures in contract and consumer law, and even standards of care in tort. But it is also possible to imagine this applied in a far greater range of scenarios that might even affect how individuals move through space, or dictate what (even potentially sometimes criminal) behaviours are permissible or forbidden in any context. Some have even explored using virtual assistants to manage the relevant techno-legal communications (sometimes called micro-directives)[15] to users.[16] As one author notes, 'in the arena of lawmaking, the next methodological frontier will most likely follow from an audacious combination of behavioural studies and data science'.[17] Such a law-making method would almost certainly involver greater participation by non-state actors capable of executing the relevant data science.[18] It also highlights the role of the user as the relevant legal subject or person, emphasizing the importance of the profile in cyber-physical systems.

Profiling is critical to these types of behavioural engineering tasks. Online behavioural advertising provides another clear example, and uses profiles as input for determining what message will be presented to a user, and in what way. Increasingly, this includes psychometric or psychographic profiling to nuance to the design and delivery of that message. As a particularly insightful piece on machine learning in behavioural advertising from *The Intercept* notes, 'Instead of merely offering advertisers the ability to target people based on demographics and consumer preferences, Facebook instead offers the ability to target them based on how they will behave,

---

[14] See e.g., Ariel Porat and Lior Jacob Strahilevitz, 'Personalizing Default Rules and Disclosure with Big Data' (2014) 112(8) *Michigan Law Review* 1417.
[15] Anthony J. Casey and Anthony Niblett, 'The Death of Rules and Standards' (2017) 92(4) *Indiana Law Journal* 1401.
[16] Christoph Busch, 'Implementing Personalized Law: Personalized Disclosures in Consumer Law and Data Privacy Law' (2019) 86 *The University of Chicago Law Review* 308.
[17] Philipp Hacker, 'Nudge 2.0 – The Future of Behavioural Analysis of Law, in Europe and Beyond. A Review of "Nudge and the Law: A European Perspective", edited by Alberto Alemano and Anne-Lise Sibony' (2016) 24 *European Law Review* 297.
[18] Andrew Verstein, 'Privatizing Personalized Law' (2019) 86 *The University of Chicago Law Review* 551.

what they will buy, and what they will think.'[19] This reminds us that the law of profiling needs to attend to a double-relation between embodied person and digital identity. On one hand, there is the interpretive space between event, phenomena, or experience, and its representation. On the other is the space between representation and subsequent action or behaviour. 'Operability', how a profile can be put to use, is thus becoming a critical concern.[20] To that end, another emerging set of legal norms must address not only the generation of profiles, but how those profiles affect embodied and informational behaviour.

Cass Sunstein's *Nudge* and Daniel Kahneman's *Thinking Fast and Slow* are now highly influential texts for technology developers.[21] Legal scholars and philosophers of technology have growing awareness that such practices are an integral dimension of contemporary information environments. In 2011, Hildebrandt and Rouvroy edited a collection on agency in the context of 'autonomic computing' – the hidden background operations that define 'smart' environments.[22] Karen Yeung, for instance, has also written about 'hypernudging', a condition whereby informational choice contexts are configured through algorithmic analysis in order to nudge user choices in directions preferred by the choice architect.[23] Others like Tal Zarsky and Ryan Calo have written lucidly about manipulation in online contexts.[24] These technological realities have prompted further philosophical reflection on what constitutes manipulation in contemporary digital contexts.[25] Daniel Susser, Beate Roessler, and Helen Nissenbaum have thus explored how manipulation, which they define as 'the process of subverting another person's decision-making power by imposing a hidden influence on them', might be reformulated in digital

---

[19] Sam Biddle, 'Facebook Uses Artificial Intelligence to Predict Your Future Actions for Advertisers, Says Confidential Document', *The Intercept* (online), 13 April 2018 https://theintercept.com/2018/4/13/facebook-advertising-data-artifical-intelligence-ai.

[20] As Antoinette Rouvroy notes,

We can give rights to individuals on their personal data, and this is necessary. But all these rights are not applicable to everything that I am describing here. Big Data is interested in categorising a quantity of persons but without being concerned about these persons individually. We by-pass the subjectivity and we thus arrive at a kind of very objective operability – a kind of machinic objectivity. Antoinette Rouvroy and Bernard Steigler, 'The Digital Regime of Truth: From the Algorithmic Governmentality to a New Rule of Law' (2016) 3 *La Deleuziana: Online Journal of Philosophy* 12.

[21] Richard H Thaler and Cass R Sunstein, *Nudge: Improving Decisions about Health, Wealth, and Happiness* (Yale University Press, 2008); Daniel Kahneman, *Thinking Fast and Slow* (Farrar, Straus, and Giroux, 2011).

[22] Mireille Hildebrandt and Antoinette Rouvroy (eds) *Law, Human Agency and Autonomic Computing: The Philosophy of Law Meets the Philosophy of Technology* (Routledge, 2011).

[23] Karen Yeung, '"Hypernudge": Big Data as a Mode of Regulation by Design' (2016) 1 *Information, Communication & Society* 19.

[24] See, e.g., Tal Z Zarsky, 'Online Privacy, Tailoring, and Persuasion' in Katherine J Strandburg and Daniela Stan Raicu (eds) *Privacy and Technologies of Identity* (Springer, 2006); Ryan Calo, 'Digital Market Manipulation' (2013) 82 *George Washington Law Review* 995.

[25] See Daniel Susser, Beate Roessler, and Helen Nissenbaum, 'Online Manipulation: Hidden Influences in a Digital World' (Working Paper, SSRN, 8 January 2019).

environments.[26] They separate manipulation from coercion or persuasion because the latter two leave the decision-maker's capacity for decision-making intact, whereas the former undermines agency with the manipulator 'taking hold of the controls', causing a person to make decisions that they cannot account for themselves.

Online manipulation implicates profiles and profiling because it operates in the space between profile and behaviour. However, the line between permissible and objectionable influence on human will is difficult to define. It is unclear whether manipulation is even a legally meaningful category. Consumer law standards like 'misleading and deceptive conduct' may be enough in this context. But the issue is complex, and there might be more at stake. Discussions of manipulation typically take human 'autonomy' for their definitional counterpoint and normative orientation. As Catriona Mackenzie specifies:

> Underpinning the normative requirement to respect another's autonomy is the presumption that autonomy confers normative authority over one's life; the authority to make decisions of practical importance to one's life, for one's own reasons, whatever those reasons might be. Autonomous persons are presumed to have the capacity, the right and the responsibility to exercise this authority, even if they do not always exercise it wisely.[27]

These capacities are what are implicated by manipulation. Mackenzie goes on to note, 'A widespread intuition in the literature is that normative authority derives in some way from the connection between autonomy and the agent's practical identity or evaluative first-person perspective.' In other words, discourses around autonomy typically put practical ideas of evaluative or narrative identity to work, assuming the possibility of a self-determining subject whose decision-making capacities, and thus sense of self, are undermined through manipulation.

On the other hand, Ryan Calo argues that autonomy is a difficult normative parameter in the context of online manipulation.[28] He notes that while thinking through autonomy, in the sense that Julie Cohen describes as 'the modality through which situated subjects advance their own contingent goals', may be instinctual, autonomy is both very difficult to define and to measure against the entire spectrum of possible incursions on human will. Calo therefore suggests the effects of manipulation (in his example in the online market) are better defined as the material construction of 'irrationality'. Put another way, the problematic dimension of market manipulation is the generating of profitable irrationality on the part of the consumer. It is unclear, however, whether this standard would be applicable to systems that exploit rational choices rather than generate irrational ones. Indeed, the

---

[26] Ibid 22.
[27] Catriona Mackenzie, 'Relational Autonomy, Normative Authority and Perfectionism' (2008) 39 *Journal of Social Philosophy* 512, 512.
[28] Calo, above n 24.

distinction between rational and irrational action may be increasingly difficult to draw, perhaps challenging the utility of rationality as a metric. Nonetheless, it does appear that the 'optimisation' of concern here takes us beyond market manipulation, and into a new type of communicative dynamic between embodied person, profile, and information environment.

Optimisation

For online manipulation, a profile is used to inform the selection of messages presented to a user, to change how that message is presented, or to make incursions into information environments through notifications – a tool made far more effective and pervasive with smart phones. In fact, there are myriad techniques for driving desirable behaviour going up and down the technology stack, from protocol design to interface design. The generic example is that the information platform communicates to the user, using the profile as ammunition for targeted messaging. However, in more speculative examples like *The Selfish Ledger*, the relationship between profiling and identity involves different and more complex communicative dynamics.

The Selfish Ledger may be a stylised and speculative account of profiling in the 'world state', but it demonstrates the thinking behind this type of behavioural optimisation, where the ledger or profile is conceptualised as a purposeful agent, and the interaction between behavioural ledger and embodied person is optimised to achieve certain behaviours. Using a virtual assistant in a personalised law application might include a similar dynamic. In these examples, the profile plays a more active role. Here, the profile or ledger is a recursive index built from sensing and tracking the actions of the embodied user, which communicates back to that user through a platform, for a particular purpose. The profile thus takes on the character of a 'smart' agent. It is considered volitional, able to design and express its own goals (or channel the goals of another entity), and execute them through recursive information flows with an embodied person. An example given in *The Selfish Ledger* video is where the ledger requires a particular category of data to achieve its goal (better health), so it contrives an advertisement for a sensing product (a bathroom scale) that would allow it to capture the necessary data to measure its progress, and thus appropriately condition the environmental pressures on an embodied subject. The degree to which this communicative dynamic occurs, and in what way, will depend, of course, on each idiosyncratic application – but it introduces a subtle and important distinction from other forms of online manipulation.

When we think about normative objections to such a practice, the concern is not that any specific behaviour is constrained or enabled through force. It may not even be that the decision-making capacities of the embodied person have been compromised in any way. Rather, it may be that the goal towards which behaviour is directed is in some way problematic. Tying this to a legal standard is difficult. What types of behavioural optimisation are sufficiently problematic to warrant legal intervention?

Answering that question is definitively beyond the scope of this book. However, the following sections describe some conceptual strategies that may help think through tools for addressing this emerging feature of informational environments.

CONTESTATION FOR ALGORITHMIC ACCOUNTABILITY

One strategy for regulating profiling in the 'world state' is to ensure that mechanisms of algorithmic accountability such as fairness and explainability (or any other mechanism capable of exposing how different calculative methods produce different outputs), are directly linked to mechanisms of contestation. If, as Hildebrandt argues, we seek to action an 'agonistic' interpretation of ourselves, or to resist being optimised in a particular way, computational contestation seems a critical requirement. This is also integral to ensure that computational implementations of algorithmic accountability adhere to desirable public functions, rather than become instruments of corporate *justification*. Put another way, challenging the epistemological position of data science requires preventing the corporate capture of what counts as fair or explanatory information or computation.

The computational applications of algorithmic accountability formulate individuals as statistical nodes rather than discursive subjects within systems of calculation. Extending this to facilitate contestation means a legal subject that still operates within the statistically defined parameters of an automated decision-making system, but has a hand in manipulating the parameters, models, representations, or optimisations by which they are computed. The legal subject as 'filter' defined in Chapter 7 as the product of the computational embedding of fairness and explainability mechanisms, thus has the potential to become a legal person capable of acting on their rights. As F.H. Lawson stated as early as 1957, 'Legal personality and legal persons are, as it were, mathematical equations devised for the purpose of simplifying legal calculations.'[29]

Numerous tools are already being developed to facilitate those types of manipulations of machine learning processes, often in the name of fairness (or anti-discrimination), typically for the purpose of algorithm design.[30] However, 'contestability' is also an emerging norm in algorithm design. Tad Hirsch and colleagues have, for instance, described the utility of contestability as a design principle for systems that evaluate human behaviour.[31] Those authors argue, using the example of machine learning evaluations of human psychological health, that contestability should be introduced off the back of increased legibility mechanisms in algorithm design. If XAI explanations are geared towards facilitating contest rather than justification, then why not also link

---

[29] F H Lawson, 'The Creative Use of Legal Concepts' (1957) 32 *NYU Law Review* 909.
[30] See Erica Du, 'Considerations for Algorithmic Fairness Auditing' (Working Paper, 25 March 2019).
[31] Tad Hirsch et al, 'Designing Contestability: Interaction Design, Machine Learning, and Mental Health' (Presented at the 2017 Conference on Designing Interactive Systems, Edinburgh, UK, 10–14 June 2017).

those explanatory outputs to mechanisms of contestation that can directly manipulate their output. One might call this 'online dispute resolution for fairness' or 'contestation by design'.

Extending dispute resolution mechanisms into platforms and computational systems is not necessarily controversial. In many ways users already operate prolifically in the dispute-resolution mechanisms of private online alternative dispute resolution. Rory Van Loo, for instance, points out in his 2016 article 'The Corporation as Courthouse' that eBay deals with approximately 60 million disputes annually (90 per cent of which are conducted entirely electronically without the intervention of an eBay employee). By contrast, the American Arbitration Association deals with about 1,500.[32] He thus suggests that 'the main institutional actor in the private consumer-facing legal system is not the arbitration tribunal, but the consumer-facing courthouse'.[33] This type of computational dispute resolution also goes beyond e-commerce. Similar mechanisms are used in disputes over intellectual property, permissible speech on platforms, and financial credit ratings. Some online dispute resolution systems are also highly institutional – for instance, the ICAAN Uniform Domain-Name Dispute Resolution Policy, the WIPO Arbitration and Mediation Centre, as well as the EU Electronic Consumer Dispute Resolution program.

Typically, online dispute resolution is conceptualised as a virtual space, within which disputants have access to various dispute resolution tools, such as negotiation support or argument organisation tools. Could similar systems include tools for manipulating machine learning classifications for fairness, or for their inclusion of inappropriate data? The biggest challenge would be ensuring such mechanisms had an institutional or at least independent character when applied to private actors, rather than simply enabling entities to evaluate their own conduct. Making such a system possible or desirable would also require structural systems for notifying an individual that a relevant decision had been made, and that such a decision was amenable for adjustment. This also means understanding which decisions are challengeable and why, and on what basis. In other words, there needs to be ongoing development in understanding the degree to which such manipulations might meaningfully express a person's right to co-determination of reading, or otherwise inform a decision system.

The normative premises for such a contest are also difficult to define. Fairness as a proxy for non-discrimination is one normative guideline, enabling different stakeholders to pursue alternative optimisations, however it may not be enough. 'Reasonableness' or 'self-image' may be other useful guidelines, though also difficult to define, especially in computational terms. What about contesting behavioural engineering or optimisation towards goals that were contrary to the user's interests? Could contestation reconfigure the goals an information environment is optimised

---

[32] Rory Van Loo, 'The Corporation as Courthouse' (2016) 33 *Yale Journal on Regulation* 547.
[33] Ibid 549.

to achieve? That would require understanding what optimisations were permitted for different types of decision-making outcomes or system designs. With respect to decision-making systems, it may be possible to prescribe what type of explanation (or XAI system) is appropriate, and what type of fairness tool, be it statistical, similarity, or causal, is more desirable, according to the context of that profile generation or decision. Criminal justice assessments are likely to require different types of contestation from credit scores. Should parolees be able to participate in the production of their risk assessment? In the domain of online retail, we typically permit optimisations designed to extract money from users as long as it does not include deception. Could these be supplemented in system to design to facilitate self-directed goals like social justice or environmentalism? In social media, we permit optimisations designed to maximise attention, but some mechanisms also enable greater control over the character of information they are exposed to. Ensuring automated decision-making systems produce contestable outcomes that are sufficiently visible for the sake of contestation, and can be meaningfully challenged through the use of online tools, is therefore a non-trivial legal and technical engineering task.

CONTEXT AS NORMATIVE PARAMETER IN THE WORLD STATE

Rather than pursuing individual rights to protect us from profiling, some have argued for structural modulation of information communication architectures to facilitate self-making and the proliferation of identities. Julie Cohen, for instance, has written about the need for 'semantic discontinuity' in technological systems as a way to produce gaps and inconsistencies within systems of meaning.[34] Presented as a counter-point to narratives of seamlessness in the design of technologies, these gaps would be designed to enable 'identity play'. Cohen also rightly identifies how contemporary interest in consumer rights and data portability enact the opposite paradigm, by instead smoothing the aggregation of identity across digital spaces. Cohen's normative positioning is premised on her account of how identity and self are generated through 'practice and play' in digital environments. In this way, privacy is figured as a capabilities-based mechanism for the protection of identity through self-establishment of boundaries within networked and informational environments. Paying attention to environmental or structural conditions, Cohen argues, 'opens up spaces of operational possibility that a narrower focus on subjects forecloses (or has enabled us to ignore), even as the benefits of such an approach rebound to those subjects. It directs our attention to the essential roles of gaps, barriers, breakdowns, and failures of translation in producing the conditions that render selves incomputable'.[35] 'Semantic discontinuity' thus becomes a way for

[34] Julie Cohen, *Configuring the Networked Self: Law, Code, and the Play of Everyday Practice* (Yale University Press, 2012).
[35] Cohen, above n 9, 21.

individuals and groups to 'push back against the particular institutional, cultural, and material constraints that they encounter in their everyday lives'.[36] Cohen has also intimated at the role of context in the creation of such discontinuity, and for privacy interventions to 'separate contexts from one another'.[37] Semantic discontinuity thus becomes another expression of the necessity of the functional differentiation of society and identity, integral to Luhmann's systems theory, or Nissenbaum's theory of privacy.

Seamlessness in the 'world state' privileges an epistemological position that sees meaning as a product of opaque protocol and mathematical operation, rather than connected to context, causation, or semantic referent. Meaning becomes the product of a *capacity* to find statistical patterns in massive unstructured datasets. While this opens a space for freedom and identity play in certain respects, those meaning-making capacities are not evenly distributed. Introducing discontinuity thus means rejecting the knowledge logic of flattening all data into meaningless inputs for machine learning transformations that, for instance, guide our financial, welfare, or policed subjectivities. Introducing (or imposing) new boundaries into information architectures has the potential to not only constrain information flow, but also constrain the computational 'grammars of action' applied to individuals within any domain.[38] In other words, it could be useful to interrupt the information flows used in contemporary profiling and machine learning model building, as well as the operationalising of those profiles to affect behaviour. This could make context a normative orientation for parameterising behavioural advertising, mechanism and interface design, or any other system of optimisation. Put another way, semantic discontinuity might be achieved by transposing the normative parameters we ascribe to particular places, social spheres, or institutions into computational registers. Work most closely approximating that translation to date are computer science applications of Nissenbaum's theory of contextual integrity.[39]

According to contextual integrity, context is defined by the five parameters: sender, recipient, subject, information type, and transmission principle (and in other formulations 'uses' and 'purposes'). Information 'types' and 'actors' are distinguished according to contextual ontology. More recent work on the theory has indicated the necessity of drawing more types of non-semantic data, sometimes called data 'primitives', such as mouse clicks, GPS coordinates, or anything else that might not have clear semantic meaning into a contextual framework.[40] In other words, it would require a radical computational implementation of semantic data-tagging. However, in so doing, it could also re-configure the information

---

[36] Ibid 12.
[37] Cohen, above n 34.
[38] Philip Agre, 'Surveillance and Capture; Two Models of Privacy' (1994) 10 *The Information Society* 101.
[39] Sebastian Benthall, Seda Gürses, and Helen Nissenbaum, 'Contextual Integrity through the Lens of Computer Science' (2017) 2(1) *Foundations and Trends in Privacy and Security* 1, 13.
[40] Helen Nissenbaum, 'Contextual Integrity Up and Down the Data Food Chain' (2019) 20 *Theoretical Inquiries in Law* 222.

environment into comprehensibly differentiated series of 'spaces', 'environments', or 'institutions', each with normatively differentiated communicative dynamics.

The production of profiles and automated decisions (i.e. what data can and cannot be included in profiling systems), how information is presented to users, and the permissible agendas animating the design of interfaces or mechanisms could similarly be parameterised by context. Those new communicative dynamics could be imposed through positivist top-down approaches, or through bottom-up autopoietic approaches.[41] But their normative content is less the subject of this investigation than the structures capable of defining the boundaries within which normativity in communicative dynamics and permissible grammars of action can emerge. Contextual integrity is hardly the only theory relevant to achieving this type of functional differentiation of society, let alone in computational environments. Indeed, the parameters of contextual integrity may not be the most useful or appropriate paradigm for that task. Others have sought to define context and semantic content using Judea Pearl's work on the importance of causality in automated decision-making systems. For instance, Sebastian Benthall has argued that causality can impose (or expose) the 'situatedness' of information, according to the 'nomic' connection (i.e. connected through probabilistic causality) to phenomena and data, for a particular classes of observers.[42] However, contextual integrity has already received a significant amount of attention from computer science – and deploys a more sophisticated and developed account of context than other computational paradigms like 'context aware computing'.[43] The complexity of the task is immense, but it may afford an important structural impediment on powerful actors and their systems of meaning-making, and could also importantly assist in determinations of how and why certain machine learning calculations ought be manipulated.

(LEGAL) IDENTITY AS INTERFACE

A final strategy for bringing contestability into the 'world state' is the design of an appropriate legal entity to bear rights and enter contestation. Why do we need a new notion of identity or legal personality here? This book has attempted to demonstrate why the model of internal and external identity and self, elaborated into the legal subject of privacy and data protection, may be of limited utility in the contemporary information regime. Arguably, new notions of identity in the 'world state' could reorient the normative boundaries of the profiling and optimisation behaviours we seek to prevent.

---

[41] See, e.g., Paul Dourish, 'What We Talk About When We Talk About Context' 2004 8 *Personal and Ubiquitous Computing* 19.
[42] Benthall 'Situated Information Flow Theory', Proceedings of the 2019 NSA HotSauce Conference (on file with author).
[43] Benthall et al, above n 39, 13.

Legal scholarship has been investigating the relationship between persons and data for a long time. Alongside the jurisdictional connections imposed by 'identifiability' in information privacy and data protection regimes, there is a long and persisting debate over the utility of property rights for constraining undesirable data processing. Indeed, there are good arguments for the imposition of property rights in this context, particularly in their capacity to be constitutive of personhood.[44] As Peter Halewood notes, 'self-ownership' means rights 'to prevent anyone, including the state, from acquiring a market interest in persons that would interfere with liberty and autonomy'.[45] In this way, property is figured as a mechanism for controlling personal data and selfhood, an intuitive form of non-regulatory control, and a highly useful economic metaphor. However, on the other side of self-constitution through property is self-commodification through property. Property rights inherently provoke marketisation of personal data, which not only inevitably favours certain actors over others, but may be normatively counter-productive in the profiling context.[46] Property rights in personal data would mean participating in the logics of what Zuboff calls 'surveillance capitalism', or what Frederick Jameson called the logic of 'late capitalism' premised on the continuing expansion of the market into hitherto uncommodified territories.[47] Going further, even if we were able to conceptualise data as a *non-alienable* property right, which many advocates of the property approach would reject, property rights in data may not adequately address the generation of knowledge, inferences, and profiles from data, at least not without some sort of analogue to 'moral rights' that could constrain downstream transformations. In other words, data as property is not, in itself, adequate for dealing with profiling in the 'world state'.

Preferred here is another way of conceptualising the relationship between person and data that may have more relevance to the emerging practices of profiling and behavioural optimisation outlined above. This involves reconfiguring identity, for the sake of law at least, along the lines of a composite of embodied person and aggregated informational output. There is a tradition of post-humanist and transhumanist thought describing human identity and subjectivity as a hybrid of embodied and informational components. Much of this thinking is premised on the idea that narratives of technology and capital have, since the Second World War especially, begun to challenge the distinction between humans and things that undergirds liberal human subjectivity. Post-humanist thinking posits the distinction between humans and non-humans as a contingent boundary, dependent on social,

---

[44] See, e.g., Peter Halewood, 'On Commodification and Self-Ownership' (2008) 20 *Yale Journal of Law and the Humanities* 131.
[45] Ibid 134.
[46] See, e.g., Jessica Litman, 'Information Privacy/Information Property' (2000) 52 *Stanford Law Review* 1283; See also Paul M Schwartz, 'Property, Privacy, and Personal Data' (2004) 117 *Harvard Law Review* 2056.
[47] Frederick Jameson, *Postmodernism, or, The Cultural Logic of Late Capitalism* (Duke University Press, 1991).

political, and technical formations. Haraway's pronouncement, for instance, that 'we are all chimeras, theorized and fabricated hybrids of machine and organism',[48] or 'permanently partial identities',[49] speaks to this new type of technological subject. From a socio-materialist perspective, Deborah Lupton has described the onto-epistemological dimensions of human-data assemblages, their relationships to bodies, and how people can best interpret and make use of them.[50] Others use terms like 'augmented subjectivity' wherein subjects are embodied simultaneously by organic flesh and digital prosthesis, as a way to destabilise the problematic boundary between 'online' and 'offline'.[51] N Katherine Hayles similarly argues that if we think of cognition as a process of interpreting information in contexts that connect it with meaning, we ought think of humans and technical systems as interconnected cognitive assemblages.[52] Peter-Paul Verbeek further suggests these accounts help us transition from thinking about humans as autonomous beings that need defending from technology, and instead as technologically mediated subjects, capable of expressing freedom with technology.[53] In other words, acknowledging the complex connections between embodied persons and data is a way to move past the idea that 'When the boundary between the human and the technological is blurred, we also appear to have to give up that which makes us most human: our autonomy, the freedom to organize our lives as we see fit.'[54]

For our purposes, the utility of thinking along these lines is how it enables us to conceptualise a rights-bearing legal entity that has more in its arsenal than replicating the subject of data protection's desire to impose its own account of the truth into a statistical world. Using the fiction of a 'composite legal identity', we may be able to redraw the line around what we see as a useful description of a communicative entity operating in the world, in a way that can sensibly constrain the conduct of others. Put another way, a composite legal identity might enable us to redraw boundaries of protection around individuals and data, not according to the jurisdictional idea of identifiability, nor through possession or property rights that inevitably introduce

---

[48] Donna Haraway, *Simians, Cyborgs, and Women* (Routledge, 1991), where the author notes: 'Late twentieth-century machines have made thoroughly ambiguous the difference between natural and artificial, mind and body, self-developing and externally designed, and many other distinctions that used to apply to organisms and machines. Our machines are disturbingly lively, and we ourselves frighteningly inert.'
[49] Ibid.
[50] Deborah Lupton, 'How Do Data Come to Matter? Living and Becoming with Personal Data' (2018) 5 *Big Data & Society*.
[51] P J Rey and Whitney Erin Boesel, 'The Web, Digital Prostheses, and Augmented Subjectivity' in Daniel Lee Kleinman and Kelly Moore (eds) *Routledge Handbook of Science, Technology, and Society* (Routledge, 2014).
[52] N Katherine Hayles, 'Cognitive Assemblages: Technical Agency and Human Interactions' (2016) 43(1) *Critical Inquiry* 32.
[53] Peter-Paul Verbeek, 'Subject to Technology: On Autonomous Computing and Human Autonomy' in Mireille Hildebrandt and Antoinette Rouvroy (eds) *Law, Human Agency and Autonomic Computing: The Philosophy of Law Meets the Philosophy of Technology* (Routledge, 2011) 27.
[54] Ibid 29.

more markets into the ecology of human behaviour, but through the communicative dynamics used in profiling and 'behavioural optimisation'. Inventiveness in the 'juridical art of personality' is not uncommon. It is part of an analytical or positivist tradition that sees the legal person as pure abstraction – a fiction or device calculated to play a role in legal relations. There is ongoing argument over the degree to which the legal person still does, in certain ways, trace the metaphysical characteristics of the natural person.[55] But that position seems harder and harder to maintain as the fiction of legal person is extended over a broader range of referents that have recently including ecological features and artificial intelligences.[56]

The idea of composite legal personality drawn on here stems from Gunther Teubner's work extending Niklas Luhmann's systems theoretical account of organisational legal personality into the non-human realm. Luhmann argued that if communications within a system (group of actors or organisation) also include communications *about* the system, i.e. it self-describes, then those communications can be attributed to the self-describing entity as actions, which can account for the provision of legal personality to those organisations (as communicative systems). Teubner takes this idea of legal personality as constituted by communication flows further, drawing on Latour's notion of 'hybrids' of human and non-human actors (and actants). He argues that composite legal persons are identifiable from empirical (rather than ontological) investigations of how an entity is defined as separate from its environment through its own communicative dynamics. Teubner argues, in the same way that '[a] state becomes a collective actor, not because it has certain natural properties or a specific organizational form' but rather because 'it is the international system of war and peace that constructs its actors and thereby forces ethnic/territorial entities to take on the form of an institutionalized state if they are supposed to participate in international politics', that a hybrid can be understood as a legal entity, premised on the specific dynamics of the flow of information that define it and separate it from the environment. These hybrids, for Teubner, are thus both feasible and necessary in contemporary technological and political ecologies.[57]

Although Teubner's legal design is expedient, it is also rooted in a specific theoretical tradition of investigation into notions of identity and self. Indeed, Teubner's systems theoretical legal person, explicitly derived from Luhmann, is strongly connected to Humberto Maturana and Francisco Varela's work on autopoiesis that, building on the ideas of Weiner and McCulloch with respect to human-machine systems defined by feedback circuits, became a critical premise of second-order cybernetics. Those ideas were highly influential in the fields of

---

[55] See Ngaire Naffine, 'Who Are Law's Persons? From Cheshire Cats to Responsible Subjects' (2003) 66(3) *Modern Law Review* 346.
[56] Connal Parsley and Edward Mussawir, 'The Law of Persons Today: At the Margins of Jurisprudence' (2017) 11 *Law and Humanities* 44.
[57] Gunther Teubner, 'Rights of Non-Humans? Electronic Agents and Animals as New Actors in Politics and Law' (2006) 33 *Journal of Law and Society* 497, 502.

'artificial intelligence' and 'artificial life', as well as Luhmann's sociological systems theory. They were also a response to the problematic effects on autonomy that Varela interpreted as a consequence of thinking about human identity through 'control systems' thinking alone.[58]

Varela's approach to biological and cognitive identity is premised on the idea that a global identity *emerges* from smaller-scale local transactions.[59] He argues that an underlying circular process gives rise to an emergent coherence, and this emergent coherence is what constitutes the self. The critical dimension of that self is therefore how it provides a surface for interaction with the world outside it. Varela thus challenges Western liberal ideas of self, instead embracing the 'virtual self' or the 'selfless self', which is emergent and exists primarily to provide this interface to the external world. On this account, identity is not the self-experience of the subject, it is the unitary quality or coherence of the organism. It is also a process – a process that creates a 'perspective' for experiencing that interaction. For our purposes, the self in this formation is what separates (and identifies) the behaving entity from its cyber-physical milieu. It is a combined human and informational 'surface' behind which the embodied entity and networks of information flow aggregate into behaviourally operative entities that interact with cyber-physical environments.

The legal identity of 'virtual persons', 'pseudonyms', and 'avatars' was subject to sophisticated analysis in the *Future of Identity in Information Society* projects a decade ago.[60] That analysis focused on questions of agency when there is no longer a simple correspondence between person and online identity, and when multiple online identities pertain to a single person. There has also been excellent work into the utility of extending ideas of legal personality to deal with problems of accountability in automated decision-making systems,[61] and ensuring that relevant entities can be located to bear sanctions.[62] The discussion of legal personality here, however, is less for the purpose of defining an accountable computational actor, than for defining an entity that can enter into legal relations for the sake of constraining the conduct of others. It is about building the interface that separates

---

[58] N Katherine Hayles, *How We Became Posthuman: Virtual Bodies in Cybernetics, Literature, and Informatics* (University of Chicago Press, 1999).

[59] Francisco J Varela, 'Patterns of Life: Intertwining Identity and Cognition' (1997) 34 *Brain and Cognition* 72; Francisco J Varela, 'The Emergent Self', in John Brockman (ed) *Third Culture: Beyond the Scientific Revolution* (Simon and Schuster, 1996) at 211: 'I don't have one identity, I have a bricolage of various identities. I have a cellular identity, I have an immune identity, I have a cognitive identity, I have various identities that manifest in different modes of interaction. These are my various selves.'

[60] David-Olivier Jacquet-Chiffelle et al, 'Virtual Persons and Identities' in K Rannenberg et al (eds) *The Future of Identity in the Information Society* (Springer, 2009) 75.

[61] Lawrence B Solum, 'Legal Personhood for Artificial Intelligence' (1991) 70 *North Carolina Law Review* 1231.

[62] Bert-Jaap Koops, Mireille Hildebrandt, and David-Olivier Jacquet-Chiffelle, 'Bridging the Accountability Gap: Rights for New Entities in the Information Society?' (2010) 11 *Minnesota Journal of Law, Science & Technology* 497.

an identity from its environment. To that end, there are questions as to the practical utility (and possibility) of this juridical move. For instance, how might this meaningfully affect the relationship between embodied persons, personal data, and controllers of information environments? How might this meaningfully reconfigure the parameters of permissible data processing? One rationale for reconfiguring legal identity this way is to ensure the connection between embodied person and data tracks through the entire processing life-cycle up into the construction of a profile, and down into the generation of behaviour. However, the primary rationale is that it affords a normative orientation for evaluating behavioural optimisation by seeing profiles as a location of distributed agency.

If we contrive a rights-bearing entity as a composite that creates an interface to the outside world, then practices influencing behavioural patterns can be reconceptualised as harms to identity. Put another way, rather than control over how an individual is represented, such a protection of identity might *preserve behavioural integrity*. Drawing on Mackenzie's insights about normative connections between autonomy and identity, there is thus value in thinking about the effects of profiling and optimisation practices in terms of impact on identity. In other words, it gives us a way of thinking about identity harms differently from those of an inaccurate or irrelevant representation, and a way to think about autonomy harms without having the capacity for decision-making undermined. This might be framed as a right to limited optimisation – the setting of one's own behavioural agenda, or as part of the boundary formation discussed in Cohen's work. It might also be a response to the possibility raised by Rouvroy, that as the 'profile' ascends in importance, 'not wanting to be profiled will mean not wanting to be oneself'.[63]

Hyo Yoon Kang argues that this is the role of legal conventions – 'fictional as they may be' – to 'stabilize and uphold the notion of human agency within the proliferating hybrid network of multiple agencies'. In describing Varela's account of identity and its extension through Teubner's hybrid legal person, she argues 'the prospect of autonomic computing of bioinformatics data affords an interesting framework in which to reconsider the notion of the bounded biological self as the locus of human agency'.[64] For Kang, there is therefore normative work performed by law in creating new embodiments. This is inevitably a major 'disjuncture between the locations of the human material body and the experience of embodiment' – one that necessarily makes traditional ideas of human agency obsolete.[65] But that might make sense in a technical environment that also seems to make older notions of agency and autonomy obsolete. For Kang, Teubner's hybrid model is thus the most appropriate

---

[63] Rouvroy, above n 20.
[64] Hyo Yoon Kang, 'Autonomic Computing, Genomic Data and Human Agency: The Case for Embodiment' in Mireille Hildebrandt and Antoinette Rouvroy (eds) *Law, Human Agency and Autonomic Computing: The Philosophy of Law Meets the Philosophy of Technology* (Routledge, 2011) 104, 106.
[65] Ibid.

legal person to do this work – to facilitate the emergence of complex subjectivities, and new relationships between individual and environment. But what type of new subjectivity are we imagining here?

Within this composite identity, what data constitutes the informational component of a person, where is it located, how is it controlled, and how does it form the necessary communicative relations? If Google can build a discrete data ledger applicable to you as an individual, can the boundary between self (or legal self) and environment be drawn to include that data? Is a police database part of such a composite even if it is a static record? Using Teubner's extension of Luhmann, this will depend on the communicative dynamics of the system. It would require a technological system generating or collecting data to include a reference to the identity of the legal entity, with which it is in dynamic relation. This itself is not controversial, many recording systems and platforms do this already. However, the existence of a composite would not be satisfied if this were a static record. There must be a meaningful communicative interaction between the profile and the person. In particular, the profile needs to act, this line of thinking is relevant for when a profile is no longer a representation but an agent. This might go beyond the way we typically think about contemporary information platforms referring to its own users. Such a 'user' is typically the platform's own artefact, actively constituting the platform rather than the person. When an existing platform modifies the presentation of information to a user in order to satisfy an optimisation, this is better thought of as the platform communicating with itself. In cases like *The Selfish Ledger*, or virtual assistants for personalised law, this communicative interaction might produce something closer to a composite. Implementing something like composite legal identity in a meaningful way would require new systems architectures and communications protocols that deal with profiles as 'smart' agents. To that end, the burgeoning thinking about blockchain and smart contracts for identity frameworks,[66] as well as the renewed interest in data co-ops and other intermediaries, speaks to the possibility and desirability of such an approach. Indeed, building appropriate online identity frameworks is an ongoing goal in the study of information architectures and the life of the internet. For a long time, thinking around identity frameworks has sought to achieve functional differentiation of society and identity that are user-centric and customisable.[67] In the same way that context tagging introduces new requirements on the semantic labelling of data, any system premised on defining identity or personality as a communicative flow within a system requires a mechanism to ensure that the production and transmission of data includes that self-referential character. The extension of this into active, agential profiles is a speculative but emerging outgrowth of these ideas.

---

[66] See, e.g., Paul Dunphy et al, 'A First Look at Identity Management Schemes on the Blockchain' (2018) 16(4) *IEEE Security & Privacy* 20; Jason Potts, Ellie Rennie, and Jake Goldenfein, 'Blockchains and the Crypto City' (2017) 59(6) *Information Technology* 285.

[67] J D Lasica, 'Identity in the Age of Cloud Computing: The Next-Generation Internet's Impact on Business, Governance, and Social Interaction' (Report, The Aspen Institute, 21 April 2009).

CONCLUSION

The last few chapters have outlined the profile as a compendium of physiology, psychology, and emotion, as both an account of past behaviour and a lever of future behaviour. In other words, as a site of distributed agency. This type of profile requires a more sophisticated role in our notion of identity than as an external representation or image. The cybernetic model of identity operationalised in data science emerges from a tradition of thinking about identity as a pattern of behaviour. Deeply embedded in this tradition is the idea of de-materialisation, that the body is an irrelevant container. Humberto Maturana and Francisco Varela have extended that thinking while at the same time insisting on embodiment as an essential character of biological and cognitive identity. The question is whether there is a way to *legally* operationalise the more sophisticated thinking about the relationship between behaviour and identity without succumbing to 'exhaustion' – the idea that the profile constitutes the totality of the person. The notion of identity described here, with the potential to inform a rights-bearing legal person that can operate in the cyber-physical environment of the 'world state', is depicted as an interface to the information world, through which interference with identity could then be measured and challenged.

Arguing for this juridical entity is a call to pay attention to how the cyber-physical realm is being structured and actioned. It is a call to contest the building of the 'world state' according to the idea that meaning is derivable from any and all data. It is about building a new juridical orientation towards data and towards the informational elements of life. This book has been about exploring what a legal subject might look like in the 'world state', what it might want from law, and how it might achieve it.

10

Law and Legal Automation in the World State

Chapter 9 argued for shifting and expanding the relationship between law and technology in terms of mechanisms and persons. This was proposed as necessary in the context of new forms of technological governance that are changing the morphology of people, places, and law, as well as challenging many of the fundamental categories long central to legal theory. What were once 'legal expert systems' using symbolic knowledge representation, are now machine learning and neural network prediction systems, using computer vision, computer audition, and other biometrics as inputs. What were once discrete software programs running on terminals in bureaucratic offices, are now the very infrastructure of governance in the world at large. Indeed, this is the space of governance and not governments. As legal norms are translated into computational applications, we generate structural, ubiquitous, and environmental techno-normative environments, governed by 'Platform Sovereignties'. We now inhabit what Benjamin Bratton describes as 'the nomos of the cloud',[1] the form of governance for which the 'Smart City' as a mesh of geographic and technological jurisdiction has become an emblem.[2] As Connal Parsley points out, these changes in technologies of governance have produced a conspicuous slippage from what was once a relation between 'law, world, and jurist' into a relation between 'norms, technology, and expertise'.[3]

On the other hand, the relationship between law and technology in the theoretical work seems to have culminated in the idea that law best regulates technology by regulating its design at the level of public institutions. In this way, the debates around *Lex Informatica*,[4] the idea that law and code might carry similar regulatory gravity,[5] were settled by diminishing the status of technological enforcements of

---

[1] Benjamin H Bratton, *The Stack: On Software and Sovereignty* (MIT Press, 2015).
[2] See, e.g., Evgeny Morozov and Francesca Bria 'Rethinking the Smart City: Democratizing Urban Technology' (2018) available www.rosalux-nyc.org/wp-content/files_mf/morozovandbria_eng_final55.pdf.
[3] Connal Parsley, 'On Office for Technological Times: From the Law without Jurists to a Jurisprudence without Law' – Presentation at 'Offices of the Jurist' at Cardozo Law School 2nd December 2018.
[4] Joel Reidenberg, 'Lex Informatica: The Formulation of Information Policy Rules Through Technology' (1997) 76 *Texas Law Review* 553.
[5] Lawrence Lessig, *Code and Other Laws of Cyberspace* (Basic Books, 1999).

legal normativity to a 'techno-regulation' – i.e. legally prepositioned technologies that implement legal rules, though with little legal significance of their own.[6] This is the law/technology hierarchy embedded in 'privacy by design', 'legal protection by design',[7] 'compliance by design',[8] and 'governance by design'. Introducing cyber-physical (legal) persons into cyber-physical environments, for which the 'mechanisms', 'interfaces', and 'grammars of action' are defined by computational rules might, however, challenge this hierarchy of technology and legality. How ought we think about these computational environments governed by automated rule systems, especially in their relationship to the chaotic real world governed by interpretive systems and moral choices? Are these governing mechanisms too distinct to reconcile, or is there a sense of cyber-physical law that can desirably be recuperated?

Some have argued that technology and law are 'shaped by distinctly different systems of logic. While policy tempers rule-based mandates with context-specific judgments that allows for interpretive flexibility and ongoing dispute about the appropriateness of rules, computer code operates by means of on-off rules. Thus, there is always a difference between "law in books" and "law in technology".'[9] But this distinction may not be sustainable. Indeed, several authors have argued that there is *no* inconsistency between the operating modes of law and computation. As Lawrence Diver, as well as Cornelia Vismann and Markus Krajewski have made clear, law is a user of media systems: 'Media technologies have to decide about the conditions under which all systems, including the legal system, think and speak. Media law must therefore reformulate itself under the same conditions established by the universal machine for so-called users. For what is the law with respect to the computer if not a user itself?'[10]

Indeed, a focus on law's procedural character exposes its function as an information processing technology in and of itself. Law translates 'noise' from the 'real' world into the symbolic register of *legal* reality.[11] These legal procedures and processes are for Vismann, the 'algorithms of law', that have now immigrated into the interior of computational architecture.[12] To that end, if the social environment is increasingly computational or cyber-physical, it is therefore time to acknowledge that the

---

[6] See, e.g., Serge Gutwirth discussing Kyle McGee's work on Latour in Serge Gutwirth, 'Providing the Missing Link: Law after Latour's Passage' in Kyle McGee (ed) *Latour and the Passage of Law* (Edinburgh University Press, 2015) 122, 141; Roger Brownsword, 'Code, Control and Choice: Why East Is East and West Is West' (2005) 25(1) *Legal Studies* 1.

[7] Mireille Hildebrandt, 'Legal Protection by Design: Objections and Refutations' (2011) 5 Legisprudence 223.

[8] Laurence Diver, 'Law as a User: Design, Affordance, and the Technological Mediation of Norms' (2018) 15(1) *SCRIPTed* 4.

[9] Deirdre K. Mulligan and Kenneth A. Bamberger, 'Saving Governance-by-Design' (2018) 106 *California Law Review* 697.

[10] Cornelia Vismann and Martin Krajewski, 'Computer Juridisms' (2007) 29 *Grey Room* 90, 101.

[11] Cornelia Vismann, 'Jurisprudence: A Transfer Science' (1999) 10(3) *Law and Critique* 279.

[12] Vismann and Krajewski, above n 10.

computer is no longer 'a matter of law, which poses certain problems for the legal order',[13] but rather that the computer, the network, code, and programming logic should be thought of as the modes and media of legal transmission, and the materiality of 'law's media dependency'.[14]

Thinking about law and technology, or physical and informational, or world and 'world state', as entirely distinct domains thus needs supplementing with thinking about how hybridisations of law and technology might effectively and desirably regulate the 'world state' and the agents within in. In other words, we need law that operates both in physical and computational space, as well as in the space between, in the translations and interactions. Maintaining the distinctions between technology and law (or defining particular actions or artefacts as 'code as law' or 'law as code') thus misses the more fundamental development – that traditional notions of positive law are hybridising with technical, coded (hyper-positivist) *legal* expressions to pluralise legality. Accordingly, images of law and code on alternate sides of a regulatory schematic need replacing with intertwined images of co-coordinating and co-constituting techno-juridisms. Indeed, the legal character of these systems may be of secondary relevance. Roger Brownsword, who defines techno-regulation as something different from law because it undermines the capacity to make moral choices, is also correct in questioning 'whether there is any point in trying to assess the applicability of rule-related legality to technologically achieved management',[15] recognising that legality may be of less relevance in the future.[16] What we need are tools for addressing how informational worlds and physical worlds operate as systems, not as separate spheres. We need to think not about how all of technology and technological mediation is law, but how law as an information technology, and potentially an automated information technology, operates in these networks of relations. We also need to update our thinking on how code as a technology governs, especially how it is conceptualised as an architecture of control.

In law's addressing of digital environments, the discussion of control has long focused on what Lessig warned of when describing 'code is law', i.e. behavioural limitation through technological and informational architectures. In other words, a type of digitally mediated 'force' operating on actors. This mode of constraining behaviour has heavily influenced theoretical work on the hierarchy of law and technology. In particular, it is reflected in the idea that automated enforcement of rules constitutes techno-regulation rather than law.[17] Ian Kerr, for instance, following Brownsword, argues that the 'shift from our current ex post facto systems of

---

[13] Ibid 92.
[14] Vaios Karavas, 'The Force of Code: Laws Transformation Under Technological Conditions' (2009) 10(4) *German Law Journal* 474.
[15] Roger Brownsword, 'Technological Management Rule of Law' (2016) 8(1) *Law, Innovation and Technology* 100.
[16] Roger Brownsword, 'In the Year 2061: From Law to Technological Management' (2015) 7(1) *Law, Innovation and Technology* 1.; Roger Brownsword, 'Field, Frame, Focus' in Rob van Gestel et al (eds) *Rethinking Legal Scholarship: A Transatlantic Dialogue* (Cambridge University Press, 2017).
[17] Brownsword, above n 15.

penalties and punishments to ex ante preventative measures', fundamentally alters the 'path of law', and undermines law's contribution to moral community through its addressing persons as moral actors with moral agency.[18]

However, this relationship between architecture and moral choice is complicated by technological systems designed to direct behaviour otherwise than by only permitting this or that specific action or transaction. Laurence Diver has deeply extended this thinking through the lens of 'affordance', and the complicated mechanisms by which technological artefacts interact with and relate to human behaviour. In information environments, there is also room for more thinking about the mediation of human conduct through 'control systems' or cybernetics thinking, not simply technological artefacts, which remind us how the design of platforms and data science optimisations facilitate agendas and teleology as well as interactions. Under the 'control systems' approach, technologies are part of environmental design optimised to produce certain objectives or behaviours. This is control in the sense that animated the thinking of William Burroughs in his 1978 article 'The Limits of Control',[19] which instigated further work on the concept by both Deleuze and Foucault.[20] Burroughs reminds us that despite technical capacities to precisely direct the behaviour and actions of individuals, words (perhaps information environments in our more contemporary context) remain the 'principal' instrument for control. Anything relying on force or direct physical control (i.e. architecture) ultimately encounters the 'limits of control', because control needs opposition, without which it becomes simply *use* of a subject. If control is total, there is nothing left to control. Deleuze took these ideas further, extending Burroughs' description of the mass media as the principle agent of control into the realm of computation, describing how control is best understood as 'modulation' not 'moulds'.[21] This control paradigm reminds us that the most significant forms of control rest in the capacity to set an agenda, and then to instrument an environment to achieve it without imposing direct force on agents. In other words, achieving an agenda is best done by enabling rational actions within a specific environment. Accordingly, we need legal thinking geared towards regulating mechanisms, operating at the level of information inputs and outputs, that achieve objectives by *underdetermining* the actions of its subjects.[22] We need thinking about how law and technology are both

---

[18] Ian Kerr, 'Prediction, Pre-emption, and Presumption: The Path of Law after the Computational Turn' in Mireille Hildebrandt and Katja de Vries (eds) *Privacy, Due Process and the Computational Turn* (Springer 2013).
[19] William S. Burroughs, 'The Limits of Control' in J. Grauerholz and I. Silverberg (eds) *Word Virus: The William S. Burroughs Reader* (Grove Press 1998) [original work published in 1975].
[20] Gilles Deleuze, 'Postscript on the Societies of Control' (1992) 59 *October* 3.
[21] Ibid.
[22] See, e.g., Jannice Käll, 'A Posthuman Data Subject: The Right to Be Forgotten and Beyond' (2017) 18(4) *German Law Journal* 1145; See also Mika Viljanen, 'A Cyborg Turn in Law?' (2017) 18(4) *German Law Journal* 1277.

capable of dissolving the barrier between subject and command, and infiltrating their subjects' 'cognitive and volitional processes'.[23]

If platforms and software are sovereign, we also need more thinking about their jurisdictions, not in terms of legal geography, but in terms of legality, legal process, and legal *technology*. Legal theory has been dealing with the empirical reality of non-state jurisdictions, like International Investment Law, for some time, by tying questions of legality more strongly to jurisdiction than to sovereignty. In the most sophisticated theories, jurisdictions are generated through the technologies that connect conduct to mechanisms or institutions of dispute resolution and enforcement. This account follows the work of, for instance, Shaunnagh Dorsett and Shaun McVeigh, as well as Gunther Teubner, who have all discussed 'non-state' jurisdictions taking shape as reiterative relationships between conduct, arbitration, and the capacities for enforcement.[24] On these theoretical accounts, law is inaugurated through jurisdiction as produced through technologies and practices, rather than positivist categories. Dorsett and McVeigh accordingly argue that jurisdiction is the 'first question of law',[25] and is brought into being by 'technologies' capable of linking (i.e. mediating) between conduct in the world and institutions of enforcement. For example, Dorsett and McVeigh describe how the technology and practices of writing produced a jurisdiction through the common law 'writ' (and how oral legal traditions used the 'plaint') by creating a grammar for conduct in the world that was comprehended and disciplined by institutions capable of enforcement. If computational conduct could similarly be linked to enforcement bodies on the basis of their own 'jurisdictional devices',[26] with new 'statuses' and 'personas' carrying legal subjectivity, according to legal 'functions' or 'programs', then this has the potential to be similarly jurisdictional. When we think along jurisdictional lines, we have an opportunity to imagine online arbitration systems not simply as corporate enforcement of Terms of Service, or as embedding utopian visions of contracting and private ordering. But rather, for providing mechanisms for the embedding of public law requirements like impartiality and procedural standardisation, and norms beyond those specified in private agreements.

PROFILING IN THE WORLD STATE

As the world and the persons in it hybridise with information environments into cyber-physical entities, law needs to do the same. As rule systems become

---

[23] Viljanen, above n 22, 1283.
[24] A good background to this phenomenon is found in the various chapters of Gunther Teubner (ed) *Global Law without a State* (Dartmouth, 1997), including Teubner's chapter 'Global Bukowina: Legal Pluralism in the World Society' at 3. For a discussion of the jurisdictions of investor–state arbitration, see for example Rudolph Dolzer, 'The Impact of International Investment Treaties on Domestic Administrative Law' (2005) 37 *International Law and Politics* 953.
[25] Shaunnagh Dorsett and Shaun McVeigh, *Jurisdiction* (Routledge, 2012).
[26] Ibid.

increasingly automated, we need to think through reconfiguring and relocating the spaces of interpretation that maintain law as an interpretive practice. As technical environments increasingly govern behaviour, we need to rethink our understandings of moral agency and autonomy. We need to think about what law is for, what law does, and what law looks like at the 'end of representation'.

Contemporary information processing environments are vastly different from those in which privacy and data protection came to life. Profiling is transitioning from the production and indexing of identity images in manually searched Habitual Criminal Registers to the production of data ledgers that operate as agents capable of influencing embodied behaviour. We've moved from photography to computer vision, from dossiers to data science, and from states to smart cities. For a long time, law has sought to protect people from profiling by deploying and defending a particular understanding of identity – a division between a narrative and categorical self – and a particular understanding of harm to identity. Privacy and data protection law, for instance, privileged the discursive truth of the narrative self as a way of avoiding the consequences of losing control of those external categorical expressions of identity. But the technological environment of profiling has moved on, and the law needs to as well.

The 'world state' is an actuarial and statistical place. The move towards statistical epistemology began around the same time as photography emerged as a knowledge-technic in the nineteenth century. Since then, the technical and statistical mechanisms for sensing, interpreting, and knowing the world have evolved together, making statistics the primary knowledge logic for the institutional assessment of people. However, those assessments can no longer be thought of as mere representations. The capture of psychology, emotion, behaviour, and associations, channelled through the weird power of neural networks, is transitioning those profiles from representations into agent. In this context, the legal strategy of privileging a discursive truth over a statistical one, while ideologically preferred by many, has become anachronistic. The liberal-self of privacy law has all but disappeared.

This book has argued for extending law's protection of identity against profiling, but premised on a different conceptualisation of identity – one that connects embodied persons and (agential) profiles as an interface to the world and 'world state' – as a way to separate entity from environment, and to create a meaningful perspective with which to face that 'world state'. To that end it has suggested the juridical art of personality be directed towards building a composite legal identity – a cyber-physical legal person. This entity is considered useful and necessary for bridging the gap between physical and informational, as well as law and technology. An identity as interface may thus have the tools necessary to navigate the legalised networks of computationally defined relations between individuals, spaces, institutions, and actors within the 'world state'.

Some of these ideas may be vulnerable to criticism as overly formal or positivist. Indeed, the addition of structural elements in cyberspace may benefit those with the power to define those structures as they wish. This is not inevitable however. The goal of implementing structure into information architectures and the data that flows through them is targeted at interrupting the knowledge paradigms that thrive on massive amounts of unstructured data. If this could be solved at the level of political economy, then these institutional measures may not be necessary. However, by bringing 'people' into the informational regimes as rights-bearing identities that constrain actors, the capacity to not only create knowledge but actively define what knowledge is, diminishes. Boundaries interrupt flow and introduce inefficiency. The challenge is doing so in a way that avoids rigidity, that encourages contestation, and promotes the proliferation of identity according to the functional differentiation of computational spheres. By creating legal entities that can inhabit the 'world state', we can resist exhaustion and saturation. By opening a space for contestation within technological architectures, we recognise that any expression of law, be it linguistic, gestural, or technological, is only an *expression* of law, and that law inevitably exceeds any single expression. By recognising the complexity of the 'world state', we insist technology cannot occupy, exhaust, or supplant all of life, or all of law.

Index

Accenture, 102
actuarial paradigm, 4, 75, 102–104, 107–108, 111, 130
Agamben, Giorgio, 8–9, 11, 15, 136
Agrawal, Rakesh, 101
algorithmic accountability, 5, 79, 97, 114–119, 158
   and the law, 117–127, 128–129
   and the legal subject, 133–134, 166
   and transparency, 107, 116–118
   implementation of, 132–133, 166–168
Aliens Register, 70
Amann v. Switzerland, 55, 62
Amazon, 12, 130, 138, 142, 151
Amazon Mechanical Turk, 135, 138
Amoore, Louise, 101–102, 110, 112
Andrejevic, Mark, 2, 144–145, 148
archives, 23, 38–41, 45, 75–76, 81, 84, 113
   and law, 42–43, 53–55, 56, 57–62, 78–79
   and mass surveillance, 65, 70, 72–73
   criminal, 21, 31, 33–34, 37
Australian High Court, 46
Automated Decision Making Guidelines, 119
Automated Personality Analysis. *See* personality computation
Automated Personality Recognition. *See* personality computation

Barocas, Solon, 95
Barthes, Roland, 8, 14, 25
Bateson, Gregory, 155
Bauman, Zygmunt, 110
Bazin, André, 25–26
behavioural advertising, 95, 115, 162–163, 169
behavioural informatics, 161
behavioural manipulation, 120
behavioural monitoring. *See* dossiers
Bengio, Yoshua, 147
Benjamin, Walter, 144
Bennet Moses, Lyria, 109

Benthall, Sebastian, 132, 170
Bentham, Jeremy, 21, 112
Bertillon, Alphonse, 8, 34–37, 45, 68, 74
Biber, Katherine, 27
Big Brother Watch v. United Kingdom, 81
big data. *See* data science
Bigelow, Julian, 155
Bigo, Didier, 110
biometrics, 8–9, 38, 42–44, 63, 76, 113, 121, 137–138, 141, 143
   jurisprudence on, 55–61
Blackstone, William, 46
Boyd v. US, 48
Boyle, James, 16
Brandeis, Louis, 45
Bratton, Benjamin, 178
Brennan, Tim, 104
Brownsword, Roger, 180
Burrell, Jenna, 116
Burroughs, William, 181
Bygrave, Lee, 85, 89, 90, 120

Calo, Ryan, 163, 164
camera obscura, 26
Canadian Dangerous Behaviour Rating Scale, 104
Caplan, Jane, 64
Carpenter v. United States, 50, 55
cartes de visite, 24
Catt v. United Kingdom, 43, 51, 52, 57–58
CCTV, 44–45, 61, 105, 142
Census Act Case, 86, 87
Chan, Janet, 109
Chopra, Samir, 17
Citron, Danielle, 118
Citron, Danielle Keats, 118
Clarke, Roger, 89
Clemens, Justin, 111
CNIL, 95

Cohen, Julie, 164, 168–169, 175
Cole, Simon, 37
COMPAS, 104, 107, 130
computational empiricism, 4, 136, 146, 149–152
computational physiognomy. *See* personality computation
computer vision, 38, 127–128, 135–138, 141–142, 143, 145–147, 151–152, 160
contextual integrity, 169–170
convolutional neural networks. *See* neural networks
Court of Justice of the European Union, 120, 122
cybernetics, 9, 20, 87, 115, 136, 152, 154–156, 173, 177, 181
cyber-physical systems, 182

dark patterns, 161
DARPA, 125
Daston, Lorraine, 25, 27
data mining. *See* data science
data protection. *See* rights of data subjects
Data Protection Directive, 95, 124
data science, 11
 challenges to, 160–161, 166, 169–170
 harms of, 109–111
 history of, 28–31
 methodologies of, 102–104, 105, 138–140, 145–149
 narratives of, 3, 143–144
 use by states, 11–12, 101–102, 109, 151–152
data shadow, 123
data triple, 78
database. *See* archive
Dawkins, Richard, 154
de Hert, Paul, 61, 81–82, 94, 109, 121
deep learning, 140, 143, 148
deep neural network. *See* neural networks
Deleuze, Gilles, 181
Directive on the Protection of Individuals with Regard to the Processing of Personal Data and on the Free Movement of Such Data, 85
Disney, 138
Distance Identification codes, 37
Distinctive Marks Register, 34–35, 105
Diver, Laurence, 133, 179, 181
Dixon J, 46
Do Not Track, 96
Dorsett, Shaunnagh, 182
Doshi-Velez, Finale, 127
dossiers, 61, 64–67, 70–74, 97
 harms of, 72–73, 76–77
Dreyfus Affair, 71–72
Du, Erica, 131–132
dynamite, 68–69

Eastman Kodak, 22
eBay, 167
Edwards, Lillian, 125
Edwards, Paul, 40, 101
Eisenstadt v. *Baird*, 48
ENIAC, 40
Entick v. *Carrington*, 47–48, 49
Eppler case, 86
EU Charter of Fundamental Rights, 90
EU Charter of Human Rights, 86
eugenics, 30, 138, 143, 153
European Convention on Human Rights, 43–44, 48, 51–58, 62, 80
European Court of Human Rights, 43, 55
explainability, 129, 132–133, 158, 166, *See* algorithmic accountability, right to explanation
explanatory Artificial Intelligence, 125–126, 128, 166, 168

Facebook, 96, 108, 138, 141, 151, 162
facial recognition, 38, 44, 54, 58–61, 76, 137–142
fairness, 107, 109, 115, 118, 129–132, 158, 166
 tools for, 167–168
Fenians, 68, 69, 76, 99
fingerprinting, 36–38
Five Eyes, 109
Floridi, Luciano, 14, 124
Flusser, Vilèm, 10, 145
Foucault, Michel, 112, 181
Fraser, Nancy, 132
Friedl v. *Austria*, 54–55
Fuster, Gloria Gonzáles, 129

Galison, Peter, 25, 27, 99, 145
Galton, Francis, 29–31, 37, 138, 140
Gardner, James, 31
Gaskin v. *UK*, 80
General Data Protection Regulation, 85, 89–91, 95, 117
 and consent, 95–96
 and explanation, 123–125
 and profiling, 119–121, 159
 as data governance framework, 82
German Constitutional Court, 86
German Federal Court of Justice, 120
Goodman, Bryce, 108
Google, 12, 95, 96, 132, 151, 153, 176
Google Spain v. *AEPD and Mario Costeja González*, 91
Goold, Benjamin, 7
Gray, John Chipman, 16
Griswold v. *Connecticut*, 48, 50
Guerra and Others v. *Italy*, 80

Guidelines on the Protection of Privacy and Transborder Flows of Personal Data, 85
Gürses, Seda, 114–115
Gutwirth, Serge, 61, 81–82, 100, 109

Habitual Criminals Act, 33
Habitual Criminals Register, 21, 33, 35, 73, 183
Hacking, Ian, 3, 28, 30, 38
Haldar, Piyel, 15, 27
Halewood, Peter, 171
Hamilton, Roger, 24, 28, 35
Haraway, Donna, 156, 172
Harcourt, Bernard, 4, 102, 103–104
Hargraves, Peter, 24, 28, 35
Hayles, N Katherine, 172
Hearn, Allison, 2
Henry, Edward, 37
Hildebrandt, Mireille, 7, 97, 109, 122, 159, 160, 163, 166
Hinton, Geoffrey, 135
Hirsch, Tad, 166
Holmes, Oliver Wendell, 40
Hoofnagle, Chris, 82
human-in-the-loop paradigm, 119, 122–123, 159
hypernudging. *See* nudging

IBM, 61, 101, 102, 132
IDEMIA, 142
identity
　and photography, 27, 34
　categorical, 58, 64, 98
　composite, 172–174, 183
　definitions of, 7–9, 17, 156
　diagnostic, 23, 58
　harms to, 8, 57, 58, 73, 76
　institutional, 23, 33–34, 55, 62, 76–77
　legal, 14–17
　narrative, 98, 152
　new forms of, 136–140, 153–154, 156–157, 172–176
　protection of, 6–7, 42–45, 78–79, 81, 168–169
　registers. *See* archives
ImageNet, 135
informational self-determination, 79, 86
INSLAW, 104
Instagram, 96
intellectual property, 117, 167
Intrudo, 108
Irish Republican Brotherhood. *See* Fenians

Jacobs, James, 49
Jäger, Jens, 28, 31
James, Henry, 69
Jameson, Fredrick, 171
Jasanoff, Sheila, 146

Jensen, RB, 36
Joh, Elizabeth, 108
Jones, Reginald Victor, 73

Kahneman, Daniel, 163
Kang, Hyo Yoon, 175–176
Kateb, George, 44
Katz v. United States, 50
Katz, Yarden, 13, 132
Kennedy J, 48
Kennedy, Helen, 2
Kerr, Ian, 180
Kirn, Walter, 12
Kitchin, Rob, 113
Kleinberg, Jon, 130
knowledge discovery in databases. *See* data science
Kominski, Margot, 119
Kommers, Donald, 87, 98
Kosinski, Michal, 141
Krajewski, Markus, 179
Krizhevsky, Alex, 135
Kroll, Joshua, 117

Lacan, Ernest, 31
Lambroso, Cesare, 30–31
Lamprey, JH, 29
Latour, Bruno, 173
Law Enforcement Directive, 90, 91–94, 120–121
Lawrence v. Texas, 48
Lawson, FH, 166
legal identity. *See* identity, legal
legal person. *See* legal subject
legal subject, 14, 16–17, 42–44, 51
　and data subject, 97–98
　of algorithmic accountability, 133–134, 166
　of data protection, 114
　of the ECHR, 62
Legendre, Pierre, 7
Leonelli, Sabina, 151
Lessig, Lawrence, 180
Lex Informatica, 178
Li, Fei-Fei, 135
Local Interpretable Model-agnostic Explanations, 126
Locke, John, 26, 47
Luhmann, Niklas, 87–88, 169, 173–174, 176
Lupker and Others v. The Netherlands, 53
Lupton, Deborah, 172

machine learning. *See* data science
machinic neoplatonism, 151
Mackenzie, Catriona, 164, 175
manipulation, 111
Martin, Paul, 46

Masquerade, 96
mass surveillance. *See* surveillance
Masumi, Brian, 101
Maturana, Humberto, 87, 173, 177
May, Thomas Erskine, 67
McCulloch, Warren, 155, 173
McQuillan, Dan, 151
McVeigh, Shaun, 182
mechanism design, 161
Metropolitan Police Special Branch, 66, 69
MG v. UK, 80
Microcensus Case, 86
Microsoft, 138, 142, 151
Mill, John Stuart, 66
Miller, Jacques-Alain, 114–113
Minow, Martha, 99
Mitchell, WTJ, 75, 112
Mittelstadt, Brett, 122, 124, 128
MK v. France, 57
Mnookin, Jennifer, 27
mugshot photos. *See* photography, criminal
Mussawir, Edward, 17

Naffine, Ngaire, 16
Napoleon II, 65
Narayanan, Arvind, 130
Nash, Adam, 111
National Commission for Informatics and Liberties, 95
NEC, 142
neo-Lamarckianism, 153–154
neural networks, 105, 135–139, 138–141
New York City Police Department, 61
Newton, Isaac, 26
Nissenbaum, Helen, 88, 89, 95, 163, 169
non-state jurisdictions, 182
Northpointe Inc, 104, 107
nudging, 163–164

Oculus, 96
Odièvre v. France, 80
OECD Fair Information Practices, 89
opacity. *See* transparency
Operations Research, 101
optimisation, 165–166

Palantir, 104–105, 109
panopticon, 1, 112
Papakonstantinou, Vagelis, 94, 121
Parsley, Connal, 14, 17, 178
Pasquale, Frank, 118, 132
pattern identification thinking, 101
Pearl, Judea, 170
Peelian Principles, 66

Peirce, CS, 26, 150
Penal Servitude Act, 39
penalogical modernism, 103–104
Pennsylvania v. Casey, 48
Perry v. The United Kingdom, 55
persona, 77
personalised law, 167
personality computation, 127, 136–142
PG v. The United Kingdom, 55
photography
 and identity, 7–8
 and law, 27, 39–40
 and phrenology, 29
 and privacy, 22–23
 as control, 24, 29, 31, 39
 history of, 21–24, 28–29, 44–46
 judicial, 21–22, 31–34
 objectivity of, 23–29, 74–75
 technologies of, 22
phrenology, 29, 38, 142–143
physiognomy, 29, 142–143, 144
 computational, 138–141, 143
Pick, Daniel, 28, 30
Pinney, Chris, 28
Pitts, Walter, 155
platforms
 and dispute resolution, 167
 and profiling, 165
 and relationship to users, 176
 cities as, 152
 sovereignty of, 9, 178, 182
policing
 history of, 65–72
Porter, Bernard, 68, 69–70
Post, Robert, 6, 45
Powles, Julia, 124
predictive analytics. *See* data science
predictive policing, 100, 104–106, 109, 121
PredPol, 106
Price Waterhouse, 101
PRISM, 108
privacy
 and jurisprudence, 63
 as absence of disclosure, 23, 49–50, 53, 54, 63, 81
 as contextual integrity, 88, *See* contextual integrity
 as opacity, 81, 82, 133, 160
 by design, 135–137, 179
 definitions of, 6–7
 differential, 133–136
procedural regularity, 117
profiling
 definitions of, 3–4, 100, 121
 harms of, 15, 107–108, 113
 jurisprudence on, 43–44

Index

R *(on the application of Wood)* v. *Metropolitan Police Commissioner*, 57
Rafter, Nicole, 142–143
RAND Corporation, 104, 106
Ravachol, 36, 68
Regulations for the Measuring and Photographing of Criminal Prisoners, 45
Ricoeur, Paul, 7
rights
  of data subjects, 6, 78–81, 88–98, 116, 119–121
  of profile creators, 89, 117
  of states, 81
  to access, 79, 89–90, 122
  to accuracy, 83
  to appeal to a machine, 123
  to be forgotten, 79, 91
  to be let alone, 45
  to co-determination of reading, 160–161, 167
  to contest a decision, 122, 168
  to data access, 82
  to data protection, 86
  to explanation, 115, 123–129
  to limited optimization, 175
  to non-discrimination, 167
  to personality, 86–87
  to privacy, 43, 49, 53, 86, 122
  to private life, 42, 44, 62, 79, 81
  to reasonable inferences, 122, 160
  to rectification, 79, 90–91
Rodotà, Stefano, 82, 98
Roe v. *Wade*, 48
Roessler, Beate, 163
rogues' gallery, 33
Rosenblueth, Arturo, 155
Rotaru v. *Romania*, 55, 62
Roth, Michael, 74
Rouvroy, Antoinette, 9, 27, 40, 109, 110, 112, 163, 175
Rubinstein, Ira, 133
Rule, James, 74, 88

S and Marper v. *United Kingdom*, 56–57
Salient Factor Score, 104
Saunders, Jessica, 106
Schafer, Burkhard, 133
Schauer, Frederick, 4
Secret Service Bureau, 70
Segerstedt-Wiberg v. *Sweden*, 55
Sekula, Alan, 11, 38–39
Selbst, Andrew, 124
Select Committee on Police, 67
Simitis, Spiros, 97
Simpson, AWB, 51, 70
Skype, 108

Smith v. *Maryland*, 50
Snowden revelations, 43
Snowden, Edward, 108
Social Darwinism, 138
Soraya case, 86
Sotomayor J, 50
spotter cards, 44
State v. *Loomis*, 107
statistical fairness, 125
Stokes, Paul, 156
Strasbourg Court. *See* European Court of Human Rights
Strategic Subjects List, 106
Sunstein, Cass, 163
surveillance, 42–45, 64–66
  techniques of, 70
surveillance capitalism, 96, 171
Susser, Daniel, 163

Tape Recording case, 86
technological governance, 11–13, 41, 82–83, 102, 109, 161–162, 178–179
TEMPORA, 108
Teubner, Gunther, 173, 175–176, 182
The European Union Charter of Human Rights, 82
The Selfish Ledger, 153–154, 165
Torpey, John, 52
Total Information Awareness, 76, 99
transparency, 97, 116–118, 124–125, 129, 133
Treaty of the European Union, 82, 92
trichotomy of signs, 26
Tuchman, Barbara, 68
Twitter, 108

United States v. *Jones*, 50
United States v. *Miller*, 50
Universal Declaration of Human Rights, 51
UpStream, 108
US Bill of Rights, 49–50
US Department of Defence, 151
US Supreme Court, 50
USA PATRIOT Act, 99

Van Loo, Rory, 167
Varela, Francisco, 87, 173–174, 175, 177
Veale, Michael, 116, 125
Verbeek, Peter-Paul, 172
VGG-Face, 141
Vismann, Cornelia, 8, 27, 82–83, 89–90, 179
Vucetich, Juan, 37

Wachter, Sandra, 122, 124, 159
Wang, Yilun, 141

Warren, Samuel B, 45
Weiner, Norbert, 154–155, 173
Westin, Alan, 44, 89
WhatsApp, 96
White Report, 72
White, Lawrence, 17
Wilkinson, Paul, 66
world state, 146–147, 158–171, 177, 180, 183
    definition of, 9–11
World War 2, 45
Wu, Xiaolin, 140

X v. *United Kingdom*, 52, 54
XAI. *See* explanatory artificial intelligence
XkeyScore, 108

Yeung, Karen, 163
YS and M and S v. Minister Voor Immigratie, 122

Zarsky, Tal, 163
Zhang, 140
Zuboff, Shoshana, 171

Lightning Source UK Ltd.
Milton Keynes UK
UKHW051416201019
351896UK00015B/40/P